AF780988

Work in a Modern Society

New German Historical Perspectives

Series Editors: Jane Caplan (Executive Editor), Timothy Garton Ash, Jürgen Kocka, Gerhard A. Ritter and Margit Szöllösi-Janze

Originally established in 1987 as an English-language forum for the presentation of research by leading German historians and social scientists to readers in English-speaking countries, this series has since become one of the premier vehicles for the dissemination of German research expertise on contemporary academic debate and of broad topical interest to Germans and non-Germans alike. Its coverage is not limited to Germany alone but extends to the history of other countries, as well as general problems of political, economic, social and intellectual history and international relations.

Volume 1
Historical Concepts between Eastern and Western Europe
Edited by Manfred Hildermeier

Volume 2
Crises in European Integration: Challenge and Response, 1945–2005
Edited by Ludger Kühnhardt

Volume 3
Work in a Modern Society: The German Historical Experience in Comparative Perspective
Edited by Jürgen Kocka

Work in a Modern Society

The German Historical Experience in Comparative Perspective

Edited by
Jürgen Kocka

Berghahn Books
New York • Oxford

First published in 2010 by
Berghahn Books
www.berghahnbooks.com

© 2010 Jürgen Kocka

All rights reserved. Except for the quotation of short passages for the purposes of criticism and review, no part of this book may be reproduced in any form or by any means, electronic or mechanical, including photocopying, recording, or any information storage and retrieval system now known or to be invented, without written permission of the publisher.

Library of Congress Cataloging-in-Publication Data

Library of Congress Cataloging-in-Publication Data

Work in a modern society : the German historical experience in comparative perspective / edited by Jürgen Kocka.
p. cm. -- (New German historical prospectives ; v. 3)
Includes bibliographical references and index.
ISBN 978-1-84545-575-0 (alk. paper)
1. Work--Social aspects--Germany--History. 2. Work--Social aspects--Europe--History. 3. Labor--Germany--History. 4. Labor--Europe--History. 5. Work--Social aspects--Germany--Historiography. 6. Work--Social aspects--Europe--Historiography. 7. Germany--Social conditions. 8. Germany--Economic conditions. 9. Europe--Social conditions. 10. Europe--Economic conditions. I. Kocka, Jürgen.
HD6957.G3W67 2009
306.3'60943--dc22

2009013892

British Library Cataloguing in Publication Data

A catalogue record for this book is available from the British Library

Printed in the United States on acid-free paper

ISBN 978-1-84545-575-0 hardback

Contents

German Historical Perspectives

Editorial Preface

The 'German Historical Perspectives' series was established in 1987 as an English-language forum for the presentation of research by German historians and social scientists to readers in English-speaking countries. Each of the volumes is devoted to a particular theme that is discussed from different points of view in separate essays by specialists. The series addresses questions that are prominent in contemporary academic debate and of broad topical interest to Germans and non-Germans alike. It is not limited to issues within Germany alone but also includes publications and individual essays covering the history of other countries, as well as general problems of political, economic, social and intellectual history and international relations, and issues in comparative history. The editors hope that the series will help to overcome the language barrier that can obstruct the rapid appreciation of German research in English-speaking countries.

The publication of the series is closely linked with the German Visiting Fellowship at St Antony's College, Oxford. This Fellowship was originally funded by the Volkswagen Stiftung, and later by the British Leverhulme Trust and by the Ministry of Education and Science in the Federal Republic of Germany. From 1990 the Fellowship has been supported by the Stifterverband für die Deutsche Wissenschaft, with special funding since 2000 from the Marga and Kurt Möllgaard-Stiftung. Each volume is based on the seminar series held annually in Oxford which the Visiting Fellow devises from his or her field of interest, in collaboration with the European Studies Centre at St Antony's College.

The editors wish to thank the Stifterverband für die Deutsche Wissenschaft and the Marga and Kurt Möllgaard-Stiftung for meeting the expenses of the original seminar series and for generous assistance with the publication. We hope that this enterprise will help to overcome national introspection and to further international academic discourse and co-operation.

Jane Caplan (Executive Editor)
Timothy Garton Ash
Jürgen Kocka
Gerhard A. Ritter
Nicholas Stargardt
Margit Szöllösi-Janze

1

Work as a Problem in European History

Jürgen Kocka

This is a broad topic for a historian: treating it within a short essay means being both very general and very selective. Why such a broad topic?

First, it allows us to bring together specialists from different fields whose contributions may appear in a new light if seen together.[1] Second, by dealing with the history of work in a general way, historians can relate to ongoing debates of the present time. In several European countries, certainly in Germany, mass unemployment and the changing nature of work under the impact of globalization and computerization have fuelled interesting debates about access to work as an economic and social resource, its political relevance and cultural meaning, about *Arbeitsgesellschaft* (labour society) and its possible alternatives if it is about to end, as some commentators think. It is against this background that it may be rewarding to reflect upon work (and labour) in a historical perspective.[2] If it can be done, third, a history of work would seem to be highly attractive, because it would have to integrate very different approaches, methods and aspects, ranging from straightforward economic history to cultural constructivism, including the analysis of institutions and politics.

But can it be done? There is reason for doubt, since the concept 'work' is not very precise, very changeable over time and between cultures and highly contested. Very often what it means is not easily separated from other human activities, but embedded, which makes its separate conceptualization appear a bit artificial and problematic. In addition, concepts like 'work' are highly aggregate and abstract; they comprise very different phenomena. This diversity makes it difficult to formulate observations valid for the whole aggregate, i.e., work in general.

Maybe this is why one knows, in fact, a lot about many single aspects of the history of work in different contexts. Some general surveys, it is true, exist.[3] But it is not yet clear what the leading questions and viewpoints structuring the history of work as a general field of research might be.

I.

I start with some remarks on *Begriffsgeschichte*, the history of the concept and problems of definition. This is the subfield with the best and most elaborate literature: although it is very much restricted to Europe, especially Western Europe, and the West.[4]

There have been many, and there still are some, cultures and languages that do not have anything like a general concept of work. In addition, cultures and languages differ with respect to which human activities they lump together under a label like 'work' in order to distinguish them from other activities. This makes comparison interesting and translation difficult.

It is, for example, reported that the Yir-Yoront, native inhabitants of Australia, use the same word for work and play, while the Dogons in Mali seem to have the same word for agriculture and religious dancing, without needing a general concept of work.[5] The Greeks of the Classical period would not have seen much sense in categorizing the manual work of slaves in the fields, the inferior work of women in the house, the production of texts by a writer and the activities of a politician under one and the same concept. They used different words for these different activities; they did not have a general concept of work.[6] In the Middle Ages the semantic situation was complex and changing, but there was a tendency to limit the meaning of *labor*, *Arbeit*, *travail* and 'labour' to physical work. Still, in Zedler's *Universallexikon*, a major German encyclopaedia of 1732, the entry on *Arbeit* does not give a general definition of the word, but its author is satisfied with the enumeration of different activities (including, however, manual work and the work of artists, as well as the travels of Paulus and the 'schwere Amts- und Erlösungsarbeit Christi', i.e., the duties of clerics).[7]

One should not be surprised to see that a general concept of work – in the sense of a purposeful application of physical and mental forces in order to fulfil needs (or something like this) – emerged only slowly and sometimes not at all. For such a concept becomes possible and meaningful only if and when different activities appear sufficiently similar or related under certain viewpoints while they are sufficiently separable from other activities as well. There were and are many constellations in which such a differentiation of activities and such a need for semantic construction did not and do not exist.

One can turn this around and ask for typical constellations in European history, which invited contemporaries to think and speak about work in general, i.e., discursive situations that contributed to the construction of a general concept of work. On the one hand, it was the context of Christian piety and theology that offered opportunities and incentives to reflect and form opinions about work in relation to industry or idleness. This occurred already in late antiquity, in the monastic movements and theological reasoning of medieval time, and particularly in the Reformation when, for example, Luther wrote about work in general, seeing it as a kind of worship and equalizing all kinds of work and activities relative to their recognition by God. On the other hand, there were governments, first in the late medieval towns, then in the early modern territorial states, which tried to fight poverty by getting people to work, by praising the virtues of work and by setting up institutions for spreading a work ethic and work discipline. Again, this discourse dealt with work in general, not only with specific trades and professions. Third, different activities were seen as comparable and formally similar with respect to their values on the market wherever capitalist mechanisms spread into the world of work. In market-related contexts, work was usually categorized as labour. 'A man's labour', Hobbes wrote in 1651, 'is a commodity exchangeable for benefit, as well as any other thing.' Finally, it was in the thinking and writing of the Enlightenment that work was perceived as a general human activity.[8]

Clearly, these were different notions of work, *travail*, *Arbeit* and 'labour', but they resembled one another in that they did not refer to very specific types of work, but to an abstraction of work in general. These were different contributions to a development, which certainly had other ingredients as well. But by the eighteenth century a general concept of work had emerged in Western languages. It differed from context to context, from speaker to speaker, remained changeable and without sharp definition. But essentially work had come to mean a human activity, which 'has an end beyond itself, being designed to produce or achieve something; it involves a degree of obligation or necessity, being a task that others set us or that we set ourselves; and it is arduous, involving effort and persistence beyond the point at which the task ceases to be wholly pleasurable.'[9] Opposite concepts were idleness, play and, increasingly, leisure. The notion of leisure emerged in the same early modern period in which the general notion of work took shape: the other side of the coin.[10]

So we have addressed processes of semantic construction in practical contexts that took place before the era of the Industrial Revolution. These were intertwined with fundamental processes: the spread of the market and industrious discipline, state building and attempts towards more regulation, as well as new ideas about progress and human identity.

The formation of a general concept of work went hand in hand with a steady revaluation of work. Again, this was a phenomenon of remarkable complexity to which I cannot do justice here, so I will limit myself to just a few points. In Greek and Roman Antiquity a sceptical assessment of most types of work predominated, corresponding to a reality of work that was largely characterized by bondage and inferiority. Work and freedom, work and citizenship, stood in deep tension with each other while one presupposed the other: like *oikos* and *polis*. The etymological roots of *Arbeit*, *travail*, 'labour' and *robot* are dark and harsh, connected with suffering, toil, hardship and punishment. A much-discussed ambivalence in many ways characterized the notion of work in the Hebrew-Christian tradition: work between curse and blessing, between punishment and divine order. Even in the most outspoken pleas in favour of recognizing work, each kind of work, as justified by God and service to God in medieval monastic rules and the writings of the sixteenth-century Reformation, there was usually a subtext implied according to which the toil and trouble of hard work had to be accepted as a sort of penance or punishment for human sinfulness ('In the sweat of thy face', Genesis 3: 17–19).

In the European towns of the Medieval and early modern periods, economically based on craft and trade, craftsmen and merchants, guilds and corporations, qualified work gained new relevance, respectability and recognition. Here, work status and citizenship were intrinsically intertwined and mutually reinforcing. This stood in sharp contrast to what had been the case in the ancient polis. Work was now central to the emerging culture of the urban bourgeoisie, and this in turn helped to upgrade the social status of work, at least of some types of work. And it was in the writings of the Enlightenment and the emerging discipline of Political Economy in the seventeenth and eighteenth centuries that a nearly emphatic upgrading of work took place: work as the major source of wealth, as well as a core element of civility, very much in a bourgeois spirit, frequently with an anti-aristocratic thrust, often supported by religious self-assuredness and a progressive mood. Hundreds of quotes could be given. Take as an example Immanuel Kant, who devalued leisure and praised work – in the broad sense of the word – as a central element of life. 'Je mehr wir beschäftigt sind, je mehr fühlen wir, dass wir leben und desto mehr sind wir uns unseres Lebens bewusst. In der Muße fühlen wir nicht allein, dass uns das Leben so vorbeistreicht, sondern wir fühlen auch sogar eine Leblosigkeit.'[11]

It would be necessary to add many differentiations, exceptions, even counter-evidence. For instance: in all the emphatic upgrading of work, sensibility for ambivalence did not disappear altogether. Take the entry for *travail* in Diderot's *Encyclopédie*, written by Diderot himself and published in a volume of 1765. He defined work (*travail*) as 'occupation journalière à laquelle l'homme est condamné par son besoin, et à laquelle il doit, en même temps, sa santé, sa subsistance, sa sérénité, son bon sens et sa vertu peut-être'. In addition, many of those intellectuals who celebrated the economic centrality and civilizing power of work also knew that, to quote Adam Smith, most labour meant 'toil and trouble', and that most people, if they had the choice, would prefer idleness. It also should be said that writers like Adam Ferguson differentiated pointedly between different types of work: some uplifting, some degrading. And what about regional differences between Protestant and Catholic Europe, between West, South and East?[12]

Still, the main trend is clear. By 1800 the originally close connection between work on the one hand and struggle, hardship and toil on the other had been loosened, and the fundamentally creative and formative dimension of work had been emphasized, giving work an unprecedented centrality as to wealth, civility and human identity. Was this upgrading of work within the discourses of intellectuals paralleled by a corresponding change in the values and attitudes, mentalities and habits of the common people?

II.

Due to problems of sources and methods, this question is hard to answer. An indirect way is provided by the study of 'utopias': utopian novels, science fiction from the sixteenth to the twentieth century, bestsellers in several European languages, widely-read books, all of which had something to say about work in an unlikely but desired utopian future. All of them gave substantial attention to problems of work.

Thomas More's *Utopia* was published in 1516. The author regarded work – or labour – as a 'service of the body'. On the island of Utopia – nowhere-land – working hours would be limited to six per day in order to have sufficient time for other 'productive tasks', for literature, scientific studies or contemplation, but also for sports and games, conversation, music and recreation. Six working hours per day would be enough. High productivity would be achieved through central planning and good organization, including an obligatory work service for men and women, collectivized consumption, the abandonment of wage work and the banning of idleness.[13]

More than one hundred years later the German novel *Insel Felsenburg* by Johann Gottfried Schnabel appeared (around 1740). It presented a similar picture of work in the future: with one novelty worth mentioning. Unlike Thomas More, this eighteenth-century author dreamt of machines and trained monkeys, which would liberate men from 'cruel troubles and labour', facilitate work and reduce working time.[14] This motive was to stay: ever more effective technical innovations maintained a central place in utopian novels, usually as signs and instruments of progress, in the twentieth century as indicators of a threatening machinery (for example, in Huxley's *Brave New World* from 1937).

Luis-Sébastien Mercier wrote in the spirit of early Enlightenment. He published a European bestseller in 1717 under the title *The Year 2440.* The story is framed as a dream. The narrator wakes up in Paris in 2440 and walks through the city. People are reasonable, diligent, thrifty, peaceful, honest and serious. The army and prostitution are abandoned. Inns and other eating-houses have been replaced by general hospitality. The theatre is a place for moral education. Physicists and astronomers serve as clerics of the highly respected religion of reason. The world of work has changed. Daily work is moderate. Breaks, games and rural dances stimulate interest in one's tasks. Labour has stopped being ugly, since it no longer resembles the lot of slaves. Since one has got rid of idlers, monks and the masses of useless servants, no class has to live in bonds to benefit another class anymore. 'Childish' luxury goods have been abandoned. Consequently, a few working hours suffice to produce more than what is necessary for fulfilling the needs of the public. But gender difference would still exist: women in domestic work, men in the fields. And the enlightened author suggested a specific solution for the most unpleasant jobs. He wrote that it was bad enough that Nature has condemned human beings to eating the meat of animals. The Parisians of the future would be spared the view of how they were slaughtered. The butchers' trade would be taken care of by foreigners who had had to leave their home countries. They would be protected by law, but not accepted as citizens. 'None of us will have to do this bloody and cruel job.'[15]

Another century later: early socialists like Saint-Simon, Fourier and Weitling dreamt of shortening the work hours and were ready to pay for it with compulsory work service, at least temporarily. A senate was supposed to decide, instead of the market. Wage work, wage labour, was to be abandoned. And there was a new utopian element in their writings: life-long careers in one and the same specialization were to be overcome. By changing the workplace every two hours, everybody would be able to pursue several occupations, several professions, several jobs side by side. Remember the young Karl Marx who in the 1840s dreamt of hunting in the morning, fishing at noon, breeding cattle in the evening, also criticizing the food: without, as he wrote, ever becoming a hunter, a fisherman, a herdsman or a critic ('wie ich gerade Lust habe').[16]

Later on, socialists were in favour of planning and efficient organization of work, as well sceptical vis-à-vis wage work, the market and idleness. They were always for shorter hours and for work regulation. Both Edward Bellamy's bestseller *Looking Backward: 2000 to 1887* and August Bebel's *Die Frau und der Sozialismus* anticipated the liberation of women and servants from household work, thanks to public laundries and communal kitchens, electrification and technical progress.[17]

So we have addressed the future of work in utopias of the past. Utopian constructions can be read as critical comments on the time in which they were formulated.[18] It is sufficiently clear what they opposed and what their authors saw as particularly unsatisfactory and unbearable in the world that they knew. It was, first of all, and without exception, the hardship of manual work, labour's toil and trouble, which was to be overcome: through the shortening of work hours, monkeys and the liberating effects of modern technology. Second, already in the eighteenth century the unequal distribution of work and its returns was to be overcome in the future. Moreover, those authors did not regard wage labour as a source of freedom but as an irritation to be replaced by organization, even at the price of limited compulsion. Finally, it was the monotony of specialized work that they wished to remedy by permanent alternation, so that work could better serve the purpose of human self-realization. One does not find this before very late in the eighteenth century.

Of course, this is only indirect evidence. No doubt, different types of work offered very different degrees of satisfaction. There was always joy in some work as well.[19] But those utopias were widely read. They must have hit a chord. In order to be good utopians, the authors had to be realistic observers. I believe they were. Their views are supported by other evidence we have, for example, by the many comments and evaluations collected in the *Oxford Book of Work*. Its editor, Keith Thomas, quotes a seventeenth-century writer: 'If it was agreeable to do anything called work, it was not really so but pleasure …It is incident to the true nature of work not to delight in it.' And Thomas continues: 'Much of this anthology is taken up with similar negative reactions to work. They evoke the dreariness, discomfort and tedium of repetitive factory work; the horrors of plantation slavery; the petty tyrannies of office life; and the major tyrannies of penal labour... [The documents] confirm the inescapable fact that, through the centuries, the lot of most of the human race has been hard toil for small reward.'[20] Pertinent folk songs and popular proverbs rarely mentioned the joy or the praise of work; rather, they expressed sympathy for rest and laziness. And when Adolf Levenstein published the first German survey based on interviews with industrials workers at the beginning of the twentieth century, they had little to say on the joy, but much on the stress and the dreariness of their work.[21]

III.

The third part of this article will deal with the 'long nineteenth century', which lasted from the French Revolution to the First World War.[22] Most evidence will come from the German case, and emphasis will be laid on structures, processes and institutions. What did the nineteenth century, the century of the industrial revolution, change?

1. On the continent, it was only after the revolutions and reforms around 1800 and with industrialization proper that the mechanisms of a capitalist market economy spread widely and thoroughly. It was only now that they became the dominant principles of the economic order, including the organization of work. Work, including work for a living, had always been performed in different institutional contexts: within houses and households, under different regimes of compulsion, in feudal and corporate settings. In most parts of Europe market-related work or labour had existed for centuries, but, with the exception of England, it had been a minority phenomenon, and the distinction between market-relatedness and non-market-relatedness had been blurred for a long time. Now, in the course of the nineteenth century, market-related work became the rule, of course in very different forms, wage work being only one of them.[23]

2. In the course of the nineteenth century, an increasing proportion of market-related work was done in manufacturing centres and workshops, factories and mines, offices and administrative agencies. There were innumerable transitions, mixtures and hybrids, certainly, but the dominant trend was to separate the workplace, where a living was earned and perhaps gains were made, from the sphere of the house and the family. Such a separation had not been the rule before, neither for peasants nor for domestic or cottage workers, neither for the artisans nor for the merchants or scholars, many of whom had worked at home or near to home (and some of them continued to do so). Work had usually been closely tied to other activities and

expressions of life. Now, the separate 'work place' emerged. Work now got its own space and its own time. Work and its products became more measurable. The distinction between work in this sense and non-work (including other activities) became clearer, easier to experience and a topic of discussion. It was against the background of this differentiation between work and non-work that the lack of work became an identifiable phenomenon, a topic, a problem. It was not before the 1880s that the concepts of *Arbeitslosigkeit*, 'unemployment' and *chômage* appeared in the dictionaries and the social discourses, and soon in legislation.[24]

3. Work had always been gender-specific to some degree. The division of work had always been gendered. Now, the connection between gender and work changed as a consequence of the increasing separation of workplace and the family/household. In the world of work, male-female inequality became more pronounced than in previous centuries.[25]

4. There had always been differences, tensions and conflicts between those who held different positions in the social system of work: between lords and peasants, masters and men or women, owners and labourers, employers and employees, and the many hybrids in between. Now, since market-related work became to some extent less embedded, more distinguishable and located in a sphere per se, such differences could play themselves out fully. Class became a major dimension of collective self-identification, class conflict one of the major topics of the century.[26]

5. For centuries, work had been regulated, one way or another, by authorities of different kinds. For a while, the breakthrough of a market economy and of legal liberalization reduced the public regulation of work, particularly in the second third and third quarter of the nineteenth century. In the last two decades of the nineteenth century a new process of legal and administrative regulation gained momentum, now dealing with a subject matter to some degree separable from other activities and expressions of life. Consequently, legal and administrative regulation of work led to a specialized legal sphere and a specialized arm of government whose impact, in return, reinforced the existence of work as a separate sphere under specific rules and regulations.

These were the five most important structural changes related to work in the century of the industrial revolution. Correspondingly, something changed in the language of work. The concept of work became narrower, got closer to 'labour', gradually narrowed down to mean work for a living and for an earning, work and work-products to be sold some way or another, market-related work, in German: *Erwerbsarbeit*. Work for wages and salaries was just one form of it, although soon the most numerous one, obviously. But *Erwerbsarbeit* also included the work of self-employed peasants, artisans and business persons, managers and entrepreneurs, professionals, politicians and soldiers, artists, intellectuals etc.: as long as they sold their services or products on markets in order to make a living or an earning. In the course of this semantic process of narrowing, some activities, which earlier had been regarded as work, ceased to be counted as work in the full sense of the word. Think of work in the house, especially woman's work in the household and in the sphere of reproduction; think of unpaid work in the civic field; think of work one does for oneself. One can document this narrowing down of the concept by analysing the categories used by statisticians, census bureaus and the like.[27]

Something else happened in the long nineteenth century. A basic contradiction became more acute, was partly politicized and became an important dynamic force. I am thinking of the tension between the emphatic concepts of work in the Western Enlightenment tradition on the one hand and the reality of work as it developed in the century of industrialization on the other. The emphatic discourse about work as a core element of human existence, as a human right and duty, continued throughout the nineteenth century and beyond. It became even more pronounced and ambitious: from Hegel through Marx to Max Weber, with many other contributors who are less well-known today. On the other hand, the reality of work was characterized by increasing division and specialization; it was mostly dependent on markets, superiors or machines, frequently hard and dreary, exhausting and miserable. This incongruity, tension or contradiction was not new, but it was coming to a point and, in the emerging civil society of the nineteenth century, it became a topic of public debate. Out of this publicly discussed contradiction emerged the sharp and mobilizing critique of work under capitalism as alienated and exploited, seen most clearly in the writings of Marx. This contradiction also helped to fuel the demands of the emerging labour movement, the socialist and social-democratic claims aiming at the recognition of work and workers, their inclusion and participation as citizens, improvement and political change. Work served as a legitimating basis for social and political claims. This was not just the content of programmes and the strategy of functionaries. By looking more closely at the grassroots level of the emerging socialist labour movement, one can see that active but ordinary workers had a demanding, ambitious understanding of their work as qualified, productive, masculine and culturally important. This understanding of work gave substance to their claims for improvement, as well as to their hostility against 'idlers' and those above them whom they pronounced idlers, because they did not work the way they knew.[28]

Take this as an example for how deeply, in the nineteenth century, the changing nature of work and the changing interpretations of work penetrated the social and political system as well as the self-identification of people. Notions of work played a central role in many other contexts as well: in the self-understanding of middle-class persons, as reflected by their autobiographies; as a topic of scientific debates, which sometimes developed biological and physics-related overtones; as a central category of the emerging social sciences; in political discourses. Take, for example, the liberal representative who stated in the Frankfurt National Assembly 1848: 'A privilege was once holy, today work is holy; free labour, diligence and activity ... is the highest honour today.' Take the debate on nation and nationalism. The widely read ethnographer Wilhelm Heinrich Riehl wrote an influential book on *Deutsche Arbeit* in 1861. Since the 1850s World's Fairs presented work and its products, distinguished by nations and tied to national aspirations. In 1875 a German professor in Prague wrote that 'work stamps a person with its essence, it forms the nation. Nationality and national work are equivalent terms'. In sharpening the distinction and constructing the relations between colonizers and natives, between the West and the rest, practices of work and statements about different attitudes towards work played an important role.[29]

Most importantly perhaps, from the 1880s onwards work in the sense of market-related work for a living and gains – *Arbeit* in the sense of *Erwerbsarbeit* – became the basis of the emerging welfare state, at least in Germany. The workers – not the poor – were the addressees of Bismarck's health, accident and old age insurances. The system, moreover, was financed by the workers' and employers' contributions, not from taxes or savings. In the course of the twentieth century the system has been perfected, elaborated and deeply anchored, so that it is hard to change. Taxes and contributions, as well as entitlements and transfer payments, became related to one's status in the system of work. In this sense, work became a major deciding factor in terms of inclusion and exclusion. What individuals contribute to and expect from the community at large has become, to a considerable degree, dependent on the work they do or lose. In many ways, work is one of the bonds, which keep our societies together.[30]

These are some elements of what has come to be called the *Arbeitsgesellschaft* (work society, labouring society) of the nineteenth and twentieth centuries. The word seems to have been coined by Hannah Arendt in 1958. Before the nineteenth century work had never been such a central pillar of the whole social, political and cultural fabric. Nowadays there is much reason to think that this pattern is running out. But one cannot be sure, nor does one see by what it can be replaced.[31]

IV.

The following articles present chapters in the history of work, particularly in Europe. On the basis of new research, Josef Ehmer shows how important work was in the value system of different social groups already in the late Medieval and early modern periods. Using German examples, he reconstructs different discourses: those of the rulers who demanded hard labour as a duty of the lower orders; those of peasants and craftsmen who drew self-confidence from the fact that they worked. In several social milieus, work was seen as part of a right and proper conduct of life. There were counter-tendencies, which the author does not neglect. One cannot speak of a general 'glorification of work' in that time. But the article makes clear that the high appreciation of work, so typical for European modernity, has roots that reach far back in our history.

Gerd Spittler reconstructs the debates of European, particularly German, social scientists, including anthropologists and ethnographers, in the 'long nineteenth century'. He traces the beginnings of the anthropology of work as a scholarly discourse. He shows the increasing centrality of 'work' and 'labour' in the writings of authors like Karl Marx, Wilhelm Heinrich Riehl, Karl Bücher, Max Weber, Karl Weule, Richard Thurnwald and Bronislaw Malinowski. It becomes clear that those European discourses about work were influenced early on by observation of work outside Europe and the West.

Thomas Welskopp shows how much the concepts of work and labour used in the nineteenth-century labour movements, and particularly in German social democracy, differed from the critical concepts of socialist master-thinkers like Karl Marx. German workers, active on the grassroots level of the emerging labour movement, in early unions and local associations, followed an artisan work ethic and cherished a positive notion of qualified work. Work had a public meaning for them. Welskopp shows how their understanding of work related to their experiences at different work places and in different social milieus. He makes clear that the workers' claims for full citizenship and participation, as well as their criticism of commerce, capitalism and exploitation, were intrinsically connected to their notion of work as part of their selves.

Karin Hausen surveys the ways in which, over the last decades, the history of work and labour was brought together with the history of women and gender. She introduces the reader to the major debates about the intersection of work and gender: from research on the spread of the family model based on the male breadwinner in the nineteenth century, through the analysis of work in the context of the changing distinction between public and private, to the gender policies of the two German states in the fields of labour and welfare legislation. German examples are central, but they are put into a broader context. The article makes clear how much the input of gender historians has enriched and transformed the study of work over the last decades.

A new approach is presented by Ute Frevert. She brings the history of trust and the history of work together. On the one hand, she makes clear how much different types of work have served as practical fields in which emotions were played out and relations of trust were established. As a consequence, one understands better some of the intrinsic mechanisms through which work helps to give coherence to modern societies. On the other hand, Frevert interprets the building and the cultivation of trust as a form of work. With this, she contributes to the broadening of the concept of work as it can be presently observed, both in public debates and in pertinent scholarship.

In a different way, Alf Lüdtke's contribution also helps to broaden the dominant concept of work. He considers whether soldiering can be seen as a form of work. Mostly on the basis of twentieth-century examples, he explores analogies and similarities between practices and experiences of work in modern industrial settings and practices and experiences in military organizations and modern wars. This article uses widely-spread ego-documents and draws our attention to the destructive implications of work, which are frequently overlooked.[32]

The history of freedom and the history of work are intrinsically connected;[33] so are the histories of work and repression. In this volume, this fundamental and complex problem is touched upon again and again. It becomes a central topic in Klaus Tenfelde's contribution. Based on new research, the article surveys the extent, the composition, the organization and the practices of forced labour in Europe under German rule during the Second World War. This is new information, which Tenfelde places in broader contexts. He relates it to the coercive elements frequently inherent in wage labour as such and registered by workers concerned. He also relates the practices of forced labour to the experiences of compulsory migration and deportation in that period of dictatorship and destruction.

Recent trends towards studying entanglements across borders and between nations, regions and cultures are about to change the emerging field of work studies. This is the note on which Karin Hausen finishes her survey of the literature on gender and work, and it is the topic of Sebastian Conrad's contribution to this volume. Conrad not only compares Protestant and Confucian work ethics in Europe and Japan. He also shows that the rise of the discourse on Confucian work ethics has been a product of transcultural interconnections, a modern construction, which relates images of tradition to recent challenges and influences both the perceptions and the practices of work.

The concluding article by Andreas Eckert demonstrates how a global perspective on the history of work and labour is about to change questions and answers in the field. It concentrates on entanglements between labour regimes, work practices and definitions of work in Europe and in other continents. It deals with free and unfree, paid and unpaid labour in different forms. Eckert relates the findings of global labour history to the present discourses on work and labour in Western societies. He rounds off the volume by offering a short and selective look at the present state of research in labour studies and the history of work.

Notes

1. Most contributions to this volume are revised versions of papers presented to a weekly seminar at St Antony's College, Oxford, in 2005. I am grateful to Jane Caplan for joining me in organizing this seminar and to the Marga und Kurt Möllgaard-Stiftung within the Stifterverband für die deutsche Wissenschaft for general financial support. A previous version of the following text was circulated to the contributors of the seminar. An extended German version of it has been published: Jürgen Kocka, 'Mehr Last als Lust. Arbeit und Arbeitsgesellschaft in der europäischen Geschichte', in *Jahrbuch für Wirtschaftsgeschichte [Economic History Yearbook]* 2005, 2: 185–206.

2. Cf. Jeremy Rifkin, *The End of Work* (New York: Little, Brown and Company, 1995); Alan Supiot (ed.), *Au-delà de l'emploi. Transformation du travail et devenir du droit du travail en Europe* (Paris: Flammarion, 1999); Jürgen Kocka and Claus Offe (eds), *Geschichte und Zukunft der Arbeit* (Frankfurt/New York: Campus, 2000); Bo Strath (ed.), *After Full Employment. European Discourses on Work and Flexibility* (Brussels: Peter Lang Publishing, 2000); *Work in the Life-Cycle. Econimic History Yearbook 2008/9* (Berlin: Akademie Verlag, 2008).
3. Cf. Frans van der Ven, *Sozialgeschichte der Arbeit*, 3 vols, (originally in Dutch,1965–68, Munich: dtv, 1972); Venanz Schubert (ed.), *Der Mensch und seine Arbeit. Eine Ringvorlesung der Universität München* (St. Ottilien: Eos Verlag, 1986); Keith Thomas (ed.), *The Oxford Book of Work* (Oxford: Oxford University Press, 1999); Josef Ehmer, 'History of Work', in *International Encyclopedia of the Social and Behavioral Sciences*, vol. 24 (London: Elsevier, 2001), pp. 16,569–16,575.
4. Cf. Werner Conze et al., 'Arbeit' in Otto Brunner et al. (eds), *Geschichtliche Grundbegriffe. Historisches Lexikon zur politisch-sozialen Sprache in Deutschland*, vol. 1 (Stuttgart: Klett, 1972), pp. 154–215; Rudolf Walther, 'Arbeit – Ein begriffsgeschichtlicher Überblick von Aristoteles bis Ricardo', in Helmut König et al. (eds), *Sozialphilosophie der industriellen Arbeit* (Opladen: Westdeutscher Verlag, 1990), pp. 3–25; Herbert Applebaum, *The Concept of Work. Ancient, Medieval, and Modern* (Albany, N.Y.: State University of New York Press, 1992); Patrick Joyce (ed.), *The Historical Meanings of Work* (Cambridge: Cambridge University Press, 1987); Adriano Tilgher, *Work. What It Has Meant to Men through the Ages* (New York: Harcourt Brace andand Co., 1977); Bénédicte Zimmermann, 'Work and Labor. History of the Concept', in *International Encyclopedia of the Social and Behavioral Sciences*, vol. 24, pp. 16,561–16,565.
5. Marshall Sahlins, *Stone Age Economics* (New York: Aldine Transaction, 1972), p. 64; Thomas (ed.), *The Oxford Book of Work*, XIV; Robert L. Heilbroner, *The Act of Work* (Washington: Library of Congress, 1985), pp. 10f.
6. Christian Meier, 'Griechische Arbeitsauffassungen in archaischer und klassischer Zeit', in Manfred Bierwisch (ed.), *Die Rolle der Arbeit in verschiedenen Epochen und Kulturen* (Berlin: Akademie Verlag, 2003), pp. 19–76; Wilfried Nippel, 'Erwerbsarbeit in der Antike', in Kocka and Offe (eds), *Geschichte und Zukunft der Arbeit*, pp. 54–66; Hans Kloft, 'Arbeit und Arbeitsverträge in der griechisch-römischen Welt', in *Saeculum* 35 (1984): 200–21. A slightly different view is presented in Winfried Schmitz, *Nachbarschaft und Dorfgemeinschaft im archaischen und klassischen Griechenland* (Berlin: Akademie Verlag, 2004).
7. Cf. Otto Gerhard Oexle, 'Arbeit, Armut, "Stand" im Mittelalter', in Kocka and Offe (eds), *Geschichte und Zukunft der Arbeit*, pp. 67–79; Wolfgang Zorn, 'Arbeit in Europa vom Mittelalter bis ins Industriezeitalter', in Schubert (ed.), *Der Mensch und seine Arbeit*, pp. 181–212, 183ff.; Verena Postel (ed.), *Arbeit im Mittelalter. Vorstellungen und Wirklichkeiten* (Berlin: Akademie Verlag, 2006). See Josef Ehmer's contribution to this volume. *Grosses Vollständiges Universal Lexicon aller Wissenschafften und Künste*, vol. 2, (Halle/Leipzig 1732), cols. 1,148–50.
8. In addition to titles given in note 4 above cf. Josef Ehmer and Peter Gutschner, 'Befreiung und Verkrümmung durch Arbeit', in Richard van Dülmen (ed.), *Erfindung des Menschen. Schöpfungsträume und Körperbilder 1500–2000* (Wien: Böhlau Verlag, 1998), pp. 283–303; Richard van Dülmen, '"Arbeit" in der frühneuzeitlichen Gesellschaft', in Kocka and Offe (eds), *Geschichte und Zukunft der Arbeit*, pp. 80–87; Rudolf Walther, 'Arbeit in Helmut König et al. (eds), *Sozialphilosophie der industriellen Arbeit*, esp. pp. 15–21.

Crawford Brough McPherson (ed.), *Thomas Hobbes, Leviathan* (1651), Harmondsworth: Penguin, 1982), p. 50.

9. With this definition I follow Keith Thomas, who proposed it after sampling a large number of texts from the early modern period and beyond: see *The Oxford Book of Work* (Oxford: Oxford University Press, 1999), p. XIV.
10. Cf. Peter Burke, 'The Invention of Leisure in Early Modern Europe', in *Past and Present* 146–149 (1995): 136–50.
11. Cf. Paul Menzer (ed.), *Immanuel Kant, Eine Vorlesung Kants über Ethik* (Berlin: Pan Verlag Rolf Heise, 1924), p. 201; 'Arbeit' in Grimm (ed.), *Deutsches Wörterbuch*, vol. 1 (1854), cols. 538–41; Manfred Bierwisch, 'Arbeit in verschiedenen Epochen und Kulturen. Einleitende Bemerkungen', in idem (ed.), *Die Rolle der Arbeit*, pp. 7–18, 8–11. Cf. the titles in notes 4 and 8 above.
12. *Encyclopédie ou dictionnaire raisonné des sciences, des arts et des métiers XVI* (Neufchatel 1765), p. 567; Adam Smith, *An Inquiry into the Nature and Causes of the Wealth of Nations*, vol. 1 (Oxford: Oxford University Press, 1967), p. 47 ; cf. Conze, 'Arbeit', p. 167–81; Josef Ehmer, 'Die Geschichte der Arbeit als Spannungsfeld von Begriff, Norm und Praxis', in *Bericht über den 23. Österreichischen Historikertag in Salzburg, Veröffentlichungen des Verbandes Österreichischer Historiker und Geschichtsvereine*, vol. 32 (Salzburg: Verb. Österr. Historiker und Geschichtsvereine, Österr. Staatsarchiv, 2003), pp. 25–44, especially notes 28–31.
13. Thomas More (1516) *Utopia: A New Translation, Backgrounds, Criticism*, Robert M. Adams, (transl. and ed.), New York: W.W. Norton, 1975), pp. 41–44.
14. Johann Gottfried Schnabel, *Insel Felsenburg*, parts I–IV (Nordhausen 1731–1743), especially part I, p. 268f. (monkeys), 270, 278; part II, pp. 86–89 (obligatory work service), 449f., 493; part III, p. 82f., 96, 290 (leisure and holidays), 366f. (women's work); part IV, p. 258, 290, 543.
15. Louis-Sébastien Mercier (1772), *Das Jahr 2440. Ein Traum aller Träume*, Christian Felix Weiße, transl. (Frankfurt am Main: Suhrkamp, 1982), title page, 92f., 94f.; English transl., *Memoirs of the Year 2500.* W. Hooper, M.D., transl., 2 vols (London: G. Robinson, 1772).
16. Wilhelm Weitling (1838/39), *Die Menschheit wie sie ist und wie sie sein sollte*, Wolf Schäfer (ed.), (Reinbek 1971), pp. 158–66; Karl Marx, *Die deutsche Ideologie* (Stuttgart: Kröner, 1932); Wolfgang Schieder, *Anfänge der deutschen Arbeiterbewegung. Die Auslandsvereine im Jahrzehnt nach der Julirevolution von 1830* (Stuttgart: Klett, 1963), pp. 248ff.
17. Edward Bellamy, *Looking Backward: 2000–1887* (New York: New American Library, 1960), pp. 58–64, 90; August Bebel, *Die Frau und der Sozialismus* (Berlin: Dietz, 1979), pp. 268–74, 511–14. Reinhart Kößler, 'Arbeit und Revolution. Sozialistische Perspektiven', in König et al. (eds), *Sozialphilosophie der industriellen Arbeit*, pp. 96–113.
18. Cf. Richard Saage, *Politische Utopien der Neuzeit* (Darmstadt: WBG, 1991).
19. Cf. Josef Ehmer's and Thomas Welskopp's contributions to this volume.
20. Thomas, *The Oxford Book of Work*, p. XVIII.
21. Cf. K. Peppler (ed.), *Die 'Deutsche Arbeitskunde'* (Leipzig: Bibliographisches Institut, 1940), pp. 432ff. Adolf Levenstein, *Die Arbeiterfrage* (Munich: Verlag Ernst Reinhardt, 1912), p. 225 and Klaus Tenfelde's contribution to this volume.
22. Cf. Jürgen Kocka, *Das lange 19. Jahrhundert. Arbeit, Nation und bürgerliche Gesellschaft* (Stuttgart: Klett, 2001).
23. Cf. Jürgen Kocka, *Arbeitsverhältnisse und Arbeiterexistenzen. Grundlagen der Klassenbildung im 19. Jahrhundert* (Bonn: Verlag J.H.W. Dietz Nachf., 1990).

24. Cf. John Burnett, *Idle Hands. The Experience of Unemployment 1790–1990* (London: Routledge, 1994), p. 3; Bénédicte Zimmermann, *La constitution du chômage en Allemagne. Entre professions et territoires* (Paris: Editions de la Maison des Sciences de l'Homme, 2001); Malcolm Mansfield et al. (eds), *Aux sources du chômage (1880–1914)* (Paris: Belin, 1994).
25. The argument is more fully developed in Jürgen Kocka, 'Mehr Last als Lust. Arbeit und Arbeitsgesellschaft in der europäischen Geschichte', in *Jahrbuch für Wirtschaftsgeschichte/Economic History Yearbook* 2 (2005), p. 196. Cf. Karin Hausen's contribution to this volume; Angelique Janssens (ed.), *The Rise and Decline of the Male Breadwinner Family, International Review of Social History*, supplement 5 (1998).
26. Ira Katznelson and Aristide R. Zolberg (eds), *Working-Class Formation: Nineteenth-Century Patterns in Western Europe and the United States* (Princeton: Princeton University Press, 1986); Gareth Stedman Jones, *Languages of Class. Studies in English Working Class History 1832–1982* (Cambridge: Cambridge University Press, 1983).
27. Some evidence in Jürgen Kocka, 'Mehr Last als Lust. Arbeit und Arbeitsgesellschaft in der europäischen Geschichte', in *Jahrbuch für Wirtschaftsgeschichte/Economic History Yearbook* 2 (2005), p. 198 (note 39). As Josef Ehmer argues in this volume, the understanding of work in the sense of 'Erwerbsarbeit' had not been totally absent in former centuries. But it was not before the nineteenth century that this definition of work became dominant. Cf. Richard Biernacki, *The Fabrication of Labor. Germany and Britain, 1640–1914* (Berkeley: University of California Press, 1995).
28. Cf. Thomas Welskopp's contribution to this volume. Also Thomas Welskopp, *Das Banner der Brüderlichkeit. Die deutsche Sozialdemokratie vom Vormärz bis zum Sozialistengesetz* (Bonn: Verlag J.H.W. Dietz Nachf., 2000).
29. Quotations from Conze, 'Arbeit', p. 190, 192f., 210; F. Thorwart (ed.), *Hermann Schulze-Delitzsch's Schriften und Reden*, vol. 2, (Berlin: J. Guttentag, 1910), pp. 235–43, 243; Wilhelm Heinrich Riehl, *Die deutsche Arbeit* (Stuttgart: Cotta, 1861); Anson Rabinbach, *The Human Motor. Energy, Fatigue, and the Origins of Modernity* (New York: Basic Books Inc., 1990), especially pp. 95ff., 179ff.; Joan Campbell, *Joy in Work, German Work. The National Debate 1800–1945* (Princeton: Princeton University Press, 1989); Sebastian Conrad, *Globalisierung und Nation im Deutschen Kaiserreich* (Munich: Beck, 2006); and Andreas Eckert's contribution to this volume.
30. Cf. Gerhard A. Ritter, *Sozialversicherung in Deutschland und England. Entstehung und Grundzüge im Vergleich* (Munich: Beck, 1983); E.P. Hennock, *The Origin of the Welfare State in England and Germany, 1850–1914. Social Policies Compared* (Cambridge: Cambridge University Press, 2007); Peter Wagner et al. (eds), *Arbeit und Nationalstaat. Frankreich und Deutschland in europäischer Perspektive* (Frankfurt am Main: Campus, 2000).
31. Cf. Hannah Arendt, *The Human Condition* (Chicago: University of Chicago Press, 1958), pp. 46, 126f., 135, 210, 3; Joachim Matthes (ed.), *Krise der Arbeitsgesellschaft? Verhandlungen des 21. Deutschen Soziologentages in Bamberg* (Frankfurt: Campus, 1983); Claus Offe, *Arbeitsgesellschaft. Strukturprobleme und Zukunftsperspektiven* (Frankfurt: Campus, 1984); Ulrich Beck (ed.), *Schöne neue Arbeitswelt* (Frankfurt: Suhrkamp, 1999); André Gorz, *Arbeit zwischen Misere und Utopie* (Frankfurt: Suhrkamp, 2000); Jürgen Kocka, 'Arbeit früher, heute, morgen. Zur Neuartigkeit der Gegenwart', in Kocka and Offe (eds), *Geschichte und Zukunft der Arbeit*, pp. 476–92; also see Andreas Eckert's contribution to this volume.
32. Cf. Lars Clausen, *Produktive Arbeit – destruktive Arbeit. Soziologische Grundlagen* (Berlin: Gruyter, 1988), pp. 54–105; Campbell, *Joy of Work*, pp. 296–309.
33. Cf. Heilbroner, *The Act of Work*.

2

Discourses on Work and Labour in Fifteenth- and Sixteenth-Century Germany

Josef Ehmer

Historians long placed the beginning of the 'modern age' at about 1500 and viewed the Reformation in particular as the turning point towards a Western work ethic and increased esteem for work, including manual labour.[1] In the past twenty years or so, however, the perspective has changed, and medieval roots of the modern appreciation for work have been continuously re-evaluated.[2] Patricia Ranft, one of the advocates of this new paradigm, wrote in a recent book: 'As the late Middle Ages descends upon Western history, medieval society is a society that advocates and respects work. Work saves the individual; work saves the community; both bring happiness and a better life in this world and the next.'[3] Despite this reassessment, however, many questions remain open. There are but few sources that provide us with a glimpse of the labour discourse of the high Middle Ages, the overwhelming majority penned by intellectuals, most of them theologians. It is not so easy to say to what extent their learned thoughts concerned society at large. Furthermore, medieval appreciation for work remained ambivalent and was not necessarily a stable, long-lasting phenomenon. The monastic tradition, for instance, appears as a sequence of waves in which reformers such as the Benedictines in the sixth century, the Cistercians in the early twelfth century and the Franciscans a hundred years later placed particular emphasis on the value of work. Once these orders were established and had achieved high social status, though, enthusiasm for manual labour seems to have waned.[4]

In the late Middle Ages the situation changed. Reflections on and discussions about labour and work now appeared in a wide range of contexts and seemed to be firmly rooted in the whole society.[5] Labour discourses had left the study halls of learned monks and become a matter of public interest and debate. The concept of work moved into the centre of economic, political and moral reasoning, and work became an important argument in class relations and social conflicts. In regard to England, it has been said that 'from the mid-fourteenth to the end of the fifteenth century, work arguably shaped social identity to a much greater extent than in either earlier or later times'.[6] A growing appreciation for work, including manual labour, was an important aspect of this development. There is broad consensus in historiography that the intensification of the labour discourse and a higher esteem for work were related to the fundamental socio-economic changes of this period; these included the transformation of agrarian class structures, the growth and spread of towns, as well as the expansion of rural crafts, proto-industry and mining.[7] Part of these processes was growing social differentiation. In Germany from the twelfth century onward, the so-called 'villication' system, in which the noble household and estate was the basic unit of agricultural production, was transformed into a system in which peasants worked autonomously within village communities and owed feudal rents or services. Rural society became increasingly divided between a peasant upper class on one hand and small landholders, cottagers or landless labourers on the other. Urban populations were even more highly stratified and included many who were impoverished. More and more people were dependent on wage labour to make a living, either as the exclusive source of their daily bread or as a supplement to other forms of income. In general, a number of new social groups had to define their place in society and their social relations, and some of them, such as the urban bourgeoisie or even guild artisans, gained political power in their respective communities. In this situation, the labour discourse served many needs, and concepts of work were used by various actors in the social arena.

An intensification of the labour discourse and a growing esteem for work can be observed in many European societies in the late Middle Ages, though not simultaneously. In economically and culturally developed regions, the new attitudes towards labour were evident in the thirteenth and fourteenth centuries; elsewhere, this took place later. In Central Europe, the fifteenth and sixteenth centuries were perhaps a watershed. It was during this period that a long-term shift in the meaning of the term *Arbeit* was finally completed and took hold. In Middle High German, *Arbeit* originally had a passive meaning in the sense of toil, tribulation and torment. In the thirteenth century, a process of transition began that culminated in *Arbeit* taking on an active meaning as an activity, the meaning that is common today. In connection with this transition, an entire set of related words – *Arbeit* (work), *arbeiten* (to work) and *Arbeiter* (worker) – took shape as a general concept (though they still implicitly referred to physicality and making an effort).[8] This shift in meaning also led in the sixteenth century to the formation of composite words such as *Arbeitslohn* (compensation for work), *Arbeitsleute* (workmen), *Handarbeit* (craftwork) and *Hausarbeit* (housework).[9]

The aim of the following chapter is to discuss the social contexts in which an intensification of the labour discourse and an increasing enhancement of the value of work took place in fifteenth- and sixteenth-century Germany. The main questions are: which concepts of work were used by various groups of actors; which strata within the social hierarchy referred to work in the construction of their identities; which interests can be identified in the labour discourse; and, lastly, what exactly people in German-speaking Europe meant when they spoke about *Arbeit* or *arbeiten* ('labour', 'work' or 'to work'). The historiography of work is obviously an international phenomenon, and research on the late Middle Ages in particular has greatly benefited from French, English and Italian scholarship. The following contribution, however, concentrates on German studies and makes use of different types of sources stemming from Central Europe: primarily historical and literary documents, as well as visual representations.

Work and the Social Order

One area of medieval thought in which consideration was given to the subject of work was the discourse surrounding the social and political order. The so-called 'order of the three estates' has often been cited as evidence for this.[10] This new trifunctional or tripartite social schema that took hold from the tenth century onward divided society into 'priests' (*oratores*), noble 'warriors' (*bellatores*) and 'workers' (*laboratores*). Georges Duby, in his masterful analysis of the 'initial appearance of the trifunctional schema' from the tenth to the early thirteenth century, pointed out that in this period it was part of a discourse that was carried on strictly within the ruling classes and had to do with relations among the king, bishops and noblemen, as well as, in a broader sense, among monks and knights.[11] It was not until later that the trifunctional schema became part of popular labour discourses. In German-speaking Europe, the schema appears in literary sources from the late Middle Ages, such as *Freidanks Bescheidenheit* ('Freidank's Modesty'), a collection of rhyming aphorisms going back to the thirteenth century that was repeatedly reworked in the fifteenth and sixteenth centuries and circulated widely as a handwritten manuscript and later as a printed book. Here, the three estates created by God – peasants, knights and clerics (*Bauern, Ritter und Pfaffen*) – were juxtaposed to a fourth estate of usurers and profiteers (*Wucherer*) invented by the Devil.[12] In the early fifteenth century the poet Oswald von Wolkenstein spoke of the three elements of the divine order: the clergy, the aristocracy and the workers (*geistlich, edel und arbaitär*).[13] In the late fifteenth and early sixteenth centuries this model also became the most popular iconographic or pictorial representation of the social structure. It spread across German-speaking Europe in the form of woodcuts and cheap prints.[14] In this period one might regard this tripartite schema and, in particular, its popular pictorial representation as expressions of a growing esteem for labour. To be sure, it assigned all working people to the lowest level of the social hierarchy; nevertheless, it made them an indispensable segment of that society.[15] In the popular pictorial images, work is more or less presented as agricultural work, hard physical labour in the form of men working the soil. One might well assume that the 'order of the three estates' strengthened the social position and the self-esteem of the agricultural upper class of independent peasants.[16] Nevertheless, the message communicated by the trifunctional schema remained ambivalent. It also implied that work was not exactly what one would call the task of the upper classes. Furthermore, it served as an argument against rebellious peasants who engaged in battle and prayer rather than in the work they were meant to do according to the schema.[17] Indeed, in the sixteenth century, the trifunctional schema served not only to legitimize social revolutionary movements, but also to stabilize the prevailing order as a model of the harmonious interaction of the estates whereby 'one served the other' ('einer dem anderen dienet').[18] The 'order of the three estates' was one of the many images of labour that were available for 'justifying but also for criticizing exploitation'.[19]

Further examples of the new attitudes towards work are the rich pictorial representations of labour on display in public spaces. In Central Italian and French cities from the thirteenth to the fifteenth century, the work of rural peasants and urban artisans appeared frequently on the façades of public buildings, such as churches, clock towers or guild halls, and one finds them even more frequently on the frescoes inside churches, chapels and town halls.[20] Reliefs on public fountains (as in Perugia) and clock towers (as in Florence) or paintings in public buildings illustrate the integration of labour into a good political order. This order was masterfully depicted in Ambrogio Lorenzetti's 1340 fresco of the *buon governo* in Siena City Hall, for example. Here, the orderly intermeshing of the work of rural peasants and sharecroppers, urban craftsmen and merchants, and the cultural pursuits and amusements of the nobility appear as the result and consummate expression of 'good government'.[21] Well-known examples from the transitional area between the Italian- and German-speaking worlds are the frescoes in the castle of the Bishop of Trento/Trient from the early fifteenth century, in which the 'Labours of the Months' glorify his good government.[22] All these images represented idealized visions of labour that served to legitimate the power of urban and rural elites.

The last example brings us to the pinnacle of the social hierarchy. The *Weisskunig* of Maximilian I is a particularly interesting source that shows how labour was viewed by the German Emperor in the early sixteenth century.[23] Maximilian commissioned a whole series of artistic and literary projects depicting his life and reign, one of which was an (auto)biographical work of prose that portrays his boyhood and education, as well as the wars and politics of the 'wise king'. This text – often referred to as a *Selbstbiographie* – was based on Maximilian's reminiscences, notes and dictations that were subsequently edited, amplified and supplemented by secretaries and then, at around 1514–16, reworked and provisionally completed by Maximilian's private secretary, Marx Treitzsaurwein, obviously in close cooperation with the emperor himself and in accordance with corrections he had made personally. In anticipation of the text's publication, Maximilian commissioned the foremost Augsburg workshops to produce a great number of woodcuts for the accompanying illustrations.

The subject of labour is addressed in the text and in the woodcuts in the second part of *Weisskunig*, which treats Maximilian's childhood, adolescence and education.[24] The theme running through this account is that 'kings who govern on their own (must) know more than the princes and the common folk in order for them to retain power'.[25] So what knowledge, insights and capabilities were deemed useful or indispensable to a ruling monarch and attributed to Emperor Maximilian I? It was an extremely wide-ranging canon that encompassed, among other fields, Latin and Holy Scripture; the 'seven liberal arts' (especially grammar, logic, medicine and astronomy); the art of government and an understanding of social rank; genealogy, history and the minting of coins; as well as several foreign languages. But it also included knowledge of other things that went beyond the immediate responsibilities and tasks of a sovereign and the social demands of life at court and had to do with the world of work of the lower classes. These included, for instance, administrative and bureaucratic activities, whereby the 'wise king' wrote more rapidly and more beautifully than his secretaries and was generally 'experienced and adept [at] carrying out the duties of a secretary'.[26] But they also included manual artisan activities. The young *Weisskunig* learned painting, constructing buildings out of stone and wood, the manufacture of armour, mining and the production of artillery and other things, and quickly surpassed his teachers in these areas. The illustrative woodcuts place all of these activities within the concrete framework of craftsmen's workshops and job sites: for example, in a painter's atelier, Maximilian peers over the shoulder of an artist who is completely immersed in his work; at a construction site, he chats with the stonemasons and uses a plumb-bob to make sure a wall is aligned; among a group of carpenters, he is seen holding a large saw in his hands; in the workshop of an armourer, he interrupts a journeyman going about his job.[27]

In these workshops, Maximilian is recognizable by his imperial attire and a laurel wreath. Even when he occasionally takes one of the tools of the trade in hand, he is not taking part in the labour itself, but he does show his familiarity with what the artisans do. The text portrays him as a man with direct, practical knowledge of the crafts and trades, as someone capable of personally taking charge of a job, checking the quality of the work being done, coming up with innovations and suggesting improvements. Artisanal work includes intellectual and manual elements, and the emperor tends to be more closely associated with the cerebral component. Nevertheless, the woodcuts depict him as a man for whom spending time in a craftsman's workshop is something taken completely for granted, one who is personally familiar with artisans and not ill at ease in the presence of masters, journeymen and common labourers doing physical work.

In the textual accounts and graphic depictions of the knowledge, insights and skills of the wise king, a variety of different influences can be seen. The compositions occupy a position within the tradition of humanistic pedagogy and the education of a prince as put forth in the *Fürstenspiegel*. They also contain views held by the emperor's friends who had received a humanistic education, and especially those of men whose roots were in the bourgeoisie of the imperial cities of Upper Germany. Furthermore, they reflect the perspectives of the emperor's scribes and secretaries, many of whom were sons of urban craftsmen and tradesmen, and, of course, the ideas of leading Augsburg artists were also on display in the woodcuts. But since the emperor exerted very considerable influence on the text and the graphic design, it is reasonable to assume that the *Weisskunig* also represents the emperor's own views. In the text, the usefulness of artisan training is mostly associated with military tasks such as fortress and bridge construction and improvements to armour and artillery. It should also be noted that the crafts and trades are addressed in only a small portion of the text and the series of illustrations; the space devoted to them is minute compared to the lengthy elaborations on war and political affairs. Nevertheless, there is nothing to suggest that Maximilian felt that training in the crafts and trades or having close contacts with physical, artisan labour was dishonourable or beneath his station. Quite the contrary: they are portrayed as an integral part of the educational canon and practise of a prince. The attitudes towards work expressed in Maximilian's *Weisskunig* are, indeed, an expression of a particular historical situation in which the reigning monarch displayed a great affinity for the urban bourgeoisie as part of an effort to break the power of the high aristocracy. With the expansion and bureaucratization of the central government administration from the late sixteenth century onward, nobles began to occupy high offices, and it was in this context that the role of the prince was also redefined.

Work, Conflict and Identity

Very often historians complain about the silence of the lower classes in respect to perceptions of labour and attitudes towards work, but specific historical situations, particularly social conflicts, seem to break the silence. Such situations appeared, for example, in the social movements and conflicts of the late Middle Ages, during which a high value was attributed to work. Over and over again during the peasants' revolts, the hard-working peasant was contrasted to the idle nobleman and the lazy monk. The well-known verse 'When Adam delved and Eve span/Who was then the gentleman' had been used in England in the late fourteenth century, and a hundred years later German versions of this rhyme were widespread as adages and verses in popular songs. Originally, it went: 'Als Adam reutte und Eva span / Wer was die Zeit da ein Edelmann?' Later, it changed to: 'Als Adam grub und Eva spann / Wo war denn da der Edelmann?'[28] The very same verse appeared during the great German peasants' revolt of 1524–25 and throughout the revolts of the sixteenth century. Widely promulgated maxims and poems derived from various passages in the Bible maintained that social inequality originated from the fact that the first noblemen were sluggish and lazy and did not want to work, which is why they had to force the poor people to produce food for them to eat ('Und wollt nit arbeiten, darumb betzwang er die armen leiten …').[29] The high regard in which work, and especially manual fieldwork, was held by Protestant clergymen was absorbed by peasant farmers and constituted a source of their self-esteem. Work thus became a symbol of their honour, a symbol that stood in stark contrast to aristocratic status symbols such as those associated with military service during wartime.[30]

Similar arguments are also to be found in the popular urban literature of fifteenth- and sixteenth-century Germany. They are particularly apparent in works that circulated among craftsmen and tradesmen, such as those by Nuremberg artisan-poets like Hans Rosenplüt, a smith who lived from about 1400 to about 1460, and the shoemaker Hans Sachs (1494–1576). In plays and poems, the manual skills of the peasants and craftsmen were portrayed as activities that were the basis for prosperity, respect and honour.[31] Rosenplüt's poem (from about 1450) *Von den mussiggengern und arbeitern* ('Of Idlers and Workers') is a song in praise of sweat-drenched labour; in it, work done by hand is depicted as the most ethically valuable activity there is.[32] Such conceptions of work were not only the stuff of dramas performed on market squares; they were also disseminated in flyers. The consummate example of this genre was a 1577 work by poet Johannes Fischart, a general apologia of work that maintained that there was nothing in the world that was so difficult that it could not be surmounted and managed by hard work:

Dann nichts ist also schwer und scharff
Das nicht die arbeit unterwarf
Nichts mag kaum sein so ungelegen
Welchs nicht die Arbeit bringt zuwegen.[33]

In the peasant movements and the literature read by the craftsmen and tradesmen in the cities, the high esteem accorded to work served as a means of setting 'the people' apart from the nobility. The spokespersons of 'the people' in these social movements and literary texts did not stem from the very bottom of the social hierarchy, but, rather, were for the most part members of the (lower) middle classes, peasants or master artisans. Work was also used as an argument in the case of conflicts within the urban crafts and trades, for instance, between master artisans and journeymen. For example, in 1529, the furriers' guild of Strasburg attempted to restrict the rights of the journeymen's confraternity and to limit the number of journeymen to three per workshop, which would have led to unemployment. The journeymen based their appeal on a divine right to work. In doing so, they supported their case with certain texts from the Bible, for instance, from the Books of Job and Genesis. One argument stated that: 'God created us human beings to work just as He created the birds to fly. And likewise did God command that we eat our daily bread in the sweat of our brow' ('Wir menschen [sind] von got zu der arbeit wie der vogel zu dem fliegen erschaffen auch von gott gebot in dem schweis unsers angesichtz unser brot [zu] essen').[34] There are two interesting aspects of these formulations by the journeyman furriers of Strasburg. First, they did not interpret the oft-cited verse from Genesis ('in the sweat of thy face shalt thou eat bread') in the sense of a Biblical curse, but, rather, as a positive assessment of work and of the right to work. Second, the furriers' argument made use of a specific and in the early sixteenth century not at all self-evident translation of the Biblical text. The Latin version was: 'Homo nascitur ad laborem, et avis ad volatum.' Martin Luther's translation of these lines of scripture into German rendered *labor* not as *Arbeit* (work), as the journeyman furriers did, but as *Unglück* (misfortune):[35] 'Sonder der Mensch wird zu unglück geborn …'.[36] I conclude from this that the Strasburg journeymen of the early sixteenth century simply did not regard work primarily as toil; instead, they considered it at least as much in a positive light: as a right, as well as an obligation. And it was precisely in the context of a social conflict that they used this positive attitude towards labour in order to strengthen their own position.

A visual expression of workers' positive sense of self can also be found in numerous mining communities at around 1500. The churches in these communities were decorated with frescoes, paintings and artistically designed altars that contained visual representations of the miners' workplaces. Among the most famous examples are Annaberg in the Erzgebirge mountains in Saxony, Kuttenberg/Kutná Hora in Bohemia, Flitsch in Carinthia and Rosenau/Roznava in Slovakia. The graphic depiction of their own world of work served to solidify the miners' identity and sense of community.[37] In the late fifteenth century, construction workers were also frequently depicted in frescoes, above all in conjunction with the legends associated with the founding of churches and monasteries. In them, manual labour was associated with the lives of saints.[38]

The Meaning of Work in Guild Documents

In historiography, medieval craft guilds very often serve as examples of associations whose members' identities were characterized by the indissoluble interrelationship between work and honour. The following section deals with guilds, but from another, linguistic, perspective. In fifteenth- and sixteenth-century Germany, guild documents were among the very few types of sources in which members of the lower and middling ranks speak directly about work, and in which the term *Arbeit* occurs in many different contexts. Guild statutes are a particularly significant source, since they can be found in huge numbers throughout German-speaking Central Europe, particularly in local town archives. A few statutes stem from the twelfth and thirteenth centuries, but from the fifteenth to the early nineteenth centuries they exist in large quantities.

Guilds statutes have a long-standing tradition in artisan and labour historiography, even if their interpretation is not that easy. In traditional historiography, they were very often overestimated and taken as pure and proper expressions of reality. In recent social and cultural historiography, on the other hand, statutes are quite often underestimated and not highly esteemed because they are considered as 'normative sources' that are thought to provide scant access to historical reality. Such a rather dichotomous notion of 'norm' and 'reality' is questionable in many respects, but obviously it does not capture the complex origins of late medieval and early modern guild statutes. Many of the first ones from the fifteenth and sixteenth centuries begin with a brief introduction that explains and describes where and when, how and why statutes were agreed upon and written down.[39] As a rule, master artisans from a particular trade and town or region assembled in order to solve a problem or a conflict. In many cases, journeymen also participated in such meetings. The norms they agreed upon were the result of a process of negotiation that depended on general contemporary ideologies and value systems, as well as on the respective situation. In order to give the settlement a permanent character, it was written down by one of the masters or – more often – the urban authorities were asked to incorporate the settlement into their records, thus making it part of urban legislation.[40]

Undoubtedly, guild statutes that made their way into urban legal codes and subsequently into the archives were 'norms', but these norms were close to and strongly interwoven with the practical needs of their creators. At least the early fifteenth- and sixteenth-century statutes were written in an idiom that was perhaps not too far removed from the everyday language of the artisans. In later periods, guild statutes seem to have lost much of their situational context. In structure and style, they became formalized and bureaucratized, less the expression of an actual situation and much more of a 'tradition'. There have been hardly any linguistic interpretations of German guild statutes so far, but I think that they offer access to the use and the meaning of 'work' and 'labour' in the language of early modern artisans.[41]

Arbeit or *arbeiten*, the German terms for work and labour (as a noun and a verb), appear frequently in guild statutes.[42] *Arbeiten* is, first of all, the activity of the master in the sense of the performance of his craft. In this context, *arbeiten* and *das Handwerk treiben* (pursuing one's trade) are used synonymously: 'whosoever ... is desirous of carrying on his handicraft' ('ein yeder, der ... das hantwerch arbaitten wil ...') or 'wants to work at and ply a trade'. However, *arbeiten* is also the activity of the *Knecht* (as the shop assistant was frequently referred to up to the fifteenth century) or *Gesellen* (journeymen, the term increasingly used from the fifteenth century on). The statutes regulate under which conditions journeymen were allowed to work (*arbaiten lassen*) or – for instance, as a result of misbehaviour – forbidden to do so (*ze arbaiten verboten*). In the case of shop assistants and journeymen – that is, employees who worked for a wage – *arbeiten* is used in these sources synonymously with 'having work' or 'being employed' (*knechts weis arbaiten* or *ainem maister arbaiten*). Journeymen may 'find' work or not (*nicht arbait fund*); travelling journeymen may like to work in the respective town or not (*hie aribaiten wolt*). Thus, for this group, *arbeiten* also means to be employed or to have a job. Activities performed by apprentices are only rarely described by the term *Arbeit*. Apprentices 'learn' or 'serve'; they must 'serve out their years of learning' (*lernjar ausdiene*).

However, in these sources, *Arbeit* also has a second meaning, namely, the piece of work that is the result or the product of this labour. The 'work done' is the finished output. This work can be good or bad, i.e., correspond (or not) to guild rules and consumer expectations. The sources speak of 'good and righteous' work (*gute und gerechte arbait*), as well as of that which is 'unrighteous and bad' (*ungerecht pöse arbait*). Commercial activities beyond the purview of the guild or contrary to its rules are also characterized as 'covert' or 'irregular work' (*ungewöhnlich arbait*), which shows very clearly the connection between work and honour. There is strong a relationship between *Arbeit* as an activity and *Arbeit* as a finished piece of work. In the guild sources, it is above all those activities that lead to the output of a product that are characterized as *Arbeit.* In the statutes I have studied, this term is not used to refer to the activities of dealers or merchants. They do not work; they vend (*vail haben*).

For masters and workers, the term *Arbeit* had a general meaning of practising a craft or trade or carrying on an occupation. In addition to the general term *Arbeit*, specialized terms were also used in the guild regulations to refer to the various steps in the particular production process such as 'to full' and 'to spread' (by cap and sock knitters), 'to sift' (by millers), etc. When guild sources mention *arbeiten* or *Arbeit,* then the reference is not to a concrete activity, but, rather, to practising a trade or occupation in general. Furthermore, what is meant thereby is more or less *Erwerbsarbeit.*

This conclusion is strengthened by contemporary gender-specific terminologies of work. Lyndal Roper has identified two meanings of *Arbeit* in sixteenth-century sources from Augsburg: on the one hand, it was an 'ideology of labour, which did not distinguish between men's and women's work'.[43] For example, quarrelling couples were officially admonished to 'work faithfully with each other' ('treulich miteinander [zu] arbaiten').[44] Nevertheless, the expression used more than any other to designate the activities undertaken jointly by the 'working couple' (*Arbeitspaar*, a term coined by Heide Wunder) was *Nahrung* (sustenance) ('... wie 2 eeleutt sich ernören ...'), which meant the way a married couple nurtured or supported one another. It was this concept of *Nahrung* that bridged 'the divide between labour within the workshop and what we might term housework – the labour of cooking, cleaning and caring for a workshop labour force. The primacy of its emphasis on feeding serves to enhance the importance of the woman's contribution, rather than seeing it as not real work in the genuine sense.'[45] On the other hand, the second meaning of 'work' accentuated the difference between the sexes and referred strictly to occupational activities and gainful employment, which was regarded as a male domain. For example, this was brought out in texts in which masters, journeymen and government officials mandated the exclusion of women from a craft or trade and established punishments for any master who set 'maids to do the work, which is fitting for journeymen to do' ('aine Magdt uber die Arbait setzt die den gesellen zu machen geburet').[46] There are other artisanal sources as well that indicate that an activity performed by women certainly could be designated as *Arbeit* as long as it was a guild-recognized occupation. For instance, this was so in the case of the manufacture of veils in Augsburg that, even in the sixteenth century, was done almost exclusively by women ('fast nur weyber arbeit').[47] This also applied to a master's widow managing her deceased husband's workshop. Some of the guild regulations from Wiener Neustadt like the tailors' in 1531 specified that 'a widow is allowed to work for only one year in our handicraft' ('ain jede wittib unseres hanndtwerch nuer ain jar arbaiten muge'). Other craftsmen demanded the complete exclusion of widows from carrying on the trade; the Augsburg goldsmiths did so in 1550 on the grounds that 'women understand nothing of the goldsmiths' work' ('frawen versteen sich nichtz auf der goldschmid arbeit').[48]

Work and Labour in the Context of Poverty, Charity and Social Policy

One of the most important areas of the labour discourse at the turn from the Middle Ages to the modern period has to do with the relations among work, poverty and charity. Throughout Europe we can observe a fundamental change in attitudes towards work and, conversely, towards not working.[49] One of the essential elements of this transformation was a radical debasement of poverty, which entirely lost any of the high spiritual esteem in which it had formerly been held and came to be regarded as a deplorable consequence of idleness and sloth. This was accompanied by a new attitude towards the poor. The giving and receiving of alms came to be viewed with disdain and replaced by social welfare policies, the aim of which was to restrict idleness and to foster, or even enforce, labour. Beggars were disparaged and their negative image contrasted to that of workers. But since poverty and beggary obviously could not be eliminated, this new approach to social welfare policymaking manifested itself in the effort to construe and juxtapose two groups of poor people. One was the group of 'idlers' who were supposedly unwilling to work and should be punished for this unwillingness. The second group included those who, according to the authorities, wished to work but could not. These persons were supported through charity or granted the right to beg (in the form of beggars' licenses and insignia to be displayed on their clothing). They were accepted as the 'dignified' poor in contrast to the 'unworthy' idlers. A second line of differentiation intended to separate the local poor, particularly long-term residents, from foreigners and those from abroad (*fremd und auslendisch*).[50] Only the locals should receive charity or the permission to beg, while foreigners should be run out of town.

These changing attitudes towards poverty and labour have been analysed throughout Europe in numerous studies. In England and France, they led to a wave of labour laws, poor laws or proclamations against beggars and vagabonds as early as the mid-fourteenth century.[51] In German-speaking Europe, the same trend occurred somewhat later. There is increasing evidence of this occurring from the second half of the fifteenth century onwards, above all in the cities where municipal authorities endeavoured to stigmatize poverty and to wage a war against foreign beggars and particularly against so-called 'strong beggars' (*starke bettler*), who were supposedly able to work. With countless regulations, the municipal authorities attempted to establish and enforce the differentiation between the supposedly 'work-shy' beggars and those who were accepted as being unable to work, for instance, due to their age or physical handicaps. These regulations were part of a wider discourse about labour and poverty, which included literary and philosophical texts, as well as theological writings, sermons, political addresses and the like.

In fifteenth- and sixteenth-century Germany, the new discourse is particularly well documented for the big cities and for urbanized regions such as the Upper Rhine Valley and Saxony, where wage labour was widespread and the problem of poverty became aggravated.[52] Here, we find manifold sources in which the terms 'labour' and 'work' play a central role. To give just a few examples: the first Nuremberg paupers' and beggars' ordinance from 1478 proclaimed that even those men and women beggars who were allowed to beg within the city walls 'ought not spend a workday lolling about begging for alms in front of the churches, but instead ought to do spinning or some other work that is within their capacity' ('sollen an keinem wercktag vor den kirchen an der pettelstat müssig sitzen, sondern spynnen oder annder arbeit, die in irem vermügen wer, thun'). It was said that children of impoverished parents, having reached eight years of age, should be given over to other people to work as domestic servants (*zu diensten*).[53] Sebastian Brant's satirical poem *Narrenschiff* ('Ship of Fools'), a work published in Basel in 1494 and widely circulated in German-speaking Europe, included among the 'fools' what the poet labelled 'unworthy' beggars, idlers, vagabonds and mendicant friars.[54] His mockery targeted those who begged in spite of being young, strong and healthy, and thus able to work.[55] In the city of Altenburg, Saxony in 1523, the preacher Wenceslaus Linck published a text entitled *Von Arbayt vnd Betteln wie man solle der faulheyt vorkommen/vnd yederman zu Arbeyt ziehen* ('On Work and Begging: How to Prevent Laziness and Get Everyone to Work').[56] Erasmus of Rotterdam, in his *Education of a Christian Prince* (published in Latin in 1516; many German translations since 1521), advised sovereigns 'either to force idlers to work or to drive them forth from the city' ('*zwing sie entweders zu arbeyten oder treib sie us auß der Stadt*').[57] The first state-wide beggars' ordinances such as the 1541 law in Saxony strove to achieve this objective and threatened 'idlers who do not want to work' with penalties or banishment from the province.[58]

There is one subject upon which the documents from the late fifteenth and early sixteenth centuries that contain contributions to the new labour discourse had astoundingly little to say: the subject of unemployment. The stark juxtaposition of the worker and the beggar suppressed the question of whether there was enough work for poor people to do. One exception was a Leipzig beggars ordinance from about 1520 that permitted poor day-labourers (*armen tagelohnern*) women as well as men – to engage in begging in winter when they were unable to obtain work ('*im wynter, so sye nicht Arbeyt haben kontten*'), but only until there was again work to be done ('*dye arebeyt angehtt*').[59] This is one of the few sources from the early sixteenth century that acknowledged fluctuations of employment, seasonal unemployment and, in general, dependency on the labour market situation, a problem of enormous importance to the lower classes.

The new urban welfare policy generated a large quantity of written testimony and, thus, historical source material in which poor people themselves had their say. Applicants for a beggars' license had to cite their reasons and describe their circumstances. Their testimony was written down and many of these documents have been preserved in municipal archives. There were frequent arrests and interrogations of numerous beggars who lacked official authorization, and their statements were recorded in writing too. These documents represent something like a dialogue between officials and members of the lower classes. They are of interest to us here, since a discussion of work was of prime importance on both sides. The authorities wanted to establish whether an impoverished person did not want to work or was unable to work, and, if so, why. Members of the lower classes cited various reasons why they could not work and were therefore forced to rely on charity or had to beg for alms. In addition to reasons like illness, injury and old age that were cited and, as a rule, accepted as justification for the individual's inability to work, there was an additional argument that assumed central significance, namely that the person 'has no work' or 'can find no work'. 'I've been out of work for half a year;' 'I have no work and no bread;' and 'I can't find work in my trade' are arguments that are cited over and over again in the relevant sources from the sixteenth to the eighteenth century.[60]

Individual testimony of this sort was summarized under the heading 'Mangel an Arbeit' (lack of work), which was also expressed in welfare policy. As mentioned previously, the top two items on this agenda were suppression and dispensing charity. However, by the early seventeenth century at the very latest, a third variant appeared in German cities: measures that could be labelled in modern terminology as labour market policy or employment policy. In areas where there was a persistent lack of work, the authorities, first and foremost municipal officials, began to think about how they could 'create work' for the poor. While the idea of the 'workhouse' in sixteenth-century Germany had more of an ideological than practical meaning, authorities in some cities had already launched elaborate building projects in order to provide relief for construction labourers and 'to give [them] work'. The city fathers of Augsburg, one of the most important sixteenth-century German centres of commerce and the crafts and trades, decided to go ahead in the early seventeenth century with extensive renovations and expansion of public facilities (including a new city hall) that would give the city a total makeover in the style of the Renaissance. One argument in favour of these construction projects, which nearly exhausted the city's finances, was that they constituted steps to alleviate the 'lack of work' and to provide work for the poor – above all, many construction labourers.[61]

The subject of unemployment and labour market instability has assumed increasing significance in recent research on labour and poverty. This provides a new way of looking at the interrelationship between work and begging, one that opposes the discourse of the fifteenth and sixteenth centuries. Studies of the lives and fates of individual beggars and labourers show that many members of the lower classes had to rely on combined income from both of these sources in order to survive. Working and begging were not so very different ways of life; rather, they were 'two facets of a single mode of existence'.[62]

Work and the Reformation

Beginning in the late fifteenth century, the discourse surrounding labour and poverty intensified in theological writings as well. Among the most frequently cited biblical passages were the words of Paul (2 Thess. 3:10: 'If any one will not work, let him not eat.') and Job (5:7: 'But man is born to trouble ...'). Martin Luther and many of his Protestant successors fiercely denounced idleness, voluntary poverty and beggary in any form, though their wrath was particularly directed against non-native beggars (*frembde betler*).[63] The labour discourse of the Lutheran Reformation strengthened the new attitudes towards labour and poverty, even if it carried with it an ambivalent perception of work. On one hand, it was rooted in a particular medieval monastic tradition that praised labour because it meant the pain, suffering and sacrifice of discipleship following Christ's passion on the cross. In this tradition, work constitutes, above all, a duty. On the other hand, the Lutheran perception implied esteem for labour, be it the physical toil of the peasants and artisans or the administrative activities of the authorities and the clergymen's ecclesiastical work. To perform one's calling was a way of serving God and the community of Christians, and, since every form of work was done for the Lord, it could also be performed with joy.[64]

Nevertheless, the prevailing opinion in recent research is that the Reformation constituted a considerably less decisive turning point in the history of labour than has long been assumed. Max Weber's approach to the relation between the Reformation and the Western concept of work, which dominated the historical discussion throughout the twentieth century, has been modified on two points. First, it is now claimed that he underestimated the work ethic and the meaning of work in the Middle Ages;[65] second, that his central thesis does not relate that much to sixteenth-century Protestantism, but primarily to Calvinism and, above all, Anglo-American Puritanism of a later period. For Weber, in seventeenth- and eighteenth-century Calvinism and Puritanism, work ultimately attained the status of an 'absolute end in itself' (*absoluter Selbstzweck*).[66] This particular form of 'Protestant ethic' promoted rational, systematic, steady and unflagging work within a strict temporal and spatial order. Work of this sort comes across as part of a 'planned regimentation of one's own life', 'continuous self-control' as the basis of 'conducting one's life in an orderly fashion' and 'rationally designing one's entire existence'.[67] In the second edition of his study, Weber limited his main thesis to radical Protestant currents, mostly in Anglo-Saxon regions, and to a 'small-scale capitalist class' made up of 'the petit bourgeoisie and farmers ... just emerging [as nascent entrepreneurs]'.[68] For these small groups, the internalization of an ascetic occupational and work ethic appears to be thoroughly plausible. In the Protestant world of sixteenth-century

8. Wolfgang Haubrichs, 'Das Wortfeld "Arbeit" und "Mühe" im Mittelhochdeutschen', in Postel (ed.), *Arbeit im Mittelalter*, pp. 91–106, esp. p. 105.
9. Konrad Wiedemann, *Arbeit und Bürgertum. Die Entwicklung des Arbeitsbegriffs in der Literatur Deutschlands an der Wende zur Neuzeit* (Heidelberg: Carl Winter Universitätsverlag, 1979), p. 49f.
10. Duby, *Die drei Ordnungen*; Oexle, 'Die funktionale Dreiteilung als Deutungsschema der sozialen Wirklichkeit in den ständischen Gesellschaften des Mittelalters', in Winfried Schulze (ed.), *Ständische Gesellschaft und soziale Mobilität* (München: Oldenbourg, 1988), pp. 19–51.
11. Duby, *Die drei Ordnungen*, p. 498.
12. Werner Lenk, *'Ketzer'lehren und Kampfprogramme. Ideologieentwicklung im Zeichen der frühbürgerlichen Revolution in Deutschland* (Berlin: Akademie Verlag, 1978), pp. 20, 179, 181.
13. Werner Conze, 'Arbeiter', in Otto Brunner, Werner Conze and Reinhart Koselleck (eds), *Geschichtliche Grundbegriffe*, vol. 1 (Stuttgart: Ernst Klett Verlag, 1972), p. 216.
14. Lipburger, '"Quoniam si quis nun vult operari, nec manducet ..."', p. 75.
15. Le Goff, *Time, Work and Culture in the Middle Ages*, pp. 53–57; Seibt, 'Vom Lob der Handarbeit', p. 164; Oexle, 'Die funktionale Dreiteilung', pp. 19–51.
16. Lipburger, '"Quoniam si quis nun vult operari, nec manducet ..."', pp. 70–75.
17. Duby, *Die drei Ordnungen*, p. 480.
18. Winfried Schulze, *Deutsche Geschichte im 16. Jahrhundert 1500–1618* (Frankfurt am Main: Suhrkamp, 1987), p. 28f.
19. Paul Freedman, *Images of the Medieval Peasant* (Stanford: Stanford University Press, 1999), p. 23.
20. Duby, *Die Zeit der Kathedralen*, pp. 163, 463–66; Postel (ed.), *Arbeit im Mittelalter*, p. 8.
21. Gerhard Jaritz, 'Der Kontext der Repräsentation oder: Die "ambivalente" Verbildlichung von Arbeit im Spätmittelalter', in Postel (ed.), *Arbeit im Mittelalter*, p. 258; Quentin Skinner, 'Ambrogio Lorenzetti: The Artist as Political Philosopher', in Hans Belting and Dieter Blume (eds), *Malerei und Stadtkultur in der Dantezeit. Die Argumentation der Bilder* (München: Hirmer, 1989), pp. 85–103.
22. Jaritz, 'Der Kontext der Repräsentation', p. 259.
23. R. Buchner et al. (eds), *Kaiser Maximilian I. Weisskunig* (2 vols, Stuttgart: W. Kohlhammer, 1956, vol. 1: text; vol. 2: illustrations). Cf. Hermann Wiesflecker, *Kaiser Maximilian I. Das Reich, Österreich und Europa an der Wende zur Neuzeit*, vol. 5 (Vienna: Verlag für Geschichte und Politik, 1986), pp. 315–17; Clemens Biener, 'Entstehungsgeschichte des Weißkunigs', in *Mitteilungen des Österreichischen Instituts für Geschichtsforschung* 44 (1930): 83–102; 'Ausstellung "Maximilian I."', *Catalog* (Innsbruck: Tyrolia, 1969), pp. 139–40; Jan Dirk Müller, 'Zwischen Repräsentation und Regierungspraxis: Transformation des Wissens in Maximilians Weiskunig', in Gerhild Scholz Williams and Stephan K. Schindler (eds), *Knowledge, Science, and Literature in Early Modern Germany* (Chapel Hill: University of North Carolina Press, 1996), pp. 49–70.
24. *Weisskunig* vol. 1, pp. 221–31; vol. 2, pp. 20–51.
25. Ibid., p. 223.
26. Ibid., p. 226.
27. Ibid., vol. 2, pp. 2, 30–32, 50.
28. Lenk, *'Ketzer'lehren und Kampfprogramme*, p. 33; Seibt, 'Vom Lob der Handarbeit', p. 175.
29. Lenk, *'Ketzer'lehren und Kampfprogramme*, p. 34.
30. Wiedemann, *Arbeit und Bürgertum*, pp. 153, 214.

31. Ibid., pp. 233–38.
32. Lipburger, '"Quoniam si quis nun vult operari, nec manducet ..."', p. 80 f.; Seibt, 'Vom Lob der Handarbeit', p. 176; Wiedemann, *Arbeit und Bürgertum*, pp. 204–6.
33. Wiedemann, *Arbeit und Bürgertum*, p. 258.
34. Based on Job 5:7 and Genesis 3:19; cf. Lipburger, '"Quoniam si quis nun vult operari, nec manducet ..."', p. 80.
35. Lipburger, '"Quoniam si quis nun vult operari, nec manducet ..."', p. 80 f.; Seibt, 'Vom Lob der Handarbeit', p. 176; Wiedemann, *Arbeit und Bürgertum*, p. 80.
36. Incidentally, the current standardized translation of the Bible reads very similarly in German: '... *der Mensch ist zur Mühsal geboren, wie Feuerfunken, die hochfliegen*' ('Man is born to tribulation like sparks flying up from a fire').
37. Jaritz, 'Der Kontext der Repräsentation', pp. 246–50.
38. Ibid., pp. 257–59.
39. This practise was by no means restricted to German-speaking Europe; see the examples from fourteenth-century Paris cited by Jacques Foviaux, 'Discipline et réglementation des activités professionelles à travers les arrêts du Parlament de Paris (1257–1382)', in Hamesse and Muraille-Samaran (eds), *Le travail au moyen âge,* p. 239.
40. Josef Ehmer, 'Traditionelles Denken und neue Fragestellungen zur Geschichte von Handwerk und Zunft', in Friedrich Lenger (ed.), *Handwerk, Hausindustrie und die historische Schule der Nationalökonomie* (Bielefeld: Verlag für Regionalgeschichte, 1998), p. 39.
41. As an example of the usefulness of linguistic analysis cf. Maarten Prak, 'Individual, Corporation and Society: The Rhetoric of Dutch Guilds (eighteenth century)', in Marc Boone and Maarten Prak (eds), *Individual, Corporate and Judicial Status in European Cities (Late Middle Ages and Early Modern Period)* (Louvain: Apeldorn, 1996), pp. 255–79.
42. The following examples stem from Viennese and Lower Austrian guild statutes from the fifteenth and sixteenth centuries. Most of them have not been edited and published yet, but there also exists a recent edition of guild statutes from Wiener Neustadt, a small town some fifty kilometres south of Vienna; cf. Martin Scheutz, Kurt Schmutzer et al. (eds), *Wiener Neustädter Handwerksordnungen (1432 bis Mitte des 16. Jahrhunderts),* Fontes Rerum Austriacarum, Fontes Juris, vol. 13 (Vienna: Böhlau, 1997).
43. Lyndal Roper, *The Holy Household. Women and Morals in Reformation Augsburg* (Oxford: Oxford University Press, 1989; German transl., *Das fromme Haus. Frauen und Moral in der Reformation,* Frankfurt am Main: Campus, 1995), p. 42.
44. Ibid., p. 41; German phrases are taken from the German translation of this book, pp. 41–45.
45. Roper, *The Holy Household,* p. 41.
46. Ibid, p. 44.
47. Claus Peter Clasen, *Die Augsburger Weber: Leistungen und Krisen des Textilgewerbes um 1600* (Augsburg: Jan Thorbecke, 1981), p. 10.
48. Roper, *The Holy Household,* p. 46
49. Geremek, 'Le refus du travail dans la société urbaine du bas moyen âge', pp. 379–94; Oexle, 'Arbeit, Armut, "Stand"' im Mittelalter, pp. 67–79.
50. Helmut Bräuer, *Der Leipziger Rat und die Bettler. Quellen und Analysen zu Bettlern und Bettelwesen bis in das 18. Jahrhundert* (Leipzig: Leipziger Universitätsverlag, 1997).
51. Geremek, 'Le refus du travail dans la société urbaine du bas moyen âge', pp. 379–94; Anthony Musson, 'Reconstructing English Labor Laws: A Medieval Perspective', in Uebel and Robertson (eds), *The Middle Ages at Work,* pp. 113–32.

52. Helmut Bräuer, 'Arbeitende Bettler? Bemerkungen zum frühneuzeitlichen Bettler-Begriff', in *Comparativ. Leipziger Beiträge zur Universalgeschichte und vergleichenden Gesellschaftsforschung* 3 (1993), pp. 70–91; Katharina Simon-Muscheid, '"in rebmesser hat sine frowe versetzt für 1 ß brotte." Armut in den oberrheinischen Städten des 15. und 16. Jahrhunderts', in Helmut Bräuer (ed.), *Arme – ohne Chance? Kommunale Armut und Armutsbekämpfung vom Spätmittelalter bis zur Gegenwart* (Leipzig: Leipziger Universitätsverlag, 2004), pp. 39–70.
53. Bräuer, Arbeitende Bettler?, p. 80.
54. Simon-Muscheid, "Ein rebmesser hat sine frowe versetzt für 1 ß brotte", in Bräuer (ed.), *Arme – ohne Chance? Kommunale Armut und Armutsbekämpfung vom Spätmittelalter bis zur Gegenwart*, p. 49 f.
55. '*Mancher dut bättlen by den joren / So er wol wercken möht und kundt / Und er jung / starck ist / und gesundt*' ('And some beg for alms year in and year out / Though able to work / young / healthy / and stout', Sebastian Brant, *Narrenschiff*, ed. Manfred Lemmer (Tübingen 1986), *lxiii.* 22–30, quoted in Simon-Murscheid 2004, p. 50. In the southwest of Germany, in addition to *arbeiten*, the term *wercken* was used synonymously (as above).
56. Bräuer, *Der Leipziger Rat und die Bettler*, p. 29.
57. Wiedemann, *Arbeit und Bürgertum*, p. 215.
58. Announcement by the City Council of Leipzig of the publication of the Provincial Beggary Ordinance enacted by Duke Henry of Saxony, April 16, 1541; in Bräuer, *Der Leipziger Rat und die Beffler*, p. 114 f.
59. Ibid., pp. 110–14, here 111.
60. Many examples in Helmut Bräuer and Elke Schlenkrich, *Armut und Armutsbekämpfung. Schriftliche und bildliche Quellen bis um 1800 aus Chemnitz, Dresden, Freiberg, Leipzig und Zwickau. Ein sachthematisches Inventar* (Leipzig: Leipziger Universitätsverlag, 2002).
61. Bernd Roeck, *Elias Holl. Architekt einer europäischen Stadt* (Regensburg: Friedrich Pustet, 1985), p.87.
62. Bräuer, Arbeitende Bettler?, p. 89
63. Expressed with particular clarity in 'An den christlichen Adel' ('Address to Christian Nobles'); Wiedemann, *Arbeit und Bürgertum*, pp. 115–52.
64. Wiedemann, *Arbeit und Bürgertum*, pp. 148–52, 158–67.
65. Ranft, *The Theology of Work*, p. 5; Lipburger, '"Quoniam si quis nun vult operari, nec manducet ... "', pp. 47–86.
66. Weber, *Die protestantische Ethik und der 'Geist' des Kapitalismus.*
67. Ibid., pp. 79–82.
68. Ibid., p. 149.
69. Oexle, 'Arbeit, Armut, "Stand" im Mittelalter', p. 79.
70. Simon-Muscheid, '"Ein rebmesser hat sine frowe versetzt für 1 ß brotte"', p. 42.
71. Herman Pleij, *Der Traum vom Schlaraffenland* (Frankfurt am Main: S. Fischer, 1997), p. 67.
72. Robert Darnton, *Das große Katzenmassaker. Streifzüge durch die französische Kultur vor der Revolution* (München: Hanser, 1989).

3

Beginnings of the Anthropology of Work: Nineteenth-Century Social Scientists and Their Influence on Ethnography*

Gerd Spittler

Introduction

When we hear of the 'anthropology of work', most of us think first of non-industrial, non-capitalist work, as it was and is studied by social anthropologists. According to this pattern, the recently published *International Encyclopedia of the Social and Behavioral Sciences* includes four articles on work, devoted to the historical, sociological and anthropological aspects. I wrote the anthropological article, which basically refers to the anthropological study of non-industrial work.[1] For many years now an anthropological research group at Bayreuth University has done extensive fieldwork in Africa, studying the work of peasants, herdsmen, artisans, factory workers and service employees.[2] Despite the diversity of topics, all these studies have one thing in common: they do not reduce work to a system, but consider the additional dimension of human action. According to this view, the performance of work requires many capabilities, such as physical strength, manual skills, knowledge, perseverance and motivation. Work brings satisfaction or frustration. The workers may be eager or unwilling. They can interpret work as meaningful or meaningless. They can see it as a purely instrumental activity or can turn into play, a struggle or an art. They can endow it with an ethical meaning (work ethic) going beyond its immediate benefit.

If we understand the anthropology of work not in the narrow sense of the social anthropology of non-industrial work, but in a broader sense, which takes anthropology as the 'science of man' seriously, then we should examine work primarily as human action and not as part of a technical, ecological or any other system. In addition to empirically-oriented social anthropology, we should also consider the tradition of philosophical anthropology. In the course of many years of intensive study in this field, I have come to the conclusion that a critical discussion of nineteenth-century scholars is necessary for two reasons: it is important for historical reasons, because the first social anthropologists who made studies of work were influenced by these scholars. It is also necessary for systematic reasons, because we can still learn from these authors today.[3]

These nineteenth-century social scientists were influenced by philosophers like Kant and Hegel, by German classical writers like Herder, Goethe and Schiller, by romantic writers like Friedrich Schlegel and Joseph Eichendorff, and by the French utopian socialist Charles Fourier. Their work adhered basically to two opposing positions. For some writers, the desire to work is part of man's nature. The most radical anthropology of work, based entirely on the principle that work is pleasant, was formulated by Charles Fourier (1772–1837). According to him, if work is properly organized, everyone can find attractive work (*travail attrayant*).[4] But for most authors, the aversion to work, the *horror laboris,* is natural to man. The question, then, was to find out what makes people want to work.

German Social Scientists of the Long Nineteenth Century

These writers had a considerable influence on social scientists, who were more empirically oriented. In Table 3.1, I give the titles of their writings relating to the subject of work. On the left is the year of first publication in German. Years in parentheses indicate that the year of publication was much later than the year of writing. On the right are the English translations with the years they were first published.

The writings of these social scientists on the subject of work can be interpreted from different perspectives. Here, I will concentrate on two questions which I consider central for a general anthropology of work: the performance problem and the rationality problem. With respect to performance, it should be stressed that work is not realized by a few select people, but has to be done by the majority. The performance of work necessitates knowledge and skills. It has to be carried out for many hours, days, weeks and even years. This requires concentration and perseverance. Work is often strenuous: how are people able to bear this strain? The rationality problem deals with efficiency. In order to be successful, work has to be done effectively, and it is effective when the desired result is achieved. But effectiveness and efficiency are different things: 'efficiency' for human work means that a job is done with a minimum expenditure of time and effort.

The most famous sentence about work in the writings of Karl Marx comes from *The German Ideology.* Here, Marx and Engels formulate their vision of the future as a 'communist society, where nobody has one exclusive sphere of activity, but each can become accomplished in any branch he or she wishes … to hunt in the morning, fish in the afternoon, rear cattle in the evening, criticize after dinner, just as I have in mind, without ever becoming hunter, fisher, herdsman or critic'.[5]

Table 3.1: German Social Scientists of the Long Nineteenth Century

Karl Marx (1818–1883)		
1844 (1932)	*Ökonomisch-Philosophische Manuskripte*	*Economic and Philosophical Manuscripts* (1959)
1845/46 (1932)	*Die deutsche Ideologie* (together with Friedrich Engels)	*The German Ideology* (1964)
1857 (1939)	*Grundrisse der Kritik der Politischen Ökonomie*	*Outlines of a Critique of Political Economy* (1959)
1867	*Das Kapital,* vol. 1	*Capital,* vol. 1 (1887)
Wilhelm Heinrich Riehl (1823–1897)		
1861	*Die deutsche Arbeit*	
Karl Bücher (1847–1930)		
1893	*Die Entstehung der Volkswirtschaft*	*Industrial Evolution* (1901)
1896	*Arbeit und Rhythmus*	
Wilhelm Ostwald (1853–1932)		
1909	*Energetische Grundlagen der Kulturwissenschaft*	
Max Weber (1864–1920)		
1904/05	*Die protestantische Ethik und der Geist des Kapitalismus*	*The Protestant Ethic and the Spirit of Capitalism* (1930)
1920/21	*Gesammelte Aufsätze zur Religionssoziologie*	
1921/22	*Wirtschaft und Gesellschaft*	*Economy and Society* (1968)

Sources: Karl Marx, *Das Kapital,* vol. 1 (Berlin: Dietz, 1867); *Capital,* vol. 1 (London: S. Sonnenschein, Lowrey 1887); *Ökonomisch-philosophische Manuskripte* (Stuttgart: Kröner, 1932; written 1844); *Grundrisse der Kritik der Politischen Ökonomie* (Moscow: Foreign Language Publishing House, 1939; written 1857/58); *Economic and Philosophical Manuscripts of 1844* (Moscow: Foreign Language Publishing House, 1959); *Outlines of a Critique of Political Economy* (Moscow: Foreign Language Publishing House, 1959); *Marx Engels Collected Works* (MECW), vol. 5: *The German Ideology* (London: Lawrence and Wishart, 1976); MECW, vol. 28: *Outlines of a Critique of Political Economy* (London: Lawrence and Wishart, 1986); Marx and Friedrich Engels, *Die deutsche Ideologie* (Stuttgart: Kröner, 1932; written 1845/46); Marx and Engels, *The German Ideology* (Moscow: Progress Publishers, 1964). Wilhelm Heinrich Riehl, *Die deutsche Arbeit* (Stuttgart: Cotta, 1861). Karl Bücher, *Die Entstehung der Volkswirtschaft* (Tübingen: Laupp, 1893; English edition, *Industrial Evolution,* New York: H. Holt and Company, 1901); *Arbeit und Rhythmus* (Leipzig: Reinicke, 1896; 4th edn 1909). Wilhelm Ostwald, *Energetische Grundlagen der Kulturwissenschaft* (Leipzig: Dr. Klinkhardt, 1909). Max Weber, 'Die Protestantische Ethik und der Geist des Kapitalismus', in *Archiv für*

Sozialwissenschaft und Sozialpolitik 20 (1904): 1–54; *Archiv für Sozialwissenschaft und Sozialpolitik* 21 (1905): 1–110; expanded version in *Gesammelte Aufsätze zur Religionssoziologie*, vol. 1 (Tübingen: Mohr, 1920), pp. 17–206; *The Protestant Ethic and the Spirit of Capitalism,* including 'Prefatory Remarks', trans. Stephen Kalberg (Los Angeles: Roxbury, 2002; 1st edn, 1930); '"Energetische" Kulturtheorien', in *Archiv für Sozialwissenschaft und Sozialpolitik* 29 (1909): pp. 575–598; reprint in *Gesammelte Aufsätze zur Wissenschaftslehre* (Tübingen: Mohr, 1968), pp. 400–426; *Gesammelte Aufsätze zur Religionssoziologie*, 3 vols. (Tübingen: Mohr, 1920/21); *Wirtschaft und Gesellschaft* (Tübingen: Mohr, 1972; 1st edn 1921/22); see also Günther Roth and Claus Wittich (eds), *Economy and Society*, 3 vols. (New York: Bedminster, 1968).

Fourier's influence is evident in this sentence; in fact, it is nothing other than a paraphrase of the daily routine of a rich man, described by Fourier in *Le nouveau monde industriel* (1829). Later on, however, Marx became more critical of Fourier. In a long paragraph in the *Grundrisse*, which gives a good introduction to Marx's concept of work, he compares pre-capitalist, capitalist and post-capitalist forms of labour:[6]

> 'Thou shalt earn thy bread in the sweat of thy brow!' was the curse which Jehovah laid on Adam. And so A. Smith conceives labour to be a curse. To him, 'rest' appears as the adequate state, as identical with 'liberty' and 'happiness'. It does not seem remotely to occur to him that the individual 'in his ordinary state of health, strength, spirits, skill, dexterity' also needs a normal portion of labour and the transcendence of 'rest'. Certainly, the volume of labour itself appears to be externally determined by the aim to be attained and the obstacles to its attainment which have to be overcome by labour. But, equally, A. Smith has no inkling that the overcoming of these obstacles is in itself a manifestation of freedom – and, moreover, that the external aims are [thereby] stripped of their character as merely external natural necessity, and become posited as aims which only the individual himself posits, that they are therefore posited as self-realization, objectification of the subject, and, thus, real freedom, whose action is, precisely, work. Of course, Smith is right that in its historical forms of slave labour, serf labour and wage labour, work is always repulsive and always appears as externally imposed, forced labour, and as against that not-work as 'liberty and happiness'. This holds doubly: it is true of this antagonistic work and of everything connected with it; it is true of work which has not as yet created the subjective and objective conditions (or also of the pastoral etc., state which has lost them) for work to become *travail attractif*, to be the self-realization of the individual, which in no way implies that work is pure fun, pure amusement, as in Fourier's childishly naïve conception. Really free work, e.g., the composition of music, is also the most damnably difficult, demanding the most intensive effort.[7]

Here, Marx criticizes Adam Smith, who – according to Marx – sees labour as a curse and does not understand its anthropological destination. Men need a normal portion of work. It is their means of attaining self-realization even when, or precisely when, there are obstacles to be overcome. In contrast to Fourier, Marx observes that self-realization through work is not the same as mere fun, but that free labour, such as is required for artistic work, is very serious, the most intense exertion. Marx admits that Smith is right in his opinion that in class societies (slave-keeping, feudal and capitalist societies), labour does appear as forced labour and non-labour as freedom and happiness. He believes that previously, for instance in pastoral societies, work was attractive and a means of self-realization. He assumes that this will also be the case in the future as soon as the necessary subjective and objective conditions exist. Capitalism itself creates the necessary preconditions for a positive future of labour. A fully developed economy makes demands which are quite different from those made by the economy of hunters, fishermen and shepherds. The difference lies, above all, in the economy of time. This affects not only the organization of the production process, but also requires of the individual an ability which the fisherman or shepherd lacks and which he only learns in capitalism: he must be able to organize his time. How does he acquire this ability? He learns it by capitalist control and by the rhythm of the industrial machinery. In the last sentence of the above-quoted paragraph, Marx characterizes the artistic work of composing as 'damnably difficult'. Here, he follows a tradition which stands in complete opposition to Fourier's idea of playful work: the tradition of German idealism. In this tradition, work is not seen as play, but as an ethical action which is basic to human education (*Bildung*).

This perspective is even more pronounced in *Die deutsche Arbeit* ('German Work'), which was written by Wilhem Heinrich Riehl at about the same time (1861). The writings of Riehl (1823–1897), a contemporary and conservative opponent of Marx, centre around the family and the people (*Volk*), not social classes. Riehl's best-known and most influential work is *Die Familie* ('The Family'), which was first published in 1854.[8] His model here is the old life and customs of the peasantry. Anyone who knows this work of Riehl will be surprised and irritated by the modernistic perspective in *Die deutsche Arbeit.* Here, the object of interest is not the old-fashioned peasant and his humdrum routine, but farmers who have been modernized by the pastor, the teacher and the policeman. Riehl concedes that the old peasant with his undeveloped labour power (*Arbeitskraft,* a term used not only by Marx, but also by Riehl) should not be despised, but the future – and Riehl's esteem – belong to the 'rational farmer', rather than to the 'real old-fashioned peasant'.

How does the change from old-fashioned peasant to rational farmer come about? For this, we have to look at the consequences of religion. Riehl refers to this as the 'Arbeitsschule des großen Stils' ('work school in the grand style'). Unlike the Reformation, which had a direct effect on craftsmen and peasants, the new movement at first only affects intellectual workers: philosophers, poets, scholars. It is not a religious movement, for its attitude to the church is indifferent, if not disapproving, but it is influenced by Protestantism in that it is based on the spirit of free research. Riehl is not so naive as to assume that the ideas of poets and thinkers can be translated easily into practice:

> The Reformation had an effect on the people, because that is where it had its roots; but literary humanism used an external lever. Thus, the former gripped the common man directly, and the latter indirectly. But it gripped him. Although the peasant did not sing Goethe's songs as he sang Luther's songs, he did learn to cultivate his field in a new way, because the thinkers and poets had learned to think and write in a new way.[9]

On the basis of these descriptions, it is hard to see why the book is entitled *Die deutsche Arbeit.* Riehl makes it clear that the spirit of work postulated by him is a new phenomenon, and in no way an old-established German model. To a certain degree, Riehl's idea of 'German work' is a programme, rather than a description of reality. Riehl wanted to contribute to national pride with his 'Predigt der Arbeit' ('Sermon on Work') by giving Germans a concept of work which unites them and ensures their political success. For in the competition between nations, efficient work counts even more than winning wars. Idle peoples have been 'worked away' by more industrious ones, even after obtaining political victory.[10]

Karl Bücher belonged to the so-called 'Historische Schule der Nationalökonomie' ('Historical School of Political Economy'). He spent the greater part of his academic career as professor of political economy (*Volkswirtschaft*) in Leipzig. As one of the pioneers of economic anthropology in the first decades of the twentieth century, he influenced Malinowski, Thurnwald, Firth, Mauss, Chayanov and Polanyi. Today he is almost forgotten, at least in anthropology. But he has been forgotten unjustly, as I intend to show, for his contributions to the anthropology of work are still fundamental today. We are interested here in that part of his work in which he discusses the economy of 'primitives' (*Naturvölker*). These questions are treated in two books: *Die Entstehung der Volkswirtschaft* (*Industrial Evolution*)[11] and *Arbeit und Rhythmus.*[12] This latter book (*Work and Rhythm*), which has never been translated into English, is of particular interest to our topic. Bücher starts from the assumption that the labour of the 'primitives' (*Naturvölker*) is particularly strenuous due to their imperfect technical implements. In addition, the primitiveness of their tools means that their work processes are very long. 'Everywhere work is performed by badly armed or unarmed hands and requires a high degree of that quality which primitive people lack most: perseverance.'[13]

What solution is offered for this apparent contradiction? In his answer, Bücher distinguishes the production of goods for permanent use from that of goods for immediate consumption (food). In a subsistence economy, the goods people produce are for their own use. The process of creation itself gives satisfaction. People even do a lot of unnecessary work – unnecessary in the eyes of the European – because hardly any objects are made without some artistic adornment, which involves additional time-consuming work processes. Most work, however, is not connected with the production of goods for permanent use, but with goods for immediate consumption (food). Here, the mechanisms we have just described are not effective. How are primitive people able to devote so much time to the production of goods for immediate consumption, which bring them no long-term satisfaction? The answer, which is already given in the title of the book, is work and rhythm.

Work that is performed rhythmically enables the worker to keep up monotonous activities for a long time. Rhythmical bodily movements performed while sowing or digging the ground help the individual to persevere in his work. In many forms of labour, the work itself does not produce a rhythm, but this can be created artificially with musical instruments and songs. At the end of his research, Bücher discovers a 'world of cheerful work': the economic principle, or the principle of the least effort, is lacking. 'Here, work is neither a burden, nor an inevitable fate, nor a marketable commodity ... everywhere, playfulness and fun, rhythm and song, companionship and willingness to lend a hand, a real economic world of child's play.'[14] Work, play, music and poetry form a single unit.

Bücher's innovation is that he takes the labour of 'primitive peoples' seriously in a way that no one had done before him. When he investigates the aesthetic form given to craft products, we are reminded of Marx's description of the medieval craftsman as a (semi-)artist. In his description of the playful character of work, he refers to Fourier. What is completely lacking in his writings is the German idealist tradition, with its stress on 'work as an ethical deed' (Riehl). What is equally lacking is the analysis of work as a rational action. For this question, we have to turn to Wilhelm Ostwald and Max Weber.

Wilhelm Ostwald, professor of chemistry in Leipzig, was awarded a Nobel Prize in 1909 for his achievements in the field of physical chemistry. What connection does this renowned chemist have with the anthropology of work? In *Energetische Grundlagen der Kulturwissenschaft* ('The Energetic Principle in the Cultural Sciences'), a series of lectures published in 1909, Ostwald attempts to set up 'energetics' as a new basis for *Kulturwissenschaften* (cultural sciences).[15] In the first lecture, 'Die Arbeit' ('Work'), Ostwald explains the physical concept of work and distinguishes it from the everyday concept. In the scientific sense (as used in physics and technology), it is a definable and measurable quantity which can be applied not only to humans and animals, but also to machines. A fundamental concept in energetics and cultural development is 'efficiency of energy use' (*Güteverhältnis*), which Ostwald explains in his second lecture. 'Cultural work' consists of improving the efficiency with which raw energy is transformed into useful energy. For example, while a paraffin lamp only converts 2–3 per cent of the chemical energy into light, a modern gas lamp converts 10 per cent.

Ostwald applies notions from energetics not only to technology, but also to 'higher' cultural phenomena. He takes law as an example. In the early stages of culture, disputes were settled by violence, and people spent the greater part of their time and energy on fighting, leaving them little time for other interests. Through law, the energy wasted in battle is turned into useful energy: efficiency of energy use is improved. In the lectures mentioned below, Ostwald broadens this notion to all cultural areas, such as language. From the point of view of energetics, the sounds of a language must be simple and easy to understand, and the words should not be too long and difficult to pronounce. The meaning of all words must be unambiguous. Since living languages cannot be made to meet these requirements, Ostwald pleads in favour of an artificial language.

At first, Ostwald's ideas do not appear to be very useful for creating an anthropology of work, even though he attaches great deal of importance to the concept of work. He deliberately removes this concept from its context of action and reduces it to efficiency. However, if one reads his book as an attempt to bring about Utopia, then it appears more interesting. For Ostwald, cultural development is nothing other than higher efficiency in any cultural field. Indirectly, though, he shows how little this principle is effective outside the technical field. For example, in his utopian demand for a rational language, he clearly shows how far removed all living languages are from this ideal. In his 'Monistische Sonntagspredigten' ('Monistic Sunday Sermons'), Ostwald tried to interest a large public in his ideas. One of these Sermons (9 August 1913) is devoted to Frederick Taylor's 'Scientific Management' (1911), because this system increases labour productivity. The systems of Taylor and Ford were in turn influenced by Ostwald's energetic principles (Herbst 1920).[16]

Of all the books treated here, there is no doubt that in addition to *Capital* by Karl Marx, Max Weber's *The Protestant Ethic and the Spirit of Capitalism* (1904) is the most famous and the best known beyond specialist circles.[17] This makes my argumentation both easier and more difficult: easier because it is possible to refer to what is already known, and more difficult because *The Protestant Ethic* is not the most important text for our topic. For more essential texts, we must also look at Weber's other works on the sociology of religion: first, *Gesammelte Aufsätze zur Religionssoziologie*, parts of which were translated into English at different places.[18] It includes the essay from 1904/5 in revised form, as well as new extensive studies on 'Confucianism and Taoism',[19] 'Hinduism and Buddhism'[20] and 'Ancient Judaism' (English, 1952).[21] In addition to these case studies, the following theoretical writings are also important: 'Prefatory Remarks' and 'Introduction to Economic Ethic of the World Religions' in 'Interim Considerations: Religious Rejections of the World and Their Directions' (all in vol. 1).[22] Second, we must look at the systematic chapter 'Religious Groups (Sociology of Religion)' in *Economy and Society*.[23]

For Weber, the decisive feature of modern capitalism is the 'rational organization of work'. It is based on a rationalized conduct of life, which is linked to two religiously based conditions: first, *Entzauberung der Welt* ('disenchantment of the world'), i.e., the elimination of magic; and second, ascetic *Weltbearbeitung* ('remaking of the world').[24] For Weber, rational behaviour is highly improbable.

If it dominates in wide areas of modern society, this is not self-evident, but something which requires explanation. Rationality has a history, and shedding light on this history is the central concern of Weber's sociology. Weber's view of humanity does not postulate man as an *animal rationale*, but exactly the opposite: man is naturally irrational, controlled by drives and passions instead of reason. Man is initially a part of nature. The achievement of culture, and of religion in particular, consists in having transformed a natural being into a cultural being. Primitive peoples still largely exist in the former state, in which magical thinking is typical. Later on, and up to the present time, this also applies to the 'masses', a term which Weber uses frequently, but never defines.

Theory and Empirical Experience

Marx and Weber share the idea that capitalism is the 'most fateful power of our modern life' (Weber). Both are therefore interested in analysing it and explaining how it arose. Both find the key to understanding capitalism in the specific character of work. However, in their explanations of the emergence of the capitalist organization of labour, Marx and Weber differ considerably. Weber considers that its cause is to be found in a specific religious ethic, Marx in the economic and technical structure of capitalism itself. It is remarkable that Weber fails to mention the aspect of joy and play in work. The tradition of Fourier and Bücher does not interest him. Weber belongs to another German tradition, which places economy and work in a religious context, like Riehl. However, Riehl's and Weber's theories are only superficially alike, in the sense that they both claim there is a connection between Protestantism and the ethic of work. For Riehl, however, Protestantism is a factor only indirectly, because it is more open to Enlightenment principles and science.

Nevertheless, Riehl sees himself as a preacher when he tries to contribute to German pride with his 'Predigt der Arbeit'. Even Wilhelm Ostwald, who was the most radical atheist among these scholars, uses the instrument of the 'Monistic Sunday Sermons' to spread his ideas on rationality. Max Weber published a long review of Ostwald's book in which he criticizes the constant mixing of empirical science with value judgements.[25] He accuses Ostwald of not limiting himself to a consideration of the 'energetical' side of culture, as he announced he would, but of simply equating cultural progress with improved efficiency of energy use.

This question leads us to the different theoretical approaches of the authors. At the end of the nineteenth century a distinction was made in Germany between the nomothetic *Naturwissenschaften* (natural sciences) and the descriptive *Geisteswissenschaften* or *Kulturwissenschaften* (humanities or cultural sciences). It is characteristic of our authors that they cannot be clearly fitted into this schema. An exception is Wilhelm Ostwald, who supported a monistic social science modelled on the natural sciences. All other authors had to struggle with the problem that, on the one hand, they recognized historical variety, but, on the other hand, did not simply describe events, but wanted to analyse them theoretically. The different attempts at solving this problem are still worth looking at today.

Marx distinguishes different historical periods which can be ordered in an evolutionist scheme. The concepts of the most developed society, namely, capitalism, are suitable for analysing the preceding periods, because what is contained only *in nuce* in earlier periods is fully developed here. This applies, for instance, to the concept of work. Only in capitalism can a general and abstract concept of work be established which smoothes out the differences between various kinds of work. This can then be used to analyse work in earlier forms of society. However, Marx voices a reservation with a reflection worthy of an anthropologist: 'The example of labour strikingly demonstrates that even the most abstract categories, despite their being valid – precisely because they are abstractions – for all epochs, are, in the determinateness of their abstraction, just as much a product of historical conditions and retain their full validity only for and within these conditions.'[26]

Bücher goes one step further: 'Every phenomenon of national economy is a phenomenon in the evolution of civilization. In scientifically defining it and in explaining the laws of its development, we must always bear in mind that its essential features and its dynamic laws are not absolute in character; or, in other words, that they do not hold good for all periods and states of civilization.'[27] This introduction to the chapter entitled 'The Rise of National Economy' is directed against the abstract, ahistorical kind of economics, as founded by Smith and Ricardo and continued by the Austrian school. However, Bücher is not defending the historical school of economics, which simply describes historical developments, while using uncritically terms taken from modern political economy. Bücher pleads for a special terminology, based on abstract notions but, in contrast to Ricardo and the Austrian school, adapted to the early forms of economy.

Of all the authors, Weber shows the greatest sympathy for the historiographical tradition. More than all the others, he presents to the reader extensive historical material, instead of only using historical examples as illustrations. But he is not just telling stories; he claims to be constructing a theoretical analysis. He finds the solution to this dilemma in his well-known 'ideal type'. At first he applies the ideal type to historical individuals (Protestant ethic, capitalism), and later also to *genera* (domestic economy, church, state). A historically comparative perspective becomes important for Weber, seen particularly in his 'Collected Essays in the Sociology of Religion'. Reconciling history and theory is easier for evolutionists than for historically oriented scholars. Marx and Bücher had fewer problems in this respect than Riehl and Weber did. But a closer look puts these differences into perspective. Marx and Bücher had a feeling for historical uniqueness and even published historical studies. Weber, who strictly rejected evolutionism in his writings and emphasized the uniqueness of historical events, is not free from evolutionist thinking when he speaks of 'stages of development' or 'stages of rationalization'.

Up to now we have spoken only of theory. What about the empirical basis of these theories? I place these authors among the social scientists, because they try to link theory and empirical experience. With the exception of Ostwald, who includes social reality only in anecdotal form, all the others base their arguments on empirical evidence. In their writings, they refer to the historical and sociological literature available at the time. Those who focus on culture in their analysis, like Riehl and Weber, do not restrict themselves to a history of ideas, but try to record the realization of these ideas in daily practice. Some authors also include their own experience and studies in their works. As Engels notes in the subtitle of his 1887 book *The Condition of the Working Class in England,* his work is based on 'personal observation and authentic sources'.[28] In the case of Riehl, many observations made in the course of his research in German folklore (*Volkskunde*) are included in *Die deutsche Arbeit.* Bücher includes childhood experiences in *Arbeit und Rhythmus.* He even suggests that students should write doctoral theses on the subject and sends questionnaires to mission societies. Weber is the only one to carry out a sociological study himself ('On the Psychophysics of Industrial Work') and devotes much space to methodological reflections.[29] However, his analyses of the development of the rational organization of work are comparative historical studies based mainly on careful reading of the available literature. The results of ethnographical research are taken into account only by Bücher. Considering the state of ethnographical research at that time, this could only be of modest assistance.

All authors present the different forms of work as contrasts and frequently as dichotomies. For Marx, capitalist labour is different from all earlier forms. Riehl compares bourgeois, urban work with the work of peasants. Bücher contrasts the cheerful work of primitive people with work in modern factories, where man has become a slave of the never-resting machine. Ostwald sees a gulf between the stupidity of primitive people and modern rational man, who is guided by science. Weber contrasts the rational conduct of life in Protestantism with various forms of irrationality. These dichotomies are suggested by theoretical premises such as evolution, or civilized versus primitive peoples. Such dichotomies are criticized by anthropologists today, not only because of the obsoleteness of the theoretical approaches, but because they represent a construction of cultural otherness which says more about the authors than about the societies they describe.

Regardless of whether or not this is true, there remains another aspect to be discussed. Scientific study always begins with alienation (*Verfremdung*) of its object. This applies to both the natural sciences and the humanities. As long as an object is close and familiar, it cannot be studied scientifically. Theoretical reflection can begin only when an object is seen from a distance. The construction of a state of nature by Locke or Rousseau may have been very far removed from historical reality, but it opened the way for radical ideas about the basis of society, ideas which are still discussed today. The same reasoning applies to the authors presented here. Their radical comparisons, their reflections on the beginnings of mankind (Bücher), their comparisons with cultures far back in history (Bücher, Weber) or with contemporary societies that are far removed culturally and spatially (Bücher), their utopian visions of *travail attrayant* within a social condition of *harmonie* (Fourier), of work as an ethical deed (Riehl) or of cultural work with the aim of improving the efficiency of energy use (Ostwald), made it possible for them to think about central elements of work such as performance and rationality. For the formation of theories, these extreme positions were fruitful, more fruitful than anthropological approaches which are wary of the construction of otherness. The social scientists of the long nineteenth century can therefore be considered as the founders of the anthropology of work, not only because they were the first, but because they created foundations which still hold today.

This theoretical justification of radical positions does not mean that empirical evidence is not important. Radical theories are not necessarily right. There is a lack of careful ethnographic studies of work in the nineteenth century, which brings us to the next section: the beginnings of an ethnography of work.

The Beginnings of an Ethnography of Work

A serious ethnography of work was started only in the twentieth century. This was due to three professional anthropologists: Karl Weule (1864–1926), Richard Thurnwald (1869–1954), and Bronislaw Malinowski (1884–1940). These three scholars began their academic career in different disciplines: Weule in geography, Thurnwald in law, Malinowski in science. Influenced by the above mentioned social scientists, they all became interested in the anthropology of work. Later on they did extensive fieldwork in Melanesia and Africa and ended up as professors of anthropology in Leipzig, Berlin and London. As a result of their own extensive fieldwork, they brought new insights to this subject. The following writings were particularly important for a newly developing ethnography of work:

Weule, *Negerleben in Ostafrika* (*Native Life in East Africa*); Weule, *Die Urgesellschaft und ihre Lebensfürsorge,* (1912);
Thurnwald, *Die Gestaltung der Wirtschaftsentwicklung aus ihren Anfängen heraus* (1923);
Thurnwald, *Werden, Wandel und Gestaltung der Wirtschaft im Lichte der Völkerforschung* (*Economics in Primitive Societies),* 1932);
Malinowski, *The Economic Aspects of the Intichiuma Ceremonies* (1912)
Malinowski, *Labour and Primitive Economics* (1925)
Malinowski, *Magic, Science and Religion* (1925)
Malinowski, *Coral Gardens and Their Magic* (1935).[30]

All three anthropologists showed an interest in the subject of work throughout their anthropological career, both in their fieldwork and in many published articles and books. As anthropologists and ethnographers, they introduced new perspectives, and yet they had close links to the social scientists discussed above.

Weule studied in Leipzig under Ratzel, and Malinowski under Bücher and Ostwald. Thurnwald and Malinowski were familiar with the writings of Max Weber. The three anthropologists understand work as an economic activity, but they distinguish real work from more diffuse activities. In an early essay, Malinowski ('The Economic Aspect of the Intichiuma Ceremonies' 1912) distinguishes 'primitive labour' and 'economic labour'. The latter is characterized by the following features: it is 'socially organized and collective, continuous, regular and periodical, performed not according to the whim of the moment or some immediate impulse, but done with forethought according to a systematic plan and with due consciousness of its aim'.[31]

The image of man on which these anthropologists base their definitions of work is the same as Bücher's. Man has a natural dislike of strenuous, regular work. He prefers spontaneous and irregular games, sports and artistic activities. In contrast to Bücher, who is obviously attracted to this 'world of cheerful work', however, the attitude of the anthropologists remains at least ambivalent, if not disapproving. This is 'primitive' and not 'economic' labour (Malinowski). Work performed 'at one's own whim' is of no use in respect to colonial labour requirements (Thurnwald) and, from an evolutionary point of view, it is also primitive. Improvements in work discipline have often only been achieved by the use of force, but Thurnwald sees this in evolutionary terms as the expression of a 'self-domestication' which helps man to gain increasing control over his environment.

Bücher's question as to how sustained, strenuous work is possible (the problem of performance) is also important for Weule, Thurnwald and Malinowski. They accept Bücher's answer (aesthetic pleasure, dance, music, rhythm), but they also bring other factors into play. Malinowski's main theme is the stabilizing and disciplining function of magic. But he is also interested in the role played by needs (hunger) and institutional structures (work in company, family relations, leadership in the village) in promoting work. Malinowski also emphasizes an aspect of performance which we normally associate with theatre or sports: the public display of work and of the results of work as an important stimulus for high performance. Since these three authors all focus on the question of the necessary conditions for strenuous, sustained work, the question as to whether work may be subject to limits recedes into the background. Only Malinowski remarks once *en passant* that sanctions may be imposed against anyone whose work reveals excessive ambition.

No one has described the different aspects of performance more precisely than Thurnwald: knowledge and skill, performance and compulsion, care and accuracy, perseverance and patience, discipline and force, diligence and laziness, effort and fatigue, devotion and indifference, ability to withstand strain, concentration and the intensification of work, intertwining of mental and physical elements, feelings of pleasure, but also of a tedious and dreary burden. The ethnographic perspective reveals an aspect of performance which was scarcely touched on by the older theoreticians: skill in the handling of simple tools. Thurnwald sums this up most clearly: 'the primitive tool is much more at the service of man than man is dependent on it'. But the most exact descriptions of skilful work performed with simple tools are given by Malinowski and especially Weule. Malinowski's account of the way gardeners use their digging sticks is an ethnographic masterpiece, but such examples are rare in his work, whereas Weule's writings are full of such descriptions.

Not only performance, but also the rationality of work is an important subject for the three anthropologists. Weule does not doubt that the work processes of primitive people are rational, taking into account their limited technical equipment. What separates 'them' from 'us' is science. Primitive people's knowledge of nature is empirical, not scientific. It is based on their concrete experience of nature. But this knowledge is affected by their magical and religious conceptions.

Thurnwald's analysis is much more thorough compared to Weule's. Any use of tools, including among primitive peoples, is based on a specific 'technical theory'. The ability to think logically is a basic property of the human mind, but each mentality has its own logic. Besides notions of causality that are similar to ours, primitives have magical and mystical ways of thinking. But this distinction is made by us, and emic analysis shows a different picture. From the emic point of view, there is no separation between technical and magical practices. The rationalization of work has a history which, for Thurnwald, does not simply begin with the separation of empirical experience and science (Weule) or with the influence of higher religions (Weber). In hunter-gatherer societies, women's work is more rational, because they strive to ensure a regular supply of food for their young children. Peasants are more inclined to face up to problems instead of fleeing like the hunter-gathers. This leads to a further rationalization of human behaviour. The cattle-keeping activities of herdsmen serve as training in 'planning how to make the best use of restricted means' and 'weighing up the expenditure of effort against benefits obtained'; this is a step forward in the process of rationalization. The distinction between work and other activities – in other words, the objectivization of work – is linked to a system of social stratification. The development of rationalization is an evolutionary process and irreversible.

Malinowski's great contribution to the rationality debate is his discussion of the relationship between magic and religion on the one hand, and work and technology on the other. His ideas in this respect changed over the years. In his early works (e.g., 'The Economic Aspect of the Intichiuma Ceremonies' 1912), religion and magic are the only forces capable of making people perform regular, coordinated and strenuous work. Primitive people do not distinguish between magic and technology. In his studies of the Trobrianders, however, Malinowski assumes that they make a strict distinction between technology and magic. Not only is this technology based on empirical experience, it is raised by Malinowski – at least in his famous essay 'Magic, Science and Religion' – to the rank of a science.[32] The role of magic is not denied; on the contrary, it fulfils its very rational functions in other areas: the timing of work, or control over good and bad luck. For Malinowski, however, the fact that work is based on empirical experience does not mean that it is organized only on the basis of technical efficiency. The 'economic principle of the maximum of effect for the minimum of effort' is true only with reservations. Rather it is the joy derived from work and artistic motives that dominates.

Malinowski's discussion of magic is interesting not only as a response to the theories of magic proposed by Frazer and Weber. Its lasting value lies above all in his unprecedented, detailed description of magic acts and their verbal transcriptions. These ethnographic descriptions are still of interest today and permit interpretations which may deviate from Malinowski's own. It can be said of all three anthropologists that their most important new contribution to the study of work is their field research. All three of them carried out fieldwork themselves. Weule's trip was the shortest (six months), while Thurnwald spent a total of seven years in the field and Malinowski spent three years. Malinowski made intensive observations over a long period and in a specific area where living among the 'natives' and a good command of the language were important. Malinowski's place in the history of anthropology rests on this research method, which later became known as 'participant observation'. Weule and Thurnwald, on the other hand, made long journeys, passing through many areas in the style of the classic expedition. Thurnwald occasionally expresses regret at this, but also finds theoretical justifications for it. His comparative perspective requires the collection of information in different places. Weule's particular methodological merit lies not in his (short) period of field research, but in his technological experiments with simple tools, which make him a pioneer in this area.

Conclusion

Instead of a conclusion I want to situate my chapter in relation to Jürgen Kocka's introduction: 'Work as a Problem in European History'. My contribution fits quite well into the part of his discussion that deals with the utopian future of work. The starting point of my research on work was not the work of the nineteenth-century scholars I have mentioned, but the fieldwork I carried out alone and with our Bayreuth-based research group in Africa. In a second phase, I read many books and articles on the anthropology of work, including the anthropology of industrial and post-industrial work. It was only then that I turned to nineteenth-century scholars and utopians. The reason was less my historical interest than a feeling that I could learn from them. The diversity of ethnographic findings concerning work could often be better interpreted by the ideas of the utopians than by those of today's scholars.

In the first part of his introduction, Kocka speaks about *Begriffsgeschichte* (the history of concepts). In this field, my contribution is certainly disappointing. Neglecting *Begriffsgeschichte* may be a sin in the eyes of historians; for most social anthropologists it is a deadly sin. As social anthropologists, we have first of all to grasp the different cultural meanings of things. We call this the emic, in opposition to the etic, perspective. We now have many ethnographic publications that concentrate on the emic meaning of work in different societies. Work may be seen as play, as a fight, as an art, as a ritual; it may be embedded in other activities or strictly differentiated from them; or there may be a specific work ethic, grounded in religion, the family or a professional group. Investigating the meaning of work is important. Our group has done a great deal of research on this issue, especially on the role of Islam in African societies. However, in my contribution I have not addressed these questions. My starting point was the fact that in all societies throughout history, most people have had to work in the sense of spending hours, days, months and years performing activities to make a living. This constitutes the performance question. The semantics of work can explain performance, but only partly. There are many other factors which have to be considered, but are neglected in current research. That is why it is worthwhile turning to the ideas of nineteenth-century scholars, who were the founders of the anthropology of work.

Notes

* This paper has been translated by Ruth Schubert.

1. Cf. Gerd Spittler, 'Work: Anthropological Aspects', in *International Encyclopedia of the Social and Behavioral Sciences* 24 (2001): 16,565–16,568.
2. For an overview, see Kurt Beck and Gerd Spittler (eds), *Arbeit in Afrika* (Münster: Lit, 1996); also Hélène d'Almeida-Topor, Monique Lakroum and Gerd Spittler (eds), *Le travail en Afrique noire – Représentations et pratiques à l'époque contemporaine* (Paris: Karthala, 2003).
3. This argument is elaborated in my book *Founders of the Anthropology of Work. German Social Scientists of the 19th and Early 20th Centuries and the First Ethnographers* (Berlin: Lit. 2008).
4. Charles Fourier, *Le nouveau monde industriel et sociétaire* (Paris: Bossange, 1829).
5. Cf. *Marx Engels Collected Works* (MECW), vol. 5, p. 47, 1976.
6. Karl Marx, *Grundrisse der Kritik der Politischen Ökonomie* (Moscow: Foreign Language Publishing House, 1939; written 1857/58).
7. Cf. MECW, vol. 28, p. 530.
8. Wilhelm Heinrich Riehl, *Die Familie* (Stuttgart: Cotta, 1854).
9. Riehl, *Die deutsche Arbeit* (Stuttgart: Cotta, 1861), p. 308.
10. Ibid., p. 62.
11. Karl Bücher, *Die Entstehung der Volkswirtschaft* (Tübingen: Laupp, 1893).
12. Bücher, *Arbeit und Rhythmus* (Leipzig: Reinicke, 1896).
13. Ibid., p. 13.
14. Ibid., p. 475.
15. Ostwald, *Energetische Grundlagen der Kulturwissenschaft* (Leipzig: Dr. Klinkhardt, 1909).
16. Edgar Herbst, *Der Taylorismus als Hilfe in unserer Wirtschaftsnot* (Leipzig: Anzengruber, third edition 1921), p. 9.
17. Weber, *The Protestant Ethic and the Spirit of Capitalism*, transl. by Stephen Kalberg (Los Angeles: Roxbury, 2002; 1st edn, 1930).
18. Weber, *Gesammelte Aufsätze zur Religionssoziologie* (Tübingen: Mohr, 1920).

19. Max Weber, *The Religion of China: Confucianism and Taoism*, ed. and trans. Hans G. Gerth (New York: The Free Press, 1951).
20. Max Weber, *The Religion of India: Hinduism and Buddhism*, ed. and trans. Hans H. Gerth and Don Martindale (New York: The Free Press, 1958).
21. Max Weber, *Ancient Judaism*, ed. and trans. Hans H. Gerth, (New York: The Free Press, 1952).
22. Weber, *The Protestant Ethic and the Spirit of Capitalism.*
23. Günther Roth and Claus Wittich (eds), *Economy and Society*, 3 vols. (New York: Bedminster, 1968).
24. Cf. Weber, *Gesammelte Aufsätze zur Religionssoziologie*, vol. 1, p. 263.
25. Weber, '"Energetische" Kulturtheorien', in *Archiv für Sozialwissenschaft und Sozialpolitik* 29 (1909), pp. 575–598, reprint in: *Gesammelte Aufsätze zur Wissenschaftslehre, third edition 1968*, pp. 400–26.
26. Cf. MECW 28, p. 42.
27. Cf. Bücher, *Industrial Evolution* (New York: H. Holt and Company, 1901), p. 83.
28. Friedrich Engels, *The Condition of the Working Class in England* (New York: Lovell, 1887).
29. Max Weber, 'Zur Psychophysik industrieller Arbeit', in *Gesammelte Aufsätze zur Soziologie und Sozialpolitik* (Tübingen: Mohr, 1908), pp. 61–255.
30. Karl Weule, *Negerleben in Ostafrika. Ergebnisse einer ethnologischen Forschungsreise* (Leipzig: Brockhaus, 1908); Weule, *Native Life in East Africa. The Results of an Ethnological Research Expedition* (London: Sir Isaac Pitman and Sons, 1909); Weule, *Die Urgesellschaft und ihre Lebensfürsorge* (Stuttgart: Kosmos, 1912); Richard Thurnwald, 'Die Gestaltung der Wirtschaftsentwicklung aus ihren Anfängen heraus', in Melchior Paly, *Erinnerungsgabe für Max Weber*, vol. 1 (München: Duncker and Humblot, 1923), pp. 273–333; Thurnwald, *Werden, Wandel und Gestaltung der Wirtschaft im Lichte der Völkerforschung* (Berlin: de Gruyter, 1932); Thurnwald, *Economics in Primitive Communities* (Oxford: Oxford University Press, 1932); Bronislaw Malinowski, 'The Economic Aspect of the Intichiuma Ceremonies', in *Festskrift tillegnad Edvard Westermarck* (Helsingsfors: J. Simelii Arvinjars, 1912), pp. 81–108; Malinowski, 'Labour and Primitive Economics', in *Nature* 116 (1925): 926–30; Malinowski, 'Magic, Science and Religion', in Joseph Needham (ed.), *Science, Religion and Reality* (London: Sheldon Press, 1925), pp. 20–84; Malinowski, *Coral Gardens and Their Magic*, 2 vols. (New York: American Book Co., 1935).
31. Malinowski, 'The Economic Aspect of the Intichiuma Ceremonies', p. 225.
32. Malinowski, 'Magic, Science and Religion', pp. 20–84.

4
The Vision(s) of Work in the Nineteenth-Century German Labour Movement

Thomas Welskopp

Karl Marx's 'Critique of the Gotha Programme'

If Karl Marx had had his way and if the German labour movement had acted as a faithful and dedicated follower of his theory, the concept of 'work' disseminated in the publications and rallies of nineteenth-century socialists in Germany would have been of a decidedly unemphatic, almost ascetic character. For Marx, 'work' was not conceivable independently of the prevailing social relations of production, which, in turn, marked specific formations of society at different stages in the history of mankind. Therefore, 'work', as an abstract notion with an ostensibly inherent value, was for Marx nothing more than an ideological phrase representing how the bourgeoisie had cut out human labour for the purposes of the capitalist economy. 'Work' could only assume this generalized meaning where it was exchangeable like any other commodity. The commodification of 'work', however, actually stripped human gainful activity from all contents and intrinsic value and reduced it to its commercial utilization. The value 'work' produced was not what the labourer had achieved in his efforts, now embodied in the product; rather, it was what the capitalist could yield by selling the product in the market.

The epic of 'work' under capitalism was a story of loss. 'Work' had become alienated from its actual performer. The workers' activities were not of their own making, but determined by employers and the machinery at their disposal. The products workers had manufactured confronted them as anonymous commodities in the market for goods, as if they had nothing to do with the workers' physical expenditure. In Marx's view, 'work' under capitalism thus was nothing more than alienation and exploitation. For him, the processes of alienation and exploitation would hopefully advance to a point at which the workers would experience these features of capitalist 'work' in their extremes. Only disillusionment with 'work' as a value in itself would prepare the proletariat for its true task: revolutionizing the relations of production by class struggle and thereby liberating 'work' from its present subjugated state.

In 1875, however, the German representatives of social democracy seemed, for Marx, to be far away from this necessary disillusionment – a prerequisite that he thought would enable the labour movement to undertake the required political action. Instead, the two social democratic party organizations that existed in Germany by that time celebrated their unification into the Socialist Workers' Party of Germany at the joint convention in Gotha with a new platform. This 'Gotha Programme' was a document of eclectic pragmatism, its prime purpose being that 'Lassalleans' and 'Eisenachers' could identify enough with its contents to consent to unification. For Marx, however, forsaking theoretical purity for broad acceptability bordered on treason, or at least ideological sell-out. Filling almost two pages, he commented furiously on the first sentence of the new programme, and his biting criticism targeted the very concept of 'work' that made up its introduction. The sentence said: 'Work is the source of all wealth and of all culture, and, since gainful work is only possible in society and through society, its unimpaired rewards rightfully belong to all members of society.'

Marx branded this formulation as bourgeois and romantic. 'The bourgeois have very good reasons to attribute to work supernatural creative abilities; for it follows just from the dependency of work on natural resources that Man, who does not possess any other property besides his own labour power, has to serve as slave to other Men, who have made themselves proprietors of the material conditions of work, under all social and cultural circumstances.'[1] Even inasmuch 'work' – as an effort of the entire society – becomes the 'source of wealth and culture', it does not produce this wealth and culture for the entire society, but 'poverty and degeneration on the side of the worker, wealth and culture on the side of the non-worker [bourgeois]'. 'This is the law of all prevailing history. Instead of making abstract statements on "the Work" and "the Society", they should have provided evidence on how, in current capitalist society, the material etc. conditions finally have been brought about that enable and force the workers to defeat this historical curse.'[2]

Yet it was neither degenerate deference to bourgeois values nor sell-out to ideological revisionists or – as Marx assumed – stubborn stupidity that had caused leading German social democrats to write a concept of 'work' into their joint programme, a programme that stressed anew work's intrinsic creative value and demanded its just remuneration. The concept of 'work' embodied in the first sentence of the Gotha manifesto appealed to the broadest possible consensus among members of the German labour movement of that time. It catered to the life experiences of journeymen and small master artisans who made up the bulk of social democratic membership and staffed the ranks of their leaders.[3] For them, the frigid logic of Marx's dialectic appeared much less plausible and attractive than the time-honoured categories of 'associational socialism' that revolved around an emotional and moral vision of 'work'. This notion of 'work' was a positive one, rich with meaning, and could not be reduced to alienation and exploitation. The artisan vision of 'work' that I will describe on the following pages was not the only vision of work in the early German labour movement, although it remained dominant at least into the 1890s. I will argue in the final sections of this article that the other visions of work circulating among German craft unions and early industrial unions embraced a positive notion of 'work' as a key to individual and group identity in a way in which the 'negative' Marxian concept did not.

The Cosmos of 'Work' in 'Associational Socialism'

Coming from an artisan background, the early social democrats in Germany shared the long-standing tradition of glorifying work that was deeply rooted in the former guild culture and ritual.[4] This is noteworthy, for the very founding of social democracy had been an explicit act of overcoming deep-seated craft and guild rivalry for the new unity of an all-embracing new 'political worker' identity. The 'workers' clubs' and 'workers' educational societies' that had sprung up during the revolution of 1848 and mushroomed again since the early 1860s were designed as the organizational form that was most distinct from the guilds. The first unions in Germany met with rejection or outright resistance by many journeymen workers. At a time when social democracy had just started to leave the old order behind, journeymen saw the unions' organization along craft lines as a regression. What makes their attachment to a guild vision of labour all the more puzzling is that young journeymen and small master craftsmen who flocked to party meetings and public rallies complained about the restrictive aspects of the eroding guild system and the disadvantageous effects it had for them, for example, in competition with the more well-off masters who controlled the guilds. The paternalistic features of guild rule appeared particularly obnoxious to the young journeymen who frequently still lodged in their masters' homes and were subjected to draconian household regimes. They suffered long hours, bad working conditions, petty exploitation and much patronizing in the shop, where the master – in contrast to the much more expanded workshop sizes in Great Britain and the United States – was still omnipresent as a co-worker and kept them under close personal surveillance.

And yet a glorification of 'work' that stood in stark contrast to these everyday experiences survived among the constituency of early social democracy. 'Work' figured as the prime masculine virtue and, in this sense, the key to the entire human universe. Given the previously cited circumstances, it must come as a surprise that this idealized notion of 'work' could actually gain even more popularity. Real working conditions were deteriorating under the influence of capitalist commercialization and the drastic overcrowding of the typical urban supply trades like tailoring, shoe making and cabinet making. The ideal of work was, moreover, not salvaged by taking refuge in an overly abstract connotation of 'work'. It began with real human activity, with the concrete practice of skilled artisan craftsmanship. In a widely circulated songbook of the 1850s and 1860s used by travelling journeymen on their tours, a verse reads:

> Briskly we are hammering, stitching and sewing away,
> And nobody twiddles his thumbs,
> For if we want to eat honest bread,
> It has to be deserved first.
> So into the praise of work
> All join in with joyful timbre,
> As [work] raises our vital spirits
> And shows what Man is worth.[5]

An artisan work ethic that placed the self-image of the skilled – and manly – craftsman at the centre of group identity thus prevailed under conditions that could not be more different. Yet it was precisely the idealization that capitalized on the abstractness of the all-embracing term 'work'. What we see here is the idea that craftsmanship in its core was a pure and noble expenditure of knowledge and diligence, nourished by virtue, producing virtue and being an inherently pleasant activity, if it was not impaired from the outside. This notion of 'work' was no representation of contemporary reality, but a vision of what skilled craftsmanship once had been and was supposed to be again in a future conceived by the labour movement. This marks a profound difference from Marx, who saw the future of 'work' embodied in the development of modern industry and decried artisan visions as hopelessly backward and naive. Yet it remained vital for the journeymen and small masters in the ranks of social democracy to link their everyday experiences to an idealized past and the dream of a future that still related to their present craftsman existence. They placed no hopes in becoming 'new men' in the future socialist production regime, but insisted on the liberation of their current beings from forces that prevented them from living up to these ideals.

'Associational socialism' did not call for state-controlled centralized industrial production, but for autonomous cooperatives combining independent craft producers. The egalitarian 'association', democratically administered, was to replace both guilds and the market. In this vision, the idealized 'work' was also linked to a future when craftsmanship would again be liberated from hostile outside forces and restored to its pure and noble core. Journeymen and small masters felt able and entitled to be the subjects and beneficiaries of this process in their current state if they acted according to the collective ethical code that placed devoted 'work' at the centre of all virtues. This semantic construction helps us to understand why these artisans were able to praise their craftsmanship as the ideal embodiment of 'work' and at the same time complain about the toil their everyday labour really was – monotony, chicanery and exploitation. They blamed all obnoxious, exhausting and disadvantageous features of their actual work life not on inherent characteristics of their trade, but on the outside forces that ostensibly prevented their dream of pure and noble 'work' from coming true.

On the one hand, these outside forces were the paralysing remnants of the eroding guild structure that rendered craft producers helpless against the challenges of the time. These challenges, on the other hand, were the free market and capitalism, the most formidable adversaries of labour. It is of utmost importance that contemporary social democrats did not portray the entrepreneur and his autocratic domination in centralized production facilities as their prime enemies, but instead focused on the merchant-financier and controller of putting-out systems. Likewise, not exploitation and alienation, but 'free competition' under a capitalist regime were seen as the impairments to pure and noble 'work'. As one programmatic statement from 1868 put it: 'We want to replace the grand splendour of private capital with the blessing of joint work, wage labour with the rewards of free work, "free competition" under the yoke of capital with the free competition within the general uplifting of our intellectual and material work capabilities.'[6]

German social democrats of that time did not see the 'free market' as a new order organizing production along capitalist rules, but as an agent that promoted the wholesale disintegration of all society. They described the 'market' in morbid metaphors of disease and decay: workers in Bavarian town of Schwabach met after the revolution of 1848 in order to 'counsel among themselves how … one should deal with capital eating away at the vitality of the labouring classes like a cancerous ulcer'. A 'Manifesto for the Metalworkers of all Countries' proclaimed in May 1869: 'Big Capital, as the exclusive proprietor of our industry, the owner of all working tools, is draining the heart's blood from the working people like a vampire.' As young locksmith Philipp Wiemer remarked in 1871, 'free competition' had 'created a situation similar to one in which thousands of men were constantly busy erecting a wall that thousands of others were simultaneously tearing down again'.[7]

In Marx's – correct – view, capital organized production and determined what would constitute valuable 'work' in the first place: work turning out goods for an anonymous market under conditions of 'free competition'. For the social democrats in Germany, in contrast, capital appeared as an outside intruder into the harmonious world of self-contained artisan production, one that hampered and blocked its healthy development. This made 'capital' not only dangerous, but superfluous and something to be replaced. 'Capital' was seen as an accumulated stock of money – 'capitalists' were metaphorically called 'money-belts' – that acted as a mechanism to divert the rewards from honest work into the coffers of the 'non-working', 'loafing' bourgeoisie. Grain merchant Wilhelm Bracke, sponsor of the Social Democratic Workers' Party in Brunswick, wrote in 1876:

> The quality of property as capital, its capitalist character, its opportunity, thereby attributed to it, to conduct the fruits of labour of diligent men to those who do nothing; the distribution of the joint rewards of work in that way we see today: that those get the greatest shares who do nothing, yet those who perform the most time-consuming and most painstaking work hardly receive the bare necessities of life; the sad straits of the great

> majority of our people and, contrasted to this, the ever increasing riches of a few people – that is what it is all about.[8]

According to this 'associational socialist' vision, 'work' alone created value by the expenditure of skill and diligence that came to be embodied in the final product, independently of its exchange value in a market distorted by 'capital', a force alien and hostile to production. 'Work', in another sense, became a synonym for 'human activity' as such. It figured as nothing less than an emblem of 'human life'; it actually represented the ontological quality of 'humanity', the meaning of life. Bracke contrasted this 'lively work' with the withered deadweight of 'capital': 'Dead property is robbing vivacious Work of its own fruits! And because Work holds the most primordial property right one can think of over these fruits, therefore dead property is an enemy of the [rightful] property of living work.'[9] Consequently, German social democrats did not call for the elimination of private ownership; they demanded that the 'good' property created by 'work' be liberated from the burden of 'capital' which made it 'bad', 'parasitic' property.

As remote from reality as this vision might appear in an era of accelerating industrialization, it did reflect the day-to-day life experiences of many petty producers, journeymen, small masters and shop owners alike. Especially those employed in the craft trades experienced capitalist commercialization and the proliferation of markets as outside forces muscling in on a sector inherently harmonious and intact. The actual sphere of work, the workshop as the site of skilled production, seemed like an entrenched strongpoint besieged by the financial storm troops of 'capital'. In this light, in a segment of the economy where capitalist commercialization long preceded the ascent of factory production, this view of 'work' and its relation to 'capital' remained plausible. August Bebel, one of the founders of the Eisenach party in 1869, for example, was at that time a small master woodturner in Leipzig. He employed one journeyman and one apprentice. His small workshop had become entirely dependent on a Leipzig merchant who had monopolized the distribution of Bebel's products, fashionable window and door handles made from buffalo horns. His sole customer let Bebel 'feel thoroughly the misery of a small master'. He reminisced:

> Goods had to be delivered on long credit, yet the wages for journeyman and apprentice, expenses and the costs of my own livelihood were due daily or weekly. Where to get the money from? I delivered my products to a merchant for cash at a price barely higher than my own costs. But when I collected my money on Saturdays, I received all the dirty paper bills Leipzig was deluged with at that time due to the commerce with the Thuringian petty states … Aside from that, I received [worthless] coupons of some dubious industrial enterprise or Ducats which the Manichean had circumcised so much that I often received, instead of 3 Thalers 5 pennies as calculated, only 3 Thalers or less from the banker who exchanged them for me.[10]

There is no doubt that the translation of this prosaic artisan existence into the exuberant one of a much admired independent craftsman entailed a great deal of illusion. In particular, the projection of craftsmanship back into the glory days of an ostensibly intact past was pure fiction, since the despised guilds had been part of this history. Yet the idealized view of worker independence, still oriented towards the independent master craftsman, survived in the vision of workers regaining their independence through voluntary association with other workers. The vision to salvage an endangered individuality – endangered by 'free competition', not collectivism – by associating with others on an egalitarian, democratically controlled basis formed the core of the political doctrine of 'associational socialism'.

'Work' as 'Self-Education' and Political Activism

This linked 'work' as actual toil and labour to a much broader concept of 'work' which encompassed the public sphere and political activism. The idea that an honourable craftsman's life should display the right balance between 'work' and 'pleasure' had a long tradition in guild culture and ritual. 'Pleasure' here, indeed, connoted 'leisure' as a way of recuperating from 'work'. This old view still informed social democrats' moral accusations against the 'bourgeois', claiming that they would not work at all, but only enjoy leisure activities while others were toiling to provide them with their luxury. Here, the balance between 'work' and 'pleasure' had become distorted; 'leisure' had become loafing and 'joy' had become 'luxury'. Society was only sound if built on a balance of 'work' and 'pleasure'. 'Loafing' and 'luxury', in contrast, meant decadence.[11]

During the nineteenth century, an interesting shift occurred in this metaphoric balance that symbolized a virtuous life: the 'pleasure' part of the balance increasingly assumed an active connotation. For German Social Democrats, 'pleasure' was no longer 'leisure', but cultural activity and political interest. Leading local party members frequently scolded their more apathetic brethren who were content to spend their dull evenings drinking beer and shooting dice. Their self-image as politically active 'workers' demanded a projection of the virtue of 'work' onto the realm of 'pleasure'. In the process, 'pleasure' became another form of 'work' – work for self-education, for cultural uplift and self-realization. Another verse in the song cited above illustrates this thinking:

> And after we have savoured work during the day,
> In the evenings the table is laid for the mind,
> Our hearts are light, our minds are bright,
> We owe it to Work.'[12]

The 'worker' in this sense did not leave work when he closed the workshop door behind him; he continued to work in a figurative sense, working for his self-education and striving for political rights. This made the 'worker' into the 'complete person' that was – in the eyes of the social democrats – entitled to full citizenship and suffrage. The inaugural speech on the party convention in Coburg in 1874 proclaimed:

> [Our adversaries] amass armed troops against us, yet they do not find us in the streets but in the workshops, and [they find] the leaders of the workers in humble chambers where they, after their heavy workday for the spoils of rich people, work on themselves, namely on their education ... This makes the present movement different from all predecessors; it is not pursued with weapons, but with our working tools; we have set out to conquer the world with our Work, and we are convinced we will prevail.[13]

A 'true' worker did not only work skilfully and diligently at his trade; through the symbolic 'work' of cultural activity, he 'earned' knowledge and refinement in arts and sciences. Through active participation, rhetorical eloquence and the bravery to defend his ideas in public, he 'earned' manly dignity and full political citizenship. Only these complementary dimensions of 'work', integrated to a holistic worldview by the basic meaning of 'work' as skilful and diligent physical expenditure, perfected the 'worker' into the accomplished 'complete person' that was the ideal. Not surprisingly, social democrats claimed that this holistic vision of the 'worker' as the exemplary citizen was superior to the narrow-minded, 'fish-blooded', 'fainthearted', 'selfish' 'bourgeois' who tried to withhold full political rights from them. A report on a Viennese rally from May 1869 stated:

> He who has given up hope of the people's energy should go to such a gathering, and he can easily convince himself that democratic blood indeed is still circulating in the people's veins. Look at these Men of Labour who, after having worked all day long, still follow the deliberations with utmost attention, giving evidence with their glances and expressions that the democratic spark has ignited their hearts. Listen to these orators who are virtually mushrooming [everywhere] and surpass in passion, force and flow of speech everything accomplished by our regular parliamentary eloquence. Here you find this truthful and excelling eloquence that is rooted in the brain, as it is in the heart.[14]

This inflated, all-encompassing, decidedly political vision of 'work' was attractive for the young journeymen and small masters in the ranks of social democracy because they could experience its validation on occasion of the numerous rallies, club meetings and festivals where they had the chance to live up to this standard. In fact, the political public was the only sphere where these young men had the opportunity to act according to high ethical standards in a self-made social environment and receive collective recognition in exchange. Actually, activism in the clubs and the wider urban public compensated for the lack of dignity they suffered in their workshops or the lack of privacy they had to endure when lodging in the master's household. Similarly, the ability to compensate the prosaic drudgery of daily toil with idealistic homologies of 'work', in the form of public political activity in workers' associations and meetings, made craftsman independence not only a political project of the future, but a task at least partially fulfilled in the present. Political activism and the vision of the liberation of 'work' in socialist associations were thus deeply entangled, and this gave early social democracy a realistic appeal. In this way, 'work' became synonymous with a whole vision of a virtuous and rewarding life.

Craft Worker Elitism: 'Work' as 'Art' Assaulted by Commerce

This 'associational socialist' understanding represented the dominant, but not the only existing view of 'work' in the nineteenth-century German labour movement. Although printers and typesetters, for example, were among the most active occupational groups in early social democracy, and an above-average number of members of this trade staffed the leading ranks of the workingmen's parties, they also founded the first German trade union in 1848. In fact, printers and typesetters constituted by far the strongest potential for unionization in Germany up to the 1890s. They reorganized their union, the German Printers Association, in Leipzig in 1866 and within a few years propelled it to the position of Germany's leading trade union organization during the 1860s and 1870s. In 1873, the organized printers won the first nationwide collective labour contract in German history. When the first survey of trade union activity in Germany was published by the social democrat August Geib in 1877/1878, the printers' and typesetters' union ranked first not in terms of membership but, more importantly, in the percentage of organized workers. Half the printers and typesetters in the German-speaking parts of Europe were cardholding trade union members at that time. This represented a very efficient degree of unionization and a capability to prevail in labour conflicts that no other German union could match.[15]

Together with the cigar makers – whose case was too different to be discussed in this context – the printers and typesetters were the only German equivalents to the contemporary craft worker elitism that prevailed in Anglo-Saxon countries at the time. In the United Kingdom and the United States, strong trade unions had formed along narrowly conceived craft lines in major handicrafts, but also in some early industries like iron and steel, coal mining or machine building.[16] In Germany, in contrast, a different course of industrialization – slow and tentative in the traditional urban trades, but even more rapid in heavy industry – had extended the life of small workshops and thereby prolonged artisan production, if on an increasingly precarious commercial basis. Consequently, a genuine craft union milieu had had only a small space in which it could strike roots in Germany. The very fact that the German labour movement constituted itself as a political party movement points to the weakness of genuine trade union potential. Social democracy largely compensated for the lack of trade union infrastructure. Aside from cigar makers, printers and typesetters represented the sole exception from the rule.

Despite their frequent double engagement in party politics and union activity, printers and typesetters did not belong to the most ideologically convinced propagators of 'associational socialism'. Unlike journeymen and small masters from the craft trades in the movement, who still heralded the independence of the master craftsman as their highest ideal – even if this required voluntary association – printers and typesetters had settled for a lifelong existence as employees of a 'principal'. German printing shops, especially in book centres like Leipzig or Frankfurt am Main, had grown to considerable sizes, equal to smaller factory establishments in other sectors of industry. Publishing and printing were both capital- and labour-intensive. Therefore, the chance for a journeyman printer or typesetter to set up shop for themselves was slim and waning fast. The owners of printing shops, in contrast, had long developed into capitalist entrepreneurs. Frequently, they were not trained printers themselves, but booksellers, publishers or editors of periodicals. There was a clear class line dividing the 'principals' from their skilled 'agents' on the shop floor. It was exactly this situation, quite different from the social background of the artisan members of the German labour movement, which translated into a rather peculiar vision of 'work'.

Printers and typesetters considered their work not only as a highly skilled trade, but as an 'art'. Their vision of 'work' did not refer to something abstract, but to a concrete and narrowly defined line of professionalism that stood out over all other forms of human labour. In glorifying their activity as 'art', printers claimed for their work the same intellectual quality attributed to the authors of the works they processed for publishing. Printers self-consciously called themselves 'the promoters of science'. They appealed to the 'sons of Gutenberg, the most intelligent element of the working classes'.[17] Stephan Born, himself a printer and co-founder of the General German Workers' Fraternity (*Arbeiterverbrüderung*) in 1848, boasted that the 'machinists and printers formed … the avant-garde, if not aristocratic elements among the workers of the city of Berlin'.[18]

The 'art' of printing entailed not only motor skills and dexterity, but intellectual aptness and literary creativity. Its practice called for responsible autonomy at the workplace and for a pace of production that left time for the reflection on the texts taking shape in the printers' hands. To become a practitioner of this 'black art' required years of training and more years of travelling in order to acquire the high degree of cosmopolitanism deemed necessary for this position. Being a printer was more than holding a skilled job; it meant belonging to an elite through habits as well as *habitus*. Printers proudly displayed their command over foreign languages; they often dressed like university students and even sported some of the college fraternities' symbols and rituals.

Yet the particular meaning this vision of 'work' as 'art' drew on the fact that printers and typesetters were dependent employees working for a wage at the same time. It was the tension between the pretensions to an 'artist' honour and an existence as lifelong wageworkers that triggered the organizational vigour of this professional group in the first place. Printers and typesetters found their elitist status challenged by the increasing strains of capitalist commercialization:

> We must not hesitate to participate in this movement, we, the sons of Gutenberg, the most intelligent element of the working classes, we must not fail, moreover, as this most intelligent element is also the most depressed one; for almost every other worker can gain independence after his travelling years, whereas the printer holds the walking stick in his hand for his entire life.[19]

'Art' was thus depicted as assaulted by commerce. The ostensible deterioration of working conditions appeared almost as an insult to the exceptional status of a workers' aristocracy. In the eyes of German printers and typesetters, their 'art' was entitled to full recognition by their employers; instead, the latter treated them as ordinary workers, not only capitalizing on their dependent position, but degrading them and hurting their honour:

> We do not want to engage in considerations whether the principals, progress or the spirit of the time, or even we colleagues [ourselves] are to blame for the fact that the order of printers has been degraded from art to handicraft, from handicraft to factory, and there even to its lowest degree; bad enough that this is reality, and we should undertake all efforts to leave this dishonourable state we are currently in as noble artists, to uplift this state and our art to the level that appertains to it and to us.[20]

The printers had never been organized in a guild. Yet an eclectic compilation of legal texts, a statute with a long tradition and only slight regional variations, the so-called *Postulat*, had guaranteed their exceptional status. It had conceded a series of rights and a range of participation to the journeymen printers that were unparalleled in any artisan guild constitution. This statute had established arbitration boards (*Einigungsämter*) where 'principals' and printers' delegates negotiated terms of employment on equal footing. It ruled that it was the journeymen's privilege to accept and train apprentices, thus giving them a large share of control over local labour markets. The *Postulat* safeguarded the printers' autonomy in administering their own funds. The statute opened up printers' learned societies for equal entitlement of membership to employers and employees. In fact, this ratified the printers' claim to intellectual equivalence with both 'principals' and writers. The *Postulat*, in sum, was a document that acknowledged the extraordinary honour of printers and typesetters as 'Gutenberg's disciples' and 'artists' rather than workers.[21]

It was from the vantage point of this privileged position that the printers and typesetters saw their 'art' degenerating into ordinary 'work'. Yet the *Postulat* had deviated from most traditional guild statutes not only in order to reward them. It actually sanctioned the liberal practices of a trade that had already for a long time developed the petty capitalist characteristics that the guilds still tried to suppress. The *Postulat* had 'bought' the 'helpers'' acquiescence to the creeping commercialization of the trade by granting them recognition and participatory rights. At the same time it had placed the 'principals' under much fewer and lower restrictions than the master artisans had to endure under the guild system. Therefore, when the *Postulat* started to erode during the first half of the nineteenth century, it was not due to the sinister machinations of 'dishonourable principals', but truly a consequence of its built-in functions to ease the way of printing into its commercial capitalist future.

Already around 1848 printers and typesetters could feel the impact of advancing commercialization: 'principals' without a background in the trade but with superior financial means had started muscling in on the ownership of printing shops. They considered printing as a lucrative business and not as an intellectual community with highly paid 'helpers'. In fact, their strategies to economize production degraded the proud status of a fully trained journeyman printer to a just-above-average ordinary workman; 'principals' took away the 'helpers'' prerogative of accepting apprentices and used them in inflated numbers as cheap unskilled or semi-skilled assistant workers. The printers labelled them, accordingly, as 'apprentice breeders' (*Lehrlingszüchter*). The introduction of the steam press transformed the printers' position into that of a machinist. Simultaneously, unskilled labour providing the menial tasks of coal shovelling and machine tending was hired in large numbers, while printers in the narrow sense of traditional hand printing increasingly took refuge in typesetting. These measures to lower the number of highly paid skilled 'helpers' and to blur skill lines were clearly intended to lower costs in a labour-intensive industry with as yet limited potential for technical productivity gains; typesetting for the time being remained the bottleneck. Such measures were flanked by attempts by 'principals' to cut wages, especially in periods of economic slumps.

As a consequence, the work of printing and typesetting bore less and less resemblance to the glorified ideal of a noble 'art' that the skilled 'helpers' of the trade still held in high esteem. Like the artisan members of the labour movement, printers and typesetters projected this ideal into a fictional past that never had been a reality anywhere. Yet only by reiterating their master narrative of printing as an 'art' could they defend their elitist esprit de corps within largely 'normalized' – and seemingly further deteriorating – employment relations. Upholding this extraordinary standard made it possible to portray employers' strategies as an outrageous assault of bare commerce on their sanctified honour. Since escape into commercial independence was not an option for printers, however, 'associational socialism' held no promise for them of a future beyond capitalism. They remained within the bounds of dependent wage work even if printing shops were run as cooperatives.

The discrepancy between their claimed status and the worsening reality of wage work translated for printers and typesetters into an obligation to organize and fight for labour's rights. They saw this as the only way to conserve an honour threatened under the assault of capitalist commerce that even drove the well-natured 'principals' into a ruinous price-reducing race for the bottom – with foreseeable results for the 'helpers'. The honour of the 'artist' was thereby transformed into the honour of 'brotherly solidarity'. A 'song for the striking printers' from August 1848 began with the verse:

> Still our banner is waving ahead
> Of the faithful men's column
> Who, conscientious of their power,
> Have pulled themselves together for the struggle
> After many a year of grief.'[22]

The printers and typesetters made very clear that their fight was no egotistical defence of narrowly conceived trade privileges. On the contrary, they saw that the extraordinariness of their honour could best be justified if they took the head position in the struggle of all workers, leading them into battle. The honour of being an elite was thereby converted into a mission to guide the working class. The printers, according to a pamphlet of 1847, 'are members of the working classes who are predestined to hurry ahead of them, as an order that is blessed with the gift of a higher education'. They should 'lead the way for all other workers with their example', a delegate by the name of Pleß claimed at the first national printers' convention in the same year. And a colleague from Neuß demanded 'that this movement not remain one-sided, but that the printers should influence the other workers beneficently, that especially the printers from all locales should join the workers' clubs, or, where such would not yet exist, should go ahead with founding such clubs, so that the considerable fund of intelligence, as is present in our association, will affect other associations in a salutary way and not be lost'.[23]

This construction of a special honour as a missionary obligation to serve as an avant-garde for the labour movement bridged the gap between the printers and typesetters and the 'less aristocratic' ranks of ordinary labour. It also bridged the tension between their political engagement in social democracy and extremely efficient craft unionism.

Skilled Work as 'Quality Work'

After the downfall of the Anti-Socialist Law in 1890, the trade union movement in Germany gained momentum, and the following decades until the outbreak of the First World War witnessed an unprecedented expansion, doubling the number of trade union members every five years. The unions finally succeeded in breaking free from domination by the Social Democratic Party, although their loyalty to the cause of social democracy remained intact. Yet the founding of a separate central umbrella organization with a political coordinating function, the General Commission (*Generalkommission*), in 1890 established the by then sixteen centralized social democratic trade unions as a formally independent force in German political culture.

The rapidly growing German trade unions were still predominantly organizations of male skilled workers. They retained an artisan core, although the largest gains in membership were now made in small and medium industrial enterprises. The unions remained organized along craft lines, but they never defined craft jurisdiction as narrowly as their British or American counterparts. In fact, the principle of centralization called for a federation of trades in single unions, which resembled branch unions rather than the craft unions of the Anglo-Saxon type. Central organization placed more weight on gross membership than on the degree of unionization or the 'union shop', a doctrine that was characteristic for Anglo-Saxon craft unions. Centralization empowered the unions by accumulating large funds that could be used for staging strategically planned and executed strikes, even in locations that were not thoroughly organized. The German trade union movement managed to stage a highly successful strike policy, coordinating more than one thousand walkouts per year all over the country in the 1890s and 1900s. Yet centralization also served the purpose of disciplining and curbing strike action. This, in turn, became the key for negotiations between employers and union leaders, especially in the small and medium industries. In an ever-increasing number of cases, it resulted in the acceptance of the union as a collective bargaining agent and in the winning of collective labour contracts (*Tarifverträge*) covering whole regions or industrial sectors.

Within this trade union environment, the prevalent vision of 'work' had changed profoundly from the days of 'associational socialism'. It had also deviated from craft worker elitism, which had been a minority phenomenon anyway, despite the fact that both concepts of 'work' still shared the common premise that dependent employment relations had to be accepted for the time being under capitalism. It was not yet clear what would replace them in case of a socialist revolution. Trade union and party publications now frequently featured etchings or prints depicting artistic allegories on 'work' or 'industry'. In these works of art, the female figures personifying 'work' or 'industry', seated on thrones overlooking neat piles of finished industrial products or shining tools, welcomed a group of male workers approaching to pay homage to them, sometimes presenting tools on laureate cushions. The workers in the picture almost without exception were portrayed as sturdy men in their thirties, bearded, with brawny, bare arms in rolled-up sleeves, sporting collarless shirts over muscular chests, long leather aprons and wooden shoes. Those workers not carrying a cushion held the tools of their trade in their hands. This semiotic ensemble was a symbolic representation of the connection between skilled 'work', as personified in the worker's figure, and 'quality work', as symbolized in the tools and products at the feet of allegoric 'industry'.

These icons of 'work' represented the prevalent self-image of the 'worker' in contemporary trade union culture. They reflected workers' high identification with their work, symbolized by the literal 'incorporation' of its physical traces in their muscular bodies or in the choice of their working clothes. Pictorial representations of social democratic workers from the artisan phase of the labour movement had shown young men in fashionable Sunday clothes, monochrome in black, their appearance alluding to a sense of respectability and full citizenship. Photographs of single workmen or entire workforces of a shop or factory after 1890, in contrast, featured more seasoned men in their distinct working outfit, complete with a selection of their trade's tools. In these photographs, the claim to respectability was present as well, yet it was derived from their status as skilled workers performing 'quality work'.[24]

The homology of skilled work and 'quality work' ran through justifications of trade union strategy and practice. The unions drove their point home time and again that their skilled clientele was entitled to a fair compensation for their labour, since it constituted 'quality' performance. If the workers were expected to live up to these standards, wages had to be raised to a level that allowed for a decent living (at that time, a male breadwinner's wage), working hours had to be cut back to ensure aptness on the shop floor and provide conditions for preserving health, and general working conditions had to be improved in order to save the workers' lives and limbs. Moreover, compensation came to mean that if workers invested their best effort in work, they were entitled to financial means and enough spare time that enabled them to participate fully in the society's cultural life. Furthermore, when collective labour contracts spread and the unions found growing recognition as collective bargaining agents on the side of employers, they claimed that workers were no longer 'industrial servants', but had risen to the status of 'industrial citizens'. Respectability as skilled workmen translated into a right to codetermine their terms and conditions of employment: 'The employer cannot decree the conditions of work any longer; the workers have their say, too. And their putting in their word is no formal matter. They have a voice [in industrial affairs].'[25]

Conclusion

The different visions of 'work' presented here also represent the development the German labour movement took over the course of the nineteenth century. The worship of an idealized 'work' as the symbol of a complete personality in the era of 'associational socialism' overlapped with the printers' elitist view of 'work' as 'art' assaulted by commerce. This view, in turn, gave way to a more down-to-earth vision of 'work' as skill embodied in 'quality work', which coloured trade union rhetoric through the late nineteenth century. The semiotic analysis has also shown how far these 'rich' concepts of 'work' as an activity with an inherent meaning and value independent from employment relations deviated from Marx's dispassionate dialectic construction of 'abstract work' as a mere function of capitalism. This difference probably contributed to the lack of revolutionary focus that Marx diagnosed in German social democracy during his time. It never had much of a realistic chance against the material lures of reformism in the future. Finally, the argument presented here has demonstrated that when discussing the labour movement, any history of 'work' inevitably becomes a history of the workers who shaped their own visions of 'work' as well. Indeed, their whole identity construction revolved around the nodal point of 'work'.

Notes

1. Karl Marx, 'Randglossen zum Programm der deutschen Arbeiterpartei' (1875), in *Karl Marx – Friedrich Engels Gesamtausgabe (MEGA),* vol. 25: *Karl Marx – Friedrich Engels Werke. Artikel, Entwürfe Mai 1875 bis Mai 1883* (Berlin, G.D.R: Dietz, 1985), p. 9.
2. Ibid., p. 11.
3. For this and many other details not documented separately, see Thomas Welskopp, *Das Banner der Brüderlichkeit. Die deutsche Sozialdemokratie vom Vormärz bis zum Sozialistengesetz* (Bonn: J.H.W. Dietz Nachf., 2000).
4. See Josef Ehmer's contribution to this volume.
5. *Liederbuch für Handwerkervereine* (1859), pp. 27f.
6. 'Was wir wollen und sollen', Part I, in *Deutsche Arbeiterhalle* 14 (27 July 1868).
7. Quotes in Thomas Welskopp, 'Markt und Klasse in der deutschen Sozialdemokratie, 1848–1878', in *Marx-Engels-Jahrbuch* (2004), pp. 9–30; esp. p. 15.
8. Wilhelm Bracke, *Nieder mit den Sozialdemokraten!* (Braunschweig: Bracke, 1876), p. 15.
9. Quoted in Welskopp, 'Markt und Klasse', p. 21.
10. August Bebel, *Aus meinem Leben* (Berlin/Bonn: J.H.W. Dietz Nachf., 1986), pp.140f.
11. Thomas Welskopp, '"Manneszucht" und "Selbstbeherrschung". Zivilgesellschaftliche Werte in der deutschen Sozialdemokratie, 1848–1878', in Ralph Jessen, Sven Reichardt and Ansgar Klein (eds), *Zivilgesellschaft als Geschichte. Studien zum 19. und 20. Jahrhundert* (Wiesbaden: VS Verlag für Sozialwissenschaften, 2004), pp. 65–88; esp. p. 70.
12. *Liederbuch für Handwerkervereine,* pp. 27f.
13. Quoted in Welskopp, *Banner der Brüderlichkeit,* p. 579.
14. *Demokratisches Wochenblatt* 18 (1 May 1869), p. 200.
15. Welskopp, *Banner der Brüderlichkeit,* pp. 279, 287, 289.
16. For iron and steel, see Thomas Welskopp, *Arbeit und Macht im Hüttenwerk. Arbeits- und industrielle Beziehungen in der deutschen und amerikanischen Eisen- und Stahlindustrie von den 1860er bis zu den 1930er Jahren* (Bonn: J.H.W. Dietz Nachf., 1994).
17. 'Beschlüsse der ersten National-Buchdrucker-Versammlung zu Mainz am 11., 12., 13. und 14. Juni 1848', in Dieter Dowe and Toni Offermann (eds), *Deutsche Handwerker- und Arbeiterkongresse 1848–1852. Protokolle und Materialien,* (Berlin/Bonn: J.H.W. Dietz Nachf., 1983), p. 423.
18. Stephan Born, *Erinnerungen eines Achtundvierzigers,* (3rd ed., Leipzig: Vorwärts, 1898), p. 65.
19. 'Beschlüsse der ersten National-Buchdrucker-Versammlung', p. 423.

20. 'Buchdruckerversammlung in Heidelberg, 23.4.1848', in *Deutsche Handwerker- und Arbeiterkongresse*, p. 393.
21. Jürgen Kocka, *Arbeitsverhältnisse und Arbeiterexistenzen. Grundlagen der Klassenbildung im 19. Jahrhundert* (Bonn: J.H.W. Dietz Nachf., 1990), pp. 383f., 387f.
22. 'For the striking printers', in *Das Volk* 30 (19 August 1848): 119f.
23. Quotes: Kocka, *Arbeitsverhältnisse und Arbeiterexistenzen*, p. 387; 'Erste National-Buchdrucker-Versammlung in Mainz, 11.–14.6.1848', in *Deutsche Handwerker- und Arbeiterkongresse*, pp. 414, 417f.
24. Joan Campbell, *Joy in Work, German Work. The National Debate, 1800–1945* (Princeton: Princeton University Press, 1989), pp. 70ff.
25. Quoted in Helga Grebing, Hans-Otto Hemmer and Gottfried Christmann (eds), *Das HolzArbeiterbuch. Die Geschichte der Holzarbeiter und ihrer Gewerkschaften*, (Cologne: Bund-Verlag, 1993), p. 80.

5

Work in Gender, Gender in Work: The German Case in Comparative Perspective*

Karin Hausen

Preliminary Remarks

Making a distinction between men and women remains the foundation and precondition for the ordering of gender relations, work and thus of societies more generally. Everyday work and the distribution of certain tasks, as well as the value placed upon them, visibly and tangibly lend the appearance of naturalness to social and cultural frameworks. Manifold images, speech and texts additionally mark and underscore the boundaries between desirable and undesirable, normal and abnormal interactions between work and gender. Such discursive boundary settings provide important assurances as long as people, both individually and in groups, repeatedly face the need to adapt the work-gender nexus to new facts and processes of historical change, not just in times of hardship or under pressure from profound changes, but also from day to day.

It is important to recall the far-reaching societal significance of the interplay between work and gender, because, as we know, social conditions only become the object of scholarly interest when they are no longer self-evident. Since the late nineteenth century feminist scholars in particular have been working to present solid empirical evidence to correct the intensely ideological public debates and political decisions on women's work and paid employment, especially the employment of married women. Their efforts had an influence on social policy. Their aim was to secure the principle of gender specificity in the welfare state, to adapt it to modern industrial capitalism and parliamentary democracy, to benefit women by anchoring a higher degree of gender justice within institutions. In 1900, however, and for decades to come, it was not yet common to cast doubt on the gender-specific division of labour, competencies, entitlements and resources themselves as allegedly indispensable principles of social order. This project was left to scholars influenced by the new women's movement beginning in the

1970s. They proceeded to scrutinize the gender-specific order closely as a socio-culturally created principle of far-reaching social distinctions and assignments of unequal opportunities, with the aim of overcoming it. With this objective, gender studies has since established itself internationally as an academic research field.

By paying heightened attention to the modes of operation and social relevance of gender orders and gender specificity, interdisciplinary research has since also unveiled highly complex relationships for gender and work. On the one hand, one is struck by the universality and persistence of the ordering process which distinguishes between male and female and men and women, interprets sexual difference hierarchically and legitimizes it as divinely ordained, natural or simply as the optimal social order. On the other hand, one can always also observe far-reaching dynamics, changes and variations with which this fundamental order is transformed by and translated into the specific conditions of time and space, economics and labour, social stratification, power and culture. Not least for that reason, gender history has been marked from the beginning both by lively debates on how to define the object of study and the appropriate and necessary theories and methods for studying it and by a readiness to engage in intensive empirical research. This research follows the intellectual challenge and the political conviction that in a globalized world, gender history can provide relevant information and insights for the present and future.

A number of critical commentaries on the state of research on gender and work in relation to gender history and labour history appeared on the occasion of the new millennium.[1] These excellent reviews of the literature show once again the extent to which, since the 1980s, English as a lingua franca and the discussions and publications relevant in the U.S.A. and Britain have promoted and channelled the development of gender history and the reception of international research findings in this area. In what follows, I will explore, with an emphasis on the working class, how historical research on gender and work has developed in Germany. In addition, focusing on a few selected aspects, I will also pursue the question of whether Germany exhibits any striking peculiarities in comparison to other countries.

The Early Years of Historical Research on Gender and Work in Germany

In the GDR in the 1960s the history of the labour movement, which was highly canonical and strongly encouraged, was supplemented by research on women's labour and emancipation. The operative concept was that, thanks to the tireless efforts of the Communist Party, socialism would solve the Woman Question once and for all. In the Federal Republic in the 1970s the history of labour and the labour movement became a booming field within social history. Important impulses came from the student movement, readings of Marx, the rediscovery of neo-Marxist debates and encounters with British Marxist historians in particular, and led to an increasingly critical reception of research in the GDR. Additional intellectual and social challenges from the new women's movement finally encouraged scholars to follow models from the U.S.A. and Britain and inaugurate women's history research as an academic project in the Federal Republic as well.[2]

In the 1970s and early 1980s historians of work and gender in the Federal Republic were primarily interested in discussing the questions raised by current feminist debates about history. They unearthed the wealth of data, knowledge and insights on women and work, as well as women in the labour movement and professional organizations, which had been published in impressive quantity and quality at the turn of the twentieth century. At the same time, women students, postgraduates, lecturers and a few professors of history set about honing their historical approaches and questions, tapping into new bodies of sources and refining their analytical concepts. Usually working alone, they developed their research topics with creativity and persistence and fought to have them accepted as themes for examinations or doctoral theses. Decisive inspiration came from international contacts, autonomously organized women's universities and conferences of women historians.

This unusual research situation promoted the thematic and methodological diversity of these early works, but also hindered the rapid expansion of this field of research. In this situation, Gisela Bock's systematic reflections on women's and gender history, which took into account international debates and scholarship, quickly assumed major significance.[3] Bock published her ideas in German for the first time in 1983 and again in 1988 in an expanded version. In 1989 and 1991 she published two updated and augmented essays in English, which now belong to the international canon of texts on gender history. Bock always criticized the tendency of scholars to fall back on biology. In 1992 she expressly rejected the apparently helpful dichotomy between sex and gender and warned against accepting uncritically the usual dichotomies of private/public, nature/culture and work/family.

Labour History as Gender History

In the mid-1980s social historians in Germany gradually began to take account of women in their research. A reliable measure of this is the planned twelve-volume *History of Workers and the Labour Movement in Germany since the End of the Eighteenth Century*, which was begun in the 1980s under the general editorship of Gerhard A. Ritter.[4] Its aim is to bring together the findings of the booming research on labour history since the 1960s and to synthesize them into a new narrative. The authors include Jürgen Kocka on the period up to 1875, Gerhard A. Ritter and Klaus Tenfelde on Wilhelmine Germany, Heinrich August Winkler on the Weimar Republic und Michael Schneider on the 'Third Reich'. In the volumes published up until now, all authors expressly also write about female workers, women's paid employment and working-class women. Their information and historical judgments, however, generally adopt nineteenth- and early-twentieth-century assessments rather uncritically.

Particularly interesting in regard to work and gender are Volumes I and II by Jürgen Kocka, which appeared in 1990.[5] Kocka takes careful account of men's and women's employment; he also expressly discusses the possibilities and relevance of an appropriate historiography of women. Nevertheless, he consistently organizes Volume II, 'Working Conditions and Workers' Lives. The Foundations of Class Formation in the Nineteenth Century' according to the 'developmental and process model of class formation'. Writing of the transition from the labouring poor of corporative society to the proletariat, he reports in Volume II how the 'patterns of inequality' in corporative society, presented in Volume I, spread beyond the corporations and their subsequent development within class society. In his analysis of proletarian class formation, he relies on the systematic distinction between class position, class identity and class agency. Surprisingly, Kocka undermines the force of his own class concept when he notes that, of course, 'no one was a member of a class only, but also a man or a woman, a German or a Pole, a Jew, Catholic, Protestant or freethinker, a citizen of Hamburg or a Bavarian, etc'. Directly following this remark, he avoids the problem just addressed in the sibylline sentence: 'The relative weight of these affiliations shifted over the course of time and represents a first-order empirical problem.'

It was precisely the 'relative weight of these affiliations', however, that has been a hotly contested issue between gender historians and labour historians since the late 1980s. While labour historians defended the primacy of class affiliation, gender historians asked whether and when it makes sense or is necessary to make such evaluations at all. In the meantime the assumption, better suited to the complex situations in which real people act, has largely won out that each person has multiple, often competing and even antagonistic affiliations. Consequently, historical scholarship has the task of discovering which affiliations are accorded priority by which persons or groups of persons in particular situations, perhaps becoming relevant for action and potentially enabling them to claim dominance over other persons.[6]

This conceptually important development, at once a precondition and an expression of the current rapprochement between labour history and gender history,[7] was barely evident in the early 1980s when Kocka was assembling the framework for Volume II. He sketched a strict hierarchy of potential class formations, took it as an outline to structure his narrative and used his empirical material to flesh it out. His account begins with that group of workers for which the potential for class formation was structurally weakest. Under the striking heading 'The Age of the Housemaid: The Changing World of Domestic Servants', he discusses feminized domestic service in bourgeois urban households. This section is followed, in a rising line of class-formation potential, by chapters on 'Agricultural Workers', 'Home Workers and Cottage Industry: Craft Tradition and Capitalist Dynamics ', 'Journeymen and Masters', 'Railway Construction Workers' and, finally, in the longest chapter and as the apex of class-formation potential, 'Wage Labour in the Centralized Industrial Enterprise'. Women who worked for wages appear in all of the chapters. Only the last chapter, however, devotes a separate sub-section to 'Women and Men, Children and Adults in the Factory'. Here, one finds statistics on gender and generational ratios in the factory, a description of the alarmed and alarming contemporary discourse since the 1840s and an account of the legislation restricting the employment of children and women.

What functions, one might ask, does the housemaid whom Kocka accords such a prominent position (generously naming an entire era after her), fulfil in his analytical concept? This chapter offers a statement on the transition 'from a domestic economy to a market economy'. This subject would have been more appropriately addressed in the previous chapter, 'An Outline of Change', more specifically in the section on 'Market and Industry'. In the housemaid chapter, however, this transition is of interest only as the reason for the diminished demand for servants and the feminization of domestic service in bourgeois families, in which housemaids occupied an exceedingly precarious legal, economic and social position because of corporative relics that persisted into the nineteenth century. Neither here nor anywhere else in Volume II does the author analyse as a significant factor in the class formation process the relationships between the domestic and market economies, which were profoundly altered in industrial society, perpetually tense and, especially for wage labourers, extremely hard to reconcile. The chapter on domestic servants also studiously avoids crossing the obvious bridge between the housemaid with her underdeveloped class formation potential and gender-typical working-class female identity. Nonetheless, in the nineteenth century it was extremely common for women to come to the city as domestic servants in early youth, leave for better working conditions and earning opportunities as soon as possible, keep an eye out for a suitable husband and, as the wives of working-class men, once again perform their household and family duties under precarious legal, economic and social conditions while earning money 'on the side'.[8]

Sonya O. Rose's 1992 *Limited Livelihoods. Gender and Class in Nineteenth-Century England* provides an impressive counter-model to Kocka's portrayal, which he builds around the concept of class formation.[9] Schooled in many years of debates on the theory and methods of gender history, Rose succeeds in bringing together the findings of empirical research on gender and work, developing an argument and presenting it all in concentrated form. With her key concept of 'livelihoods', Rose underlines the fact that people work to live, and that they do most of that living in family households and thus in families, neighbourhoods and communities: not in sites of commodity production. Rose draws our attention to the diversity of social positions, experiences, and meanings, pursuits of interests, actions and struggles. Unlike Kocka, she does not focus solely on the relationships between classes, which are antagonists according to economic logic. Rather, she pays equal attention to the relationships within the classes of wage workers and capitalist entrepreneurs. She examines the wide variety of relationships between different groups of men, different groups of women and women and men. Her aim is to illustrate and explain historically how a developmental dynamic arose out of struggles over the implementation and acceptance of changes in conditions of production, work and life, as well as over resistance to those changes. This dynamic did not proceed in a single linear development in history, but recognizably set many developments in motion. For Rose, gender is a 'multi-faceted concept'[10] that, in a social order based on gender difference, ensures that people, with their social relations and personal identity, assume their proper places as social beings. Gender is at once norm and experience, but also a cultural production whose meaning must repeatedly be adapted via language to changes in social and economic conditions.[11]

Like other gender historians before her, Rose explained once again in 1993,[12] with labour historians in mind and with extensive references to gender history research, why 'the dominant paradigms in labour history continue to be reproduced as though neither women nor gender were particularly relevant'. She diagnoses the 'foundational assumptions of the discipline' as the cause and elucidates her thesis in three stages. She begins by discussing the construct of the public-private dichotomy and separate public and private spheres, which emerged in the Enlightenment and in the nineteenth century was inscribed into social theories and policies with growing self-evidence by liberals, as well as by Marx and Engels. According to this construct, the public is associated with masculinity and men, politics and paid employment, and the private with femininity and women, the family and sexuality. This dominant construct made it appear logical to ignore the multiple links and overlaps between public and private and to portray what one ignored as ahistorical and unnatural.

She stresses, secondly, that the public-private division in the nineteenth century by no means guided theoretical models alone, but also influenced everyday life, first in the middle class and later in the working class as well, affecting perceptions, values and conduct. In addition, the social policy of both state and non-state institutions affirmed and shaped the public-private division. Gender relations were shot through with the pattern of separate spheres. The public man was equipped with appropriate masculinity and the private woman with suitable femininity. Accordingly, a man gained respect as a citizen and family breadwinner, and a woman as a wife, housewife and mother. If a man failed as a breadwinner, it damaged his public reputation. A woman lost face when she neglected her family calling and did not acknowledge the marginalization of the female sex in the public sphere. In the nineteenth and twentieth centuries, working-class men translated these normative notions into the language of their own interests, trade unions and class struggles.

Thirdly, Rose criticizes existing labour history as 'ideological work', which gives the impression of being gender-neutral by failing to reveal that by virtue of its arbitrary boundaries, the very concept of the working class is exclusive and particular. It also consistently conceals labouring women's agency by continuing to reduce female wage workers, who crossed the borders between public and private, to the private sphere of the family and neglecting to ask 'how women's identities as workers and their political activities have been shaped at the workplace'. According to Rose, an account of how 'work was constitutive of women's identities as workers and how family was constitutive of the work and political identities of men', is long overdue.

In closing, Rose calls for a new labour history which would abandon the concept of separate spheres and arrive at a 'gendered understanding of the significance of work and family in the lives of women and men'. It must also engage in close linguistic analysis, as language is constitutive of political and social life. The assumption that interests are derived directly from social positions and are merely reflected in rhetoric is erroneous. Interests are, rather, generated in the context of struggles and formulated through political rhetoric. Only a heightened analysis of language can reveal how 'gender, race and sexuality have been imbricated in the intertwined cultural, socio-economic and political formation of modernity'. Finally, working-class men at work and in the labour movement should be studied more closely from the standpoint of masculinity, male identity and competition with men and women, as well as processes of inclusion and exclusion, adaptation and resistance. 'By integrating questions of gender in labour history, and by attending to how meanings are constructed, and with what consequences, historians will be better able to address how and why events happened the way they did.'

In 1992 Kathleen Canning astutely demonstrated the inadequacy of the class concept prevalent in German labour history.[13] The international discussion on the linguistic turn apparently passed German labour historians by, along with the debate on the necessity of bringing together gender history and labour history, which was provoked in particular by Joan Scott's acute critique and theses of 1986.[14] German labour history continues to favour the rigid concept of class formation, which implies a disregard for gender. Canning develops her critique using empirical examples from the Rhenish-Westphalian textile industry and the German Textile Workers' Union for the period between 1880 and 1930. Her argument follows the four levels of the class concept: the structure of the site of capitalist production and workplace, class position, class-consciousness and class agency. Using her examples, she elucidates for each level the effects of the presence of women and men, relations between the sexes and the constant alterations in these relationships wrought by economic, technological, political and social factors. She also demonstrates the conflicts and competitions of interest between the sexes and shows that not just men, but also women, interpreted and processed their own understanding of class identity through words and actions in the workplace. She shows, above all, that communication about the meaning and purpose of individual and collective action was a never-ending process even for industrial workers – both male and female – who saw themselves as part of the working class. Canning argues overall for an understanding of 'class formation as a series of short-lived resolutions, new destabilizations, and redefinitions in which gender both shapes and contests class'.[15]

I myself have suggested that when bringing together gender and labour history, we should reduce the focus on class formation still further and devote more attention to the principle of gender hierarchy, which is effective across class lines.[16] In the nineteenth and twentieth centuries in the older industrial nations, against all economic rationality, the male sex unquestioningly enjoyed advantages in every respect, but, above all, in paid employment. This applies to their entitlement to jobs and wage income and to the higher prestige enjoyed by their workplaces and the tasks they performed, as well as to their self-evident assumption of supervisory and managerial functions. The claim to priority was legitimized and bolstered by the chorus of voices about men as breadwinners and protectors of women and children. The implicit counter-image was that of the defenceless woman incapable of supporting herself. As long as the principle of male priority went unchallenged, it defused the competition between men and women over jobs and earned incomes. At the same time, however, entrepreneurial efforts to improve market opportunities by lowering wage costs, introducing mechanization and altering product ranges kept the dynamic of change moving. One of the aims was to reshuffle the gender-specific cards and profit more strongly from socio-culturally accepted low female wages. Stubborn persistence on the one hand and the dynamics of change on the other are as effective in the individual workplace as they are in the labour market more generally. Securing advantage for the male sex in working life, both in a given case and in the long term, always requires difficult and conflict-ridden processes of negotiation. The long-term successes are considerable, though, and find eloquent structural expression in gender-segregated occupations, workplaces and labour market segments.

German Peculiarities in Histories of Work and Gender

By 1990 German gender historians had succeeded in intensifying their communication with each other and gaining more attention and acceptance for gender history research within the profession. Important studies appeared on the history of work and gender in nineteenth- and twentieth-century Germany. All of these gender history studies were conceived within the broader context of society. Most of them cover longer time spans, transcending the periods associated with political history. Their focus is on women's work, both paid labour and household and family work. Research on women's work pays close attention to the frequently fluid boundaries and close relationships between the working class and the middle class. Even when they address women workers, working-class women and the labour movement, the analyses avoid using a strict concept of class. Rather, they proceed from the assumption that a gender order of work and life is in operation everywhere and at all times, both normatively and actually, and that female and male actors alike constantly refer to this order. Studying women's work from a gender history perspective thus means incorporating men's history. Instead of introducing the publications in the field individually, I would like to focus on a few aspects and address the question of whether German labour history exhibits any striking peculiarities in regard to work and gender.

The Breadwinner Model

It would be hard to dispute the high degree of acceptance enjoyed by the breadwinner model in all industrialized capitalist nations during the nineteenth and twentieth centuries.[17] The model foresaw that men who worked for wages outside the family household would earn enough to support themselves, their wives and children, while women would work exclusively as housewives and mothers to meet the family's everyday needs. This model responded to the drifting apart of paid employment and the family household. As a vision, it was accepted for many decades, in an unusually broad socio-political consensus, by men and women, the middle and working classes and members of different religions and political parties. The model corresponded to the public-private division, which had been labelled as normal. It served as a yardstick for measuring the negative side-effects of social change. It provided reassurance that, despite the terrors of absorption by the machinery of capitalist market production, it was still important and possible to work for a good life within the family and to ensure continuity from one generation to the next. It proved a useful point of orientation, legitimating for demands for just wages for men, as well as for the formulation and implementation of a gender politics bent on a firmer structural anchoring of the desired gender order of labour, with its clear separation of women's and men's tasks.

The breadwinner model was widespread, but in those countries where freedom of occupation had been introduced and guilds robbed of their privileges early on, it was probably elaborated less emphatically than in Germany. The model appears to have become particularly effective in Germany for two further reasons. The highly developed German bureaucracy employed large numbers of civil servants whose work and family situations conformed very closely to this model. In addition, since the founding of the German Empire in 1871, universal male suffrage had been introduced on the national level. This decisively influenced the development not just of the German labour movement, but also the legislation relevant to gender politics. When it came to legislative initiatives affecting the breadwinner model, the basic societal consensus could make it easier to obtain an otherwise often elusive parliamentary majority.

The German Mother: Her Household and Family Tasks

A joy to some, a red flag to others, the German mother retains a special aura even today. In recently reunited Germany, a small spark ignited an intense row when West German women accused their East German sisters of neglecting their children, and East German women countered that West German mother hens were insufferable. Before 1989 GDR women had had no choice but to accept employment as a self-evident part of their lives and to make use of the all-day schools and the ample supply of institutions caring for children of all ages. Women in the Federal Republic, in contrast, had decades of practice in coping with the absence of childcare options and all-day schools and,[18] as soon as their prospects for employment as mothers of young children vanished, were compelled to re-invent themselves as the indispensable and satisfied maternal centre of their own, often single-child, world.

Shortly after the founding of Imperial Germany, the German mother was placed under the protection of the state.[19] In 1878 the numerically extremely small sub-group of female workers in manufacturing enterprises of more than ten employees, whose very existence nonetheless fed social anxieties, came to enjoy the initially dubious effects of protective legislation for mothers. Employers were forbidden to employ new mothers, but the young women were offered no compensation for wages lost as a result. From this nucleus there developed over time Germany's increasingly effective protective labour laws for mothers, which, however, did not offer all-important protection against dismissal until 1927.

To draft mothers into service as indispensable to children's well-being, and to expect at the same time that they would devote themselves wholeheartedly to housework is a programme with which middle-class women found themselves confronted in the nineteenth century, and working-class women encountered in the twentieth century at the very latest. The teachers and curricula of the mandatory elementary schools and, later, the further education schools were not the only useful propagandists of this programme, which was also deployed as a solution to the social question. The churches, civic associations, the labour movement, the print media and, increasingly, product advertising also played their parts. From the early twentieth century onward, mothers also increasingly received support from specialized public welfare agencies for new mothers, babies, toddlers and schoolchildren. In this field, which was expanded on the national level with particular intensity during the Weimar Republic, Karen Hagemann has reconstructed the everyday life of working-class women in Hamburg in the Weimar years.[20] Her account ranges from housework, living standards, housing and family work to paid employment and the involvement of working-class women in the Social Democratic milieu in the form of consumer cooperatives, trade unions, the women's movement and the Party.[21] Entrepreneurs, too, were increasingly willing to invest in family housing, medical treatment and domestic science training, at least for their permanent workforce. In her study of Siemens, Carola Sachse shows how the company began offering family-oriented measures as a form of war relief for the numerous women who worked for the company during the First World War.[22] In the Weimar and National Socialist periods Siemens further developed company social policy as family and gender policy, using it during the Second World War either to privilege or discriminate against workers based on racial policy.

Factory Workplaces, Entrepreneurs and Unions

Studies of working conditions in individual sectors also underline the importance of the gender politics discussed and practised in Germany as a whole. To be sure, the strict legal regulation of labour relations typical for Germany was particularly effective in large industrial enterprises. In the Weimar Republic, in addition, for the first time, special legislation was enacted to regulate the collective wage agreements between employers and unions. Another important German peculiarity is that as early as 1900, labour and management, with their effective organizations, were able to coordinate interests, conflicts and objectives beyond the individual workplace and town.

For the period up until the First World War, Kathleen Canning has studied the textile industry, which was the most important large-scale industrial employer of women in Wilhelmine Germany.[23] The thread running through her book is the excessive public discussion of the Woman Question and the social question, at the centre of which was the figure of the female factory worker and, upon closer scrutiny, the female textile worker. Canning contrasts this torrent of words with accounts of the changing demand for female and male workers in the textile industry and with a detailed examination of which women worked in the factories, what conditions they faced, what the women themselves had to say about their work in the factories and the family and how they sought to improve their working conditions with or without unions.

Brigitte Kassel takes us up to 1933, exploring the rather different world of women in the German metalworking industry and in the German Metalworkers' Union, which was founded in 1891.[24] The number of women employed in this male industry rose from some 60,000 in 1895 to around 136,800 in 1907. In addition to the older iron, steel and hardware industries, in the 1890s a large number of new workplaces arose in the electrical industry and in mechanical engineering, which were defined from the outset as segregated female jobs. Here, women were employed almost exclusively as unskilled workers. In a subtle analysis, Kassel shows that the male workers put up massive resistance to their female co-workers. Women, while theoretically welcome as union members, were rarely elected to union office and seldom spoke out. There is no reliable information on women's participation in spontaneous or union-organized strikes. Incidental information indicates that female workers fought to improve their working conditions by various means, both with and without the union. The metalworkers' union newspaper, however, mainly trumpeted the persistent complaints about the impossibility of organizing the female sex and the comforting claim that man's best female comrade-in-arms was not his co-worker, but his stay-at-home wife.

Ursula Nienhaus's study of female employees of the German postal service up to 1945 casts an especially harsh light on the economically calculated deployment of the breadwinner and family model.[25] The Post Office was not a factory, but a service institution organized in factory fashion. In Imperial Germany it was middle-class, not working-class, women who worked at switchboards as telephone operators. Their employer was the state, which decided to hire women late and against strong resistance from male employees. Young, educated women were recruited to operate the switchboards, a task described as naturally female. The women were not hired as salaried employees, because since 1889 they would have had to pay into the state pension system. They were called civil servants, but denied the privilege of permanent tenure granted to other civil service postal workers, since the ability to hire and fire at short notice made it possible to react swiftly to fluctuating demand for telephone services. In addition, the forced termination of female civil servants upon marriage, which persisted until 1919, enabled the postal service to hire young women and avoid paying for the long-term physical damage common after years of work as a telephone operator. As to the rapid changes in the postal service and the employer-state, Nienhaus does not study class struggle, but she does examine conflicts over the conditions of gender-segregated employment. In order to improve their professional situation, female postal workers risked tough conflicts not just with their employer, the state, but also – in contrast to class-conscious female wage workers – with male colleagues.

Significant Influence: The State and Politics

All recent research on women's labour in the German working class underscores the outstanding significance of the state and politics. Whether they are studying a specific occupation, a branch of industry or an enterprise, historians consistently stress the relevance of state intervention, regulations, benefits or sanctions, as well as general developments in the German states typical of the era. Given the current state of comparative research, it is difficult to tell whether this is a peculiarity of the research or of the conditions being studied. The latter appears to be more likely. The particularly early development and specific nature and scope of the German welfare state probably permitted it to attain an especially high degree of influence as an instrument and medium of gender politics.

Sabine Schmitt has studied direct state intervention in factory conditions for Wilhelmine Germany.[26] She focuses on protective labour legislation for female workers, which was established in 1878 with amendments to the Imperial Industrial Code and expanded in 1891 and 1908. Initially, it affected only factory workers, but it was later extended to other groups of employed women. The protective legislation ultimately included prohibitions on the employment of pregnant women and new mothers, on hiring women to work in certain workplaces or at night and mandated a maximum working day of ten hours, the right to extended midday breaks and shorter working hours before Sundays and holidays. Industrial inspectors supervised the observance of protective regulations and contributed to reports published annually. The special regulations, which were presented as necessary for the maintenance of morality, were intended to protect the indispensable functions of mothers and housewives. They hindered women's access to jobs and no longer left it up to the workers, as seems to have been common otherwise, to negotiate special conditions in the workplace suited to their individual situations when the need arose. For industrialists, special exceptions mitigated the imposed legal requirements. Before the First World War, the protective regulations affected only a small number of female workers de facto, but a growing one in the long term. According to Schmitt, the chief success of protective labour legislation before 1914 was that the annual reports and political debates on the extension of the legislation led to a constant discourse about female workers as 'in need of protection', thus singling them out as a separate female group in the factory workforce.

A gender history of later developments in protective labour legislation remains to be written. The same is true of a detailed gender history of the social insurance system established in the 1880s for wage workers and in 1911 for salaried employees, which attracted a good deal of international attention.[27] Over many decades, this national system of laws and regulations shored up the breadwinner model with increasing efficiency. Now, wives and children profited not only from the income from husbands' continuous, skilled and well-paid factory work. If he became incapable of acting as breadwinner because of sickness, injury, death or (in later years) unemployment, the family was still entitled to his social insurance benefits. In the twentieth century, wives and children also acquired their own entitlement to benefits in addition to the husband's health insurance.

In the wake of developments in population policy and social and racial hygiene, different groups campaigned vigorously in Imperial Germany and the Weimar Republic for further improvements to social and labour legislation in the hope of making marriage, the family and children more secure and stabilizing a modernized gender order of work.[28] The established regulations proved effective and lasting. To be sure, they did not slow the growing female participation in the workforce. Nonetheless, for decades to come, women in Germany would remain primarily committed to family work, and their earned income would be treated as supplementary to the breadwinner's wages or salary.

The First and Second World Wars temporarily changed things. Ute Daniel and Birthe Kundrus have studied the female side of the home front.[29] During the First World War the departure of male workers for the Front and the concentration of all productive capacities in wartime industry revolutionized economic and social conditions. Women entered workplaces and occupational sectors that had been reserved for men before the war. With the exception of stipulations concerning maternity, protective labour legislation for women workers was suspended. Since state support for the families of soldiers was lower than the men's previous incomes, the daughters and wives of wage workers were not the only women forced to seek paid employment. In 1916 compulsory labour service for women was introduced. At the same time, despite public control of the economy, the scarcity of consumer goods made it more difficult and expensive to supply the population with everyday necessities. With falling living standards, essential household and family tasks cost increasing amounts of time, energy and money. The rapid rise in the number of dead and wounded soldiers brought further burdens. The growing hardships faced by working mothers became a public issue. The state, municipalities and war relief organizations responded by increasing assistance, not least in the vain hope of salvaging the home front and the morale of the troops. During the Second World War the National Socialists applied lessons about the home front learnt from the First World War. They drew only reluctantly upon married 'Aryan' German women for war work, instead exploiting male and female forced labourers and foreign labourers all the more brutally as workers lacking any rights whatsoever.[30] In order to motivate married 'Aryan' German women to join the workforce, the government established a programme to relieve them of everyday household and family chores.

At the end of the First World War the authorities tackled the task of demobilization. Susanne Rouette analysed in great detail the underlying ideas, policies and practice.[31] In a post-war era marked by revolution, the highest political priority was accorded to the re-employment of returning soldiers in their old workplaces. With the strong support of workers' councils in the factories, state and municipal offices used regulations and, if necessary, coercive methods to remove women from those jobs they still occupied. Businesses were loath to dismiss female workers because of the lower wage costs. The reintroduction of protective labour legislation for women proved an effective means here. Unmarried women workers in particular, large numbers of whom had abandoned low-wage female workplaces in agriculture and consumer goods manufacturing during the war for better paid jobs in armaments production, were seldom willing to give up their positions voluntarily to demobilized soldiers. Women who refused to return to their pre-war domiciles risked exclusion from the unemployment relief benefits that had been paid since the end of the war.

After 1945 the Federal Republic and the GDR, although equally committed to gender policy, embarked on very different paths.[32] GDR policy was to employ all women, including wives and mothers, as full members of the workforce. The Federal Republic, in contrast, once again promoted the project of the housewife and mother freed from the necessity of paid employment.[33] Using the case of the history of the free housework day, Carola Sachse has written a fascinating comparison of the different state systems.[34] During the Second World War, the National Socialists allowed employed women with their own households to stay home from work one day a month to do their household chores. After the war the housework day was stubbornly defended, first, as a necessity for women forced to cope simultaneously with professional and family duties, and, later, as a social achievement. Despite persistent conflicts over who belonged to the group of entitled persons, the housework day continued in East Germany until the end of the GDR. In West Germany, the housework day was mandated by law in only a few federal states and produced numerous suits in the labour courts. The issue became moot when the trade unions succeeded in gaining Saturday as a day off.

The Federal Republic clung to the idea that paid employment was undesirable for married women and mothers even in the 1950s, when demand for labour far outstripped supply. In this situation, labour market policy and the state labour administration pursued two strategies. First, an ingenious process was devised for the official recruitment of workers in Italy, Spain, Greece, Yugoslavia and Turkey. This involved intergovernmental agreements, a recruitment bureaucracy and a process, agreed upon by the labour administration and the trade unions, for integrating the new labour force – whose members were granted temporary work permits and assigned to a particular employer – into the West German social security and wage system on equal terms. Monika Mattes has recently studied how the many female labour migrants, a group largely neglected by scholars but strategically important for the politics of recruitment, came to Germany.[35] Their recruitment made it possible to continue to pay low wages for tasks classified as female. The programme of recruiting women proved unsuccessful initially. Numbers only rose significantly with the recruitment of married couples and the offer – which particularly appealed to Turks – that migrants could bring their spouses to Germany. This paved the way for the permanent settlement of families, however, which planners had not foreseen and which later blocked political intentions to deport the 'guest workers' in response to rising unemployment.

The second strategy, part-time employment, was established as a new mode of work, especially for married women with children, and elaborately imbedded in existing legal regulations concerning the civil service, labour, wages, social insurance and taxation. Why, how and along which lines of conflict and consensus this social and labour politics of part-time employment ultimately took hold has been examined by Christine von Oertzen for numerous aspects, participating institutions, organizations and groups of individuals.[36] Interviews revealed that wives who sought paid employment out of interest rather than pure economic necessity promised their husbands that they would continue to fulfil all of their family responsibilities, so that he and the children need not fear any changes.

Conclusions

I have offered a rough outline here of research developments and the theoretical and empirical measurement of gender and work, as well as a brief account of research findings selected for purposes of comparison. An outline is ill-suited to brilliant flights of erudition and critique. It demands setting clear accents. The first accent I wanted to set was to slowly tease out the hesitant process of integrating gender history into the history of work and the labour movement. As a second accent, it was important for me to pinpoint which bulwarks of the gender order of labour, along with their hierarchically interpreted differences, were defended against social change. My third accent stressed the state, politics and the workplace as fields of power within which working-class women and men organized their lives and work, seeking to use it to their advantage and – by their actions, interpretations and individual and collective struggles – to improve it. I have left out a fourth, central accent. In order to draw our attention to the tensions and dynamics that keep gendered work from ever becoming a stable, permanent order, the outline I have sketched would need to be supplemented by the technologies and the forms of labour organization and market relations used in the production and distribution of goods and services.[37] The technological change accelerated by industrialization continually transformed gendered work in agriculture and manufacturing, as well as in family households.

As to historical comparisons, which I have merely touched on here, they are useful and, indeed, indispensable for European history. They presuppose the existence of a reliable body of research, however. If we aspire to do more than merely bind a pile of heterogeneous studies between two book covers and ensure that we actually compare the comparable, we need to develop more precise questions and approaches which allow us to discuss heterogeneous findings and observations. In addition, comparisons between nations should not enjoy more prestige than those between various other entities.

In closing, I would like to address the justified criticisms of Eurocentrism and ethnocentrism that have been raised for a number of years now. With the exception of studies of Nazi racial policy, this critique also applies to German research on gender and work. Today, the critique is undergoing an urgent further development. In 2004 Alice Kessler-Harris, a pioneer in the field of gendered labour history, called for women's labour history to adopt a global perspective in the face of transnational corporations and the globalized migration of working people.[38] All over the world growing numbers of women are increasingly visible in paid employment for the market, while still being relegated to unpaid household and family work and, despite better training, low-wage and routine jobs. According to Kessler-Harris, the 'global turn' she is calling for will force us to distance ourselves from decades of research practice guided by Western perspectives, categories and values and to recognize the particularity of Western culture, thus gaining new possibilities for more radical international comparisons. She elucidates the challenges of the global turn for the four areas of 'ideology and culture, sexual division of labour, labour-migration or the flow of labour and issues of power and status'. I share her expectation that the shaping of working conditions all over the world will continue to be closely connected with processes of constructing and reconstructing gender. How historical research and writing might cope with the sheer complexity of a gendered history of work from a global perspective and the multiplication of meaningful questions and, inevitably, of answers remains a completely open question.

Notes

* I would like to thank Pamela Selwyn for translating so excellently my German manuscripts into English.

1. See especially Efi Avdela, 'Work, Gender and History in the 1990s and Beyond', *Gender and History* 11,3 (1999): 528–41; Alice Kessler-Harris, 'Reframing the History of Women's Wage Labor: Challenges of a Global Perspective', *Journal of Women's History* 15,4 (2009): 186–206.
2. See Ute Frevert, Heide Wunder and Christina Vanja, 'Historical Research in the Federal Republic of Germany', and Petra Rantzsch and Erika Uitz, 'Historical Research in the German Democratic Republic', in Karen Offen, Ruth Roach Pierson and Jane Rendall (eds), *Writing Women's History. International Perspectives* (Bloomington and Indianapolis: Indiana University Press, 1991), pp. 291–331 and pp. 333–53; Ute Frevert, 'Klasse und Geschlecht – Ein deutscher Sonderweg?', in Logie Barrow, Dorothea Schmidt and Jutta Schwarzkopf (eds), *Nichts als Unterdrückung? Geschlecht und Klasse in der englischen Sozialgeschichte* (Münster: Verlag Westfälisches Dampfboot, 1991), pp. 259–76.
3. Gisela Bock, 'Historische Frauenforschung. Fragestellungen und Perspektiven', in Karin Hausen (ed.), *Frauen suchen ihre Geschichte. Historische Studien zum 19. und 20. Jahrhundert* (Munich: C.H. Beck, 1983), pp. 22–60; 'Geschichte, Frauengeschichte, Geschlechtergeschichte', *Geschichte und Gesellschaft* 14,3 (1988): 364–91; 'Women's History and Gender History. Aspects of an International Debate', *Gender and History* 1,1 (1989): 7–30; 'Challenging Dichotomies. Perspectives on Women's History', in Offen, Pierson and Rendall (eds), *Writing*, pp. 1–23.
4. Gerhard A. Ritter (ed.), *Geschichte der Arbeiter und der Arbeiterbewegung in Deutschland seit dem Ende des 18. Jahrhunderts* (Bonn: Dietz Verlag, 2002). Volumes already published: Jürgen Kocka, vols i and ii (1990), Gerhard A. Ritter and Klaus Tenfelde, vol. v (1992), Heiner August Winkler, vols ix, x, xi (1984, 1985 and 1987), Michael Schneider, vol. xii (1999), Christoph Kle*ß*mann (2007).
5. Jürgen Kocka, vol. 1: *Weder Stand noch Klasse. Unterschichten um 1800* (Bonn: Dietz, 1990); vol. 2: *Arbeiterverhältnisse und Arbeiterexistenzen. Grundlagen der Klassenbildung im 19. Jahrhundert* (Bonn: Dietz, 1990). What follows refers to vol. 1, pp. 33–35, quotation p. 39.
6. See Ava Baron, 'Gender and Labor History. Learning from the Past, Looking to the Future', in Ava Baron (ed.), *Work Engendered: Toward a New History of American Labor* (Ithaca and London: Cornell University Press, 1991), pp. 1–46; Marcel van der Linden (ed.), *The End of Labour History?: International Review of Social History*, supplement 1 (Cambridge: Cambridge University Press, 1993); Gabriella Hauch (ed.), *Geschlecht–Klasse–Ethnizität, 28. Tagung der Historikerinnen und Historiker der Arbeiterinnen- und Arbeiterbewegung* (Vienna and Zurich: Europaverlag, 1993); Eileen Yeo, 'Gender in Labour and Working-Class History', in Lex Heerma van Voss and Marcel van der Linden (eds), *Class and Other Identities: Gender, Religion, and Ethnicity in the Writing of European Labour History* (New York: Berghahn, 2002), pp. 73–87; Alice Kessler Harris, 'Two Labour Histories or One?', in ibid., pp. 133–49; Eileen Boris and Angélique Janssens (eds), 'Complicating Categories: Gender, Class, Race and Ethnicity', *International Review of Social History*, supplement 7 (Cambridge: Cambridge University Press, 1999). For the anxious and sceptical German debate, see Thomas Welskopp, 'Klasse

als Befindlichkeit? Vergleichende Arbeitergeschichte vor der kulturhistorischen Herausforderung', *Archiv für Sozialgeschichte* 38 (1998): 301–36.

7. For his involvement in these discussions, see, for example, Jürgen Kocka (ed.), 'Klasse und Geschlecht', *Geschichte und Gesellschaft* 18,2 (1992).
8. See, for example, Leonore Davidoff, 'Mastered for Life. Servant and Wife in Victorian and Edwardian England' (1974), reprinted in Leonore Davidoff, *Worlds Between. Historical Perspectives on Gender and Class* (London: Polity, 1995), pp. 18–40.
9. Sonya O. Rose, *Limited Livelihoods: Gender and Class in Nineteenth-Century England* (Berkeley: University of California Press, 1992).
10. Rose, *Livelihoods*, p. 11.
11. Ibid., p. 10.
12. Sonya O. Rose, 'Gender and Labour History. The Nineteenth-Century Legacy', in van der Linden (ed.), *The End*, pp. 145–62, quotations on pp. 147, 158–62.
13. Kathleen Canning, 'Gender and the Politics of Class Formation. Rethinking German Labor History', *American Historical Review* 97,3: (1992), pp. 736–68. See also her essay collection *Gender History in Practice: Historical Perspective on Bodies, Class, and Citizenship* (Ithaca: Cornell University Press, 2006).
14. Joan Wallach Scott, 'Gender: A Useful Category of Historical Analysis', *American Historical Review* 91,5 (1986): 1053–75, reprinted in Scott, *Gender and the Politics of History* (New York: Columbia University Press, 1988), pp. 28–50.
15. Canning, 'Gender and the Politics', p. 768.
16. Karin Hausen, 'Wirtschaften mit der Geschlechterordnung. Ein Essay', in Karin Hausen (ed.), *Geschlechterhierarchie und Arbeitsteilung. Zur Geschichte ungleicher Erwerbschancen von Männern und Frauen* (Göttingen: Vandenhoeck and Ruprecht, 1993), pp. 40–67; the reader contains German case studies on this topic. See also Angelika Wetterer, *Arbeitsteilung und Geschlechterkonstruktion. 'Gender at Work' in theoretischer und historischer Perspektive* (Konstanz: UVK, 2002).
17. See Angélique Janssens (ed.), *The Rise and Decline of the Male Breadwinner Family?, International Review of Social History*, supplement 5 (Cambridge: Cambridge University Press, 1998); Karin Hausen, 'Frauenerwerbstätigkeit und erwerbstätige Frauen. Anmerkungen zur historischen Forschung', in Gunilla Budde (ed.), *Frauen arbeiten. Weibliche Erwerbstätigkeit in Ost- und Westdeutschland nach 1945* (Göttingen, Vandenhoeck and Ruprecht, 1997), pp. 19–45.
18. See Karen Hagemann, 'Between Ideology and Economy: The "Time Politics" of Child Care and Public Education in the Two Germanys', *Social Politics: International Studies in Gender, State and Society* 13,2 (2006): 217–60.
19. See Teresa Kulawik, *Wohlfahrtsstaat und Mutterschaft. Schweden und Deutschland 1870–1912* (Frankfurt and New York: Campus, 1999); Gerda Neyer, 'Die Entwicklung des Mutterschutzes in Deutschland, Österreich und in der Schweiz von 1877 bis 1945', in Ute Gerhard (ed.), *Frauen in der Geschichte des Rechts. Von der Frühen Neuzeit bis zur Gegenwart* (Munich: C.H. Beck, 1997), pp. 744–58; Gisela Bock and Pat Thane (eds), *Maternity and Gender Policies. Women and the Rise of the European Welfare States 1880s–1950s* (London and New York: Routledge, 1991).
20. Karen Hagemann, *Frauenalltag und Männerpolitik. Alltagsleben und gesellschaftliches Handeln von Arbeiterfrauen in der Weimarer Republik* (Bonn: J.W.H. Dietz Nachf., 1990).
21. See also Christiane Eifert, *Frauenpolitik und Wohlfahrtspflege. Zur Geschichte der sozialdemokratischen 'Arbeiterwohlfahrt'* (Frankfurt and New York: Campus, 1993).

22. Carola Sachse, *Siemens, der Nationalsozialismus und die moderne Familie. Eine Untersuchung zur Sozialen Rationalisierung in Deutschland im 20. Jahrhundert* (Hamburg: Rasch und Röhrig, 1990).
23. Kathleen Canning, *Languages of Labor and Gender. Female Factory Work in Germany, 1850–1914* (Ithaca and London: Cornell University Press, 1996).
24. Brigitte Kassel, *Frauen in einer Männerwelt. Frauenerwerbsarbeit in der Metallindustrie und ihre Interessenvertretung durch den Deutschen Metallarbeiter-Verband 1891–1933* (Cologne: Bund, 1997).
25. Ursula Nienhaus, *Vater Staat und seine Gehilfinnen. Die Politik mit der Frauenarbeit bei der deutschen Post 1864–1945* (Frankfurt and New York: Campus, 1995).
26. Sabine Schmitt, *Der Arbeiterinnenschutz im deutschen Kaiserreich. Zur Konstruktion der schutzbedürftigen Arbeiterin* (Stuttgart and Weimar: J.B. Metzler, 1995); and '"All these Forms of Women's Work Which Endanger Public Health and Public Welfare": Protective Labor Legislation for Women in Germany, 1878–1914', in Ulla Wikander, Alice Kessler-Harris and Jane Lewis(eds), *Protecting Women. Labor Legislation in Europe, the United States, and Australia, 1880–1920* (Urbana and Chicago: University of Illinois Press, 1995), pp. 125–49.
27. For a tentative sketch, see Karin Hausen, 'Arbeiterinnenschutz, Mutterschutz und gesetzliche Krankenversicherung im Deutschen Kaiserreich und in der Weimarer Republik. Zur Funktion von Arbeits- und Sozialrecht für die Normierung und Stabilisierung der Geschlechterverhältnisse', in Gerhard (ed.), *Frauen*, pp. 713–43.
28. Eva Schöck-Quinteros, 'Heimarbeiterschutz für die "Mütter des arbeitenden Volkes". Deutschland 1896–1914', *L'Homme. Zeitschrift für Feministische Geschichtswissenschaft* 9,2 (1998): 183–215; Cornelie Usborne, *The Politics of the Body in Weimar Germany. Women's Reproductive Rights and Duties* (London: Macmillan, 1992).
29. Ute Daniel, *Klassengesellschaft in der Kriegsgesellschaft* (Göttingen: Vandenhoeck and Ruprecht, 1989); Birthe Kundrus, *Kriegerfrauen. Familienpolitik und Geschlechterverhältnisse im Ersten und Zweiten Weltkrieg* (Hamburg: Christians, 1995).
30. Rüdiger Hachtmann, 'Industriearbeiterinnen in der deutschen Kriegswirtschaft 1936–1944/45', in *Geschichte und Gesellschaft* 19,3 (1993): 332–61; Gisela Bock, 'Gleichheit und Differenz in der nationalsozialistischen Rassenpolitik', in ibid., pp.277–310; Gisela Bock, 'Antinatalism, Maternity and Paternity in National Socialist Racism', in Bock and Thane (eds), *Maternity*, pp. 233–55.
31. Susanne Rouette, *Sozialpolitik als Geschlechterpolitik. Die Regulierung der Frauenarbeit nach dem Ersten Weltkrieg* (Frankfurt and New York: Campus Verlag, 1993).
32. For comparisons, see Gunilla Budde (ed.), *Frauen arbeiten. Weibliche Erwerbstätigkeit in Ost- und Westdeutschland nach 1945* (Göttingen: Vandenhoeck and Ruprecht, 1997), and Hagemann, 'Between Ideology and Economy'.
33. See Robert G. Moeller, *Protecting Motherhood. Women and the Family in the Politics of Post-war Germany* (Berkeley, Los Angeles and Oxford: University of California Press, 1993); Merith Niehuss, *Familie, Frau und Gesellschaft. Studien zur Strukturgeschichte der Familie in Westdeutschland 1945–1960* (Göttingen: Vandenhoeck and Ruprecht, 2001), with chapters on social policy and married women's work; Wiebke Kolbe, *Elternschaft im Wohlfahrtsstaat. Schweden und die Bundesrepublik im Vergleich 1945–2000* (Frankfurt and New York: Campus, 2002).
34. Carola Sachse, *Der Hausarbeitstag. Gerechtigkeit und Gleichberechtigung in Ost und West. 1939–1994* (Göttingen: Wallstein, 2002).

35. Monika Mattes, *'Gastarbeiterinnen' in der Bundesrepublik. Anwerbepolitik, Migration und Geschlecht in den 50er bis 70er Jahren* (Frankfurt and New York: Campus Verlag, 2005).
36. Christine von Oertzen, *Teilzeitarbeit und die Lust am Zuverdienen. Geschlechterpolitik und gesellschaftlicher Wandel in Westdeutschland 1948–1969* (Göttingen: Vandenhoeck and Ruprecht, 1999), translation, Berghahn Publishers, 2007; Christine von Oertzen and Almut Rietzschel, 'Das "Kuckucksei" Teilzeitarbeit. Die Politik der Gewerkschaften im deutsch-deutschen Vergleich', in Budde, *Frauen arbeiten*, pp. 212–51.
37. See, for example, Gertjan de Groot and Marlou Schrover (eds), *Women Workers and Technological Change in Europe in the Nineteenth and Twentieth Century* (London: Taylor and Francis, 1995).
38. Alice Kessler-Harris, 'Reframing the History of Women's Wage Labor: Challenges of a Global Perspective', in *Journal of Women's History* 15,4 (2004): 186–206.

6
Trust as Work

Ute Frevert

This article is about trust and confidence, but also about work and labour. At first glance, the relation may not seem self-evident. We normally tend to dissociate trust and work by defining trust as an irrational emotion and by stripping work of its emotional and cultural context. This kind of reductionism, however, runs counter to scholarly opinion. As Jürgen Kocka has argued convincingly, the concept of work historically has much broader ramifications than the ones implicit in the modern notion of paid, market-related employment. Even activities like sports and war, consumption and play contain elements of work (generally defined as the 'purposeful application of physical and mental forces in order to fulfil needs').[1] On the other hand, psychologists and sociologists no longer regard trust as a given – or absent – emotion; instead, it is perceived as an attitude that can be acquired by a laborious process of social networking, advertisement and sustained experience.[2]

More complex and sophisticated definitions thus enable us to discover a relationship between work and trust that escapes narrower perceptions. This relationship can be observed on two levels: first, trust forms a vital component of work and labour relations; it is part and parcel of each and every economic transaction and work process. Without trust, those transactions and processes would either not occur, or would occur at much higher costs. Second, trust is itself the outcome of work. It does not come about work-free and gratuitously. In order to build trust, you have to invest in trustworthiness, which demands long-lasting efforts both material and immaterial. Trust is work and has come to be acknowledged as such. In fact, the modern Western lexicon includes the terms 'confidence work', *Vertrauensarbeit, travail de confiance, lavoro di confidenza,* meaning all kinds of activities that establish bonds of trust among people and institutions.[3]

Emotionwork

The very existence of this term presents an interesting phenomenon. In his introduction to this volume, Jürgen Kocka mentioned the process of upgrading that took place since the early modern period in Western societies and transformed work into a central feature of wealth, civility and human identity. In its broader sense of activity and occupation, work was increasingly seen as 'the main purpose of man and the source of his felicity', as the popular German philosopher Christian Garve quoted common opinion in 1798.[4] This adoration of work is reflected in the ever-growing number of composites like (in German) *Gedankenarbeit, Bildungsarbeit, Beziehungsarbeit* and, for our sake, *Vertrauensarbeit.* To claim that something is work obviously adds to its value. It serves as a kind of ennoblement and thus testifies to the powerful status of work as a main marker of social identity in modern times.

This trend of conscious and intentional inclusion quite evidently counteracts the reverse development that characterizes Western modernity: the constriction of the concept of work and its narrow definition as paid employment. As Kocka and others point out, this definition gained currency in the nineteenth century, accompanying the transformation of European societies into capitalist market economies. Compared to the medieval or early modern period, 'work' now tended to be reduced to its marketable function, thereby excluding most of women's work in the household and in reproduction (encompassing their 'labour' of giving birth or *Gebärarbeit,* as it used to be called). At the same time, the process of commodification proved all-pervasive and reached more and more segments of society. As much as the division of labour intensified, activities that had formerly been performed within the household moved out and were turned into professional work. As such, they immediately acquired a reputation of being rational, time-conscious, skilful and transparent, standing in marked contrast to those mainly female tasks that remained within the much contracted realm of family and household. What women were left doing in the (middle-class) household was not considered work any more; rather, it was seen as the natural consequence of their feminine destiny. Born to love and please and serve their loved ones, they seemed to be driven by emotions only. The services they rendered to their husbands, children and extended family were thus both thoroughly naturalized and emotionalized.

Emotions, though, held a bad reputation in a culture that became heavily influenced by the Enlightenment's gospel of reason and progressive self-improvement. Modern Western common sense has come to identify emotions as biological and feminine, adding up to a highly negative view. Drawing on classical notions, emotions have been thought of as something spontaneous and transmitted through the body (showing arousal, a change of colour, transpiration). For a short period of time, the late eighteenth century tried to make use of these actions and reactions in a positive, constructive way. Sentimentalism emerged as a powerful social and cultural mood that was considered morally superior and critical of the armoured, false and cheating culture of aristocratic and court society. The nineteenth century, however, quickly closed this chapter of emotional emancipation. Instead, it created and popularized a gendered anthropology that reserved emotions for women only. First, women were perceived as more biological beings anyway, tied to and fettered by their reproductive organs. As such, they were affected by emotional disturbances to a much higher degree than men. Second, and equally importantly, women were allowed, sometimes even encouraged to display their emotions, in contrast to men, who, if they had any at all, were expected to hide them and control their expression. Women being overwhelmed by their emotions and showing this through their bodily behaviour (fainting, shedding tears, blushing) were thus a common sight, while men had to keep their temper, show emotional restraint and pretend to be cold-blooded even in situations that made their blood boil (the duel, for example).

These different emotional regimes governed both the private and the public sphere. Male power in the household and the family depended on the father and husband being in complete control of his senses and emotions, while women and children demonstrated their structural weakness (which could, under certain conditions, be turned into a situational strength) by their emotional behaviour. As for the public sphere, even political regimes that drew heavily on emotional support and arousal (like fascism with all its mass rallies and devotional practices), made sure that this support was given as a gendered response: men goose-stepping and forming strong columns, women frantically cheering, screaming and reaching out to the *Führer* to have their babies kissed or patted.

It is exactly this gendered perception of emotions that has prevented emotions from becoming an academic topic for a very long time. Only from the 1970s onwards has this changed. The feminist movement has successfully used women's alleged emotionality for political action. Anger has thus become a powerful and carefully orchestrated weapon; love, taken to be women's ultimate destiny, was denounced as a tool of women's oppression. In this way, the emotional field was completely re-cultivated. Vice versa, men have been called upon to become more emotional and to free themselves from the demand not to display love and caring, especially in their role as fathers.

The culture of psychological therapy that has pervaded Western societies since the 1960s has taken up and consolidated this general emancipation of emotions for both genders.[5] At the same time, it has added its own professional interests, which are best revealed by the attempts to label emotions as work. Mourning, love, building and sustaining relationships, coming to terms with disappointment and fear, all these activities became semantically associated with work.[6] Quite evidently, this adds seriousness to what therapists and their patients do, namely 'working through' a problem. As is well-known, the phrase was invented by Sigmund Freud, who deliberately employed the notion of work to link philosophical, economic and scientific issues. According to Freud's psychoanalytical approach, sweat and tears had to be shed in order to get to the core of the unease or disease that troubled a patient. Furthermore, the process had to go on for an extended time and needed regularity and discipline. The notion of work as it was used in psychoanalysis – and, from there, in other branches of psychotherapy – makes it very clear that emotions were and are not about spontaneous and happily anarchic play, pleasure and pastimes, but about continuous, goal-related investment of time and energy.

Identifying emotions as (and at) work did not remain confined to therapeutic circles, though. The new semantics soon invaded common talk and were picked up by sociologists. For them, the term 'emotionwork' means 'the attempt of an acting person to adjust his feelings and their expression to the ruling norms'.[7] This rests on the assumption that 'rules about feeling' actually determine what kind of emotions can be expressed in what way and in what kind of situation. It does not preclude that people might have completely different (and, by definition, inappropriate) feelings that do not comply at all with those rules. In this case, 'emotionwork' or 'emotion management' has to set in.[8]

Sociologists generally have chosen not to bother about the long-term dispute that troubles their colleagues in psychology and anthropology, namely, the old question of nurture versus nature. Even if they acknowledge the biological or, to be more precise, neurological dimension of emotions, they are more interested in their social and cultural emanations. They seem to be supported by a growing number of psychologists who no longer regard emotions as biologically pre-programmed responses to certain events and interactions. Rather, emotions are seen as operating like overlearned cognitive habits, deeply influenced by goals, strategies and mechanisms of mental control.[9] Anthropologists have eagerly taken up this idea and used it in their own fieldwork. An eloquent majority considers emotions to be embedded in 'discourses' that enable people to express and thereby feel certain experiences. Feelings and their expression are thus interpreted as social practices deeply tied to 'relations of power as well as to sociability'.[10] They are supposed to carry, above all, relational value enabling and continuing communication among people.

For historians, the constructionist and relational approach has much to offer. Even if we give credit to the contention that all emotions have a biological or bodily substance, we might still concentrate on their expression and on the cultural code (or 'discourse') that gives meaning to expressive gestures. Among the first who took up the challenge were historians Carol and Peter Stearns. They coined the term 'emotionology', meaning emotional styles and standards that define the production and perception of emotions in a given society.[11] William Reddy, an eminent scholar of modern France, prefers to talk about 'emotional lexicons' that offer individuals ways of thinking and speaking about their feelings. These lexicons contain emotional norms that are embedded in social practices. The complex of practices, which also sanction those who break the norms, is called an 'emotional regime'. Every society imposes such a regime on its members, and thus allows for a specific mixture of constraints and liberties.[12]

This way of thinking about emotions can easily be linked with the notion of work. Emotional regimes are established, popularized and contested by people and their activities and can thus be studied 'at work', in progress. Furthermore, to build up these regimes, to keep them going, to sanction misdemeanours requires time, energy/force and skills, and as such conforms to the common definition of work. Even on an individual level, emotions and their expression (including the adjustment of feeling and expression to regimental norms) fall under this definition.

Confidence Work

At this point, we can approach trust and confidence as emotionally grounded attitudes that are achieved, upheld and altered through constant processes of individual and collective effort. As we saw earlier, this effort is contemporaneously called and acknowledged as work. But what role precisely does trust play in the emotional lexicon of modern societies? And why should we be interested in the work of trust (combining the notion of trust as work and trust at work)? Why choose trust? And what is trust, after all?

There are multiple definitions of trust, and they vary according to which disciplines are involved. The philosopher Annette Baier talks about trust as an attitude that entrusts something of great value to another person's (or institution's) safekeeping. The level of trust then rises with the worth of what is entrusted and the risk of losing it. It is the moral dimension, the expectation of goodwill on the part of the trusted, which for Baier distinguishes conscious trust from simple reliance and dependence.[13] A similar distinction is suggested by sociologist Niklas Luhmann, who also connects trust to risk and intentional risk-taking and, by contrast, attributes confidence to those who do not consider alternatives. Confidence, then, is the positive expectation of a future behaviour that cannot directly be influenced by one's own actions (like weather, traffic and the Dow Jones). Trust, however, presupposes a situation and a conscience of risk. It depends on the perception that a person's decisions can have unexpected and unpleasant consequences; trust allows the person to make the decision hoping that bad consequences will not occur. The degree of unpleasantness directly refers to the amount of trust that has to be invested in the transaction.[14]

Luhmann was not the first sociologist to be interested in the phenomenon of trust and confidence. As early as 1908 Georg Simmel wrote about trust as a psychological mechanism bridging the gap between knowing and not-knowing. According to him, somebody who knew everything did not need trust; somebody who did not know and could not control the consequences of his actions had to trust. Trust was thus thoroughly linked to risk, insecurity and the future. And it was, for Simmel as well as for Luhmann, closely associated with modern conditions. Primitive societies, Simmel argued, in which everybody knew everybody could do with much less trust than modern, highly differentiated systems whose members saw each other as strangers. Luhmann shared this view when he talked about trust as a reduction of complexity. Since complexity is seen as a characteristic feature of modern societies in contrast to pre-modern ones, trust is a functional necessity in modern societies and basically irrelevant in earlier types.[15]

This argument seems to be supported by what we observe in everyday life: trust talk is ubiquitous. The Google search engine offers ample evidence coming up with millions of results for 'confidence', *confiance*, *Vertrauen*. Bankers, business people and politicians continuously demand trust or claim that the services that they render can be trusted. Trust thus appears to be a scarce resource heavily sought after by many different people and institutions that obviously cannot do without it. A lack of trust is seen as a major calamity endangering the psychic stability of individuals as much as the smooth functioning of economic transactions and political communication.

The ever-present trust talk underlines and testifies to the value that modern Western societies attach to trust. Trust has to be 'at work', has to function and successfully operate as what has been named a central 'lubricant of a social system'.[16] Trust brings about patterns of behaviour that are crucial and vital for civil societies. It engenders civility, respect, cooperation; it enables consumers to buy and producers to sell. But trust is not something that can be automatically expected or relied on. It is volatile and sensitive; it demands effort and investment. It has to be nurtured and actively produced, which is implied in the notion of 'trust as work'.

It is precisely this qualification that makes trust interesting and rewarding for social scientists to analyse. Because trust is an emotional attitude that is acquired, rather than genuinely present, it lends itself to procedural examination. Trust is based on experiences and connected to expectations that are more often voiced than not. It is verbalized, not to the same degree as love is, but still sufficiently to be studied. Unlike love, it is a multi-area emotion, meaning that it is not confined to private and intimate relations, but works in the public sphere as well. As such, trust connects economics, politics, society and culture: something hard to find among other emotions or emotional attitudes.

At the same time, there are clear limits of exploring trust and trust work, particularly from a historical perspective. Above all, it is impossible to say anything about the 'real' existence of trust as a felt emotion. How people experienced trust in former times escapes our knowledge. What we can study, instead, is the status that trust held in a given society. As historians working with texts and, sometimes, pictures, we can find out about social expectations, emotional regimes and lexicons that prescribed or recommended a certain behaviour connected to trust or distrust. We can investigate how much societies or groups of people within a society valued trustful relations and expected their members to engage in them, and if we are lucky, they might even tell us about their motivations to do so.

What can be expected from a historical analysis, then, are insights into the cultural codes that societies apply to trust. Self-evidently, those codes are highly normative. At the same time, though, trust talk translates norms into practice. It functions as a performative speech act: whenever somebody refers to trust (or distrust), he or she is making a statement about an emotional claim ('Trust me'; 'I distrust you').[17] This statement occurs in a specific scenario and is meant to have an effect on it. It is designed to evoke certain actions and reactions (motivate the other person, for example, to prove his or her trustworthiness). The language of trust thus cannot easily be dismissed as purely prescriptive or ideological. Those who use it do something: they invoke reciprocity, construct social or political relations, and appeal to the compliance and mutuality of the people involved. Speaking about and of trust is to do trust work.

What kind of material do we have to discover trust and trust/confidence work as part of emotional lexicons and social practices? To start with, we find definitions and contextual descriptions of trust basically since the mid-eighteenth century. At around this time, the first encyclopaedias were published collecting common knowledge and passing it on to their readers. They tell us about a growing – and shifting – concern that the moderns have about trust. Comparing different entries from the age of Enlightenment till recent times, it becomes clear that trust ranks high on modern societies' cultural, political and social agendas. This is particularly obvious when looking at the very first entry available in German, from 1746. Its author, Johann Heinrich Zedler, talks at length about trust (*Vertrauen*), but 90 per cent of his article deals with trust in God, which is taken to be the most fundamental type. This surely reflects the strong Lutheran tradition, Luther having warned his audience against trusting people, since only God deserved trust.[18] Furthermore, it reflects pre-modern conditions of basic insecurity and contingency. First, most of the dangers threatening individuals seemed to be out of human control, like famine, disease, catastrophic weather, ubiquitous death. Only God could help here, and this is why it was He (and not people) who had to be trusted. Second, there was little stability in political and economic relations; legal safeguards were still underdeveloped and did not offer much support. Social trust was thus an equally scarce resource. Zedler mentioned and approved of it only once reserving it for the relationship between doctor and patient. Here, trust was functional, necessary and possible. In other respects, the author recommended being careful and watching out. He ferociously attacked those whom he called *Erneuerte*: the modernists, adherents of progress and the Enlightenment. He did not share their positive anthropology, but considered men to be 'fragile' and 'unstable', untrustworthy. To recommend more trust among people, as did the *Erneuerte*, displayed weakness, not strength.[19]

Zedler's warning went unheard, though. Throughout the nineteenth century, the dimension of social trust increased, to the detriment of trust in God, which virtually disappeared from the encyclopaedia articles. Trust among export merchants, between soldiers and their officers, between the poor and the rich, between servants and masters, among friends and family was mentioned time and again. At the same time, composite words proliferated, testifying to the increasing charms of trust. *Vertrauensstaat*, *Vertrauensmänner*, and *Vertrauensarzt*: the list grew steadily. For entrepreneurs and businessmen, trust and 'credit' translated into immediate economic gains. Citizens used trust to claim more political rights;

politicians demanded to be trusted and pretended to be trustworthy. Pedagogical literature converted trust into a cornerstone of the teacher-student relationship. Above all, it focused on the crucial role of the nuclear family to provide conditions of trust. Here children were to be taught that they could rely on their parents, for better or worse. At the same time, they were to find out that they themselves were trusted by their parents, who obviously considered them trustworthy. This experience was held to be crucial for their own ability to build self-confidence: a word newly emerged in the emotional lexicon of the nineteenth century and closely linked to trust in others.[20]

Trust, we may sum up, was considered a valuable asset for the new society that emerged after the late eighteenth century. In many ways, it embodied a powerful critique of pre-modern conditions that were seen as characterized by relations of distrust, by violence, by individual falseness and fraud. Trust, in contrast, was linked to ideas of mutuality and reciprocity, of openness and transparency.

Trust and Economic Transaction

Apart from politics, economic relations proved to be most susceptible to the new trust talk invented during the nineteenth century. Businessmen and professionals had to be very careful about constantly proving trustworthy for clients, partners and creditors alike. Trust for them was a major means of doing business and realizing continuous and long-term gains. This was clearly acknowledged and emphasized by the German entrepreneur Robert Bosch (1861–1942) when he said: 'I'd rather lose money than trust. The inviolability of my promises, the belief in the value of my goods and in my word to me always seemed more valuable than momentary gains.'[21] In this famous quote, Bosch testified both to the general necessity of trust and to the prerequisites that had to be met in order to earn trust. Trust for him was crucial to achieve the kind of economic success that he went after: not short-term and momentary, but sustained and dependable.

Economic trustworthiness was, however, only partly achieved on its own terms. The 'value of goods' was not enough to produce it, as Bosch and his colleagues surely knew. To make customers and partners believe in their 'promises' and 'word', they had to build up a reputation that drew on other sources as well. When these sources were lacking, as it often happened to the first generations of industrial entrepreneurs, the latter had to rely on kinship ties (where trust was a given matter) for financial credit and economic expansion.[22] Many used family members to set up branches in foreign countries, like Werner von Siemens, whose brother Carl ran the St. Petersburg office. Even in the British case, which is normally seen as the prime example of individualistic entrepreneurship, economic historians have recently stressed the 'collective nature of business diversification'. Active networking in social, cultural and business associations, so the argument goes, helped to build up trust and trustworthiness among potential partners and investors. This was hard work, demanding time, money and personal effort, as the

Manchester cotton merchant Benjamin Braidley pointed out in his memoirs. In 1824, when he was about to co-found the Manchester fire insurance office, he spent over thirty-six hours each week 'on matters totally unconnected with my own business', including committee meetings, correspondence, social calls and charitable and educational work. This extended networking helped him to gain a good reputation as being respectable, solid and trustworthy. His partners' trust in him thus relied on how they judged his general conduct and his adherence to common values like probity and independence.[23]

Only recently has this conspicuous triangle of reputation, trust and economic cooperation come to the fore in economic theory and history. While neo-classical economists generally paid little attention to non-economic influences and frames of reference, new institutional economics have acknowledged them as a crucial factor of economic stability and growth. Trust is increasingly seen as an element inherent in each and every commercial transaction that greatly reduces the costs of that transaction and thus proves indispensable even in narrowly defined economic terms. Without trust, cooperation of business partners and industrial enterprises would be endlessly complicated, time-consuming and expensive. Trust relations can dispense with contracts and legally administered sanctions; they make communication smoother, more informal and thus more productive. Instead of negotiating, litigating, enforcing formal regulations, trust enables economic cooperation at much lower costs.[24]

This said, economists and economic historians have started to look more closely at the processes and structural conditions that render trust possible. They have eagerly picked up the concept of social capital defined by James Coleman.[25] Trust here appears as a specific form of social capital that can be accumulated through social networking within a given set of societal norms and cultural prescriptions. Benjamin Braidley's behaviour would be a case in point: by investing time and money in social and cultural activities, by connecting to people in matters not directly related to his economic interests, he presented himself as trustworthy to potential business partners. Another prime example of social capital formation would be the numerous cooperative societies that sprang up during the nineteenth century. Especially mutual credit associations that banded together people of limited financial resources relied heavily on reciprocal trust among their members. At the same time, they served to consolidate trust relations by engaging in continuous operations of borrowing and lending money at relatively low interest rates. Assisted by auditors who checked the associations' accountancy, they obviously worked so successfully as to stand up to the competition of newly emerging alternative institutions like savings banks.[26]

Trust thus formed a major prerequisite for economic cooperation and was largely accumulated before cooperation started. It depended on social knowledge acquired through politics of reputation. On the other hand, cooperation helped to generate, stabilize and increase trust by providing common experience of trustworthy behaviour in economic interaction. Empirical case studies have amply proven how trust-based communication among business partners enhances their respective gains and enables efficient, long-term cooperation allowing for continuous learning and adjustment processes. The more cooperation is needed in a capitalist economy with an ever-faster growing division of labour, the more trust is valued and cherished.[27]

Trustful relations are not restricted, however, to economic cooperation between companies and enterprises. They also occur between professional experts and their clients. Doctor-patient-relationships are as dependent on mutual trust as the contact between lawyers and their clients. Generally speaking, the expanding service sector (including the money market and insurances) cannot function without trust and is extremely vulnerable to the perceived danger of losing trust. The same holds true for consumer markets that depend heavily on generating trust and long-lasting emotional allegiance among customers. Since the 1870s, putting trademarks on goods proved to be a highly successful means of building trust among prospective buyers. The trademark functioned as a 'trust mark' suggesting accountability and reliability. By promising constant quality control, it lowered the risk of transaction for the customer.[28]

Apart from principal-agent and customer relations, trust also played a role in labour relations, between employers and employees, capitalists and their workers. Even though modern industrial production completely changed the traditional patterns of work and work relations, many first-generation entrepreneurs tried to hold on to structures of authority that emphasized cohesion and loyalty. Alfred Krupp time and again praised the 'old trust' that reigned in his thriving company. He demanded unconditional allegiance from his workers and in return promised to care for them in good and bad times.[29] Other factory owners equally attuned to the merits of trustful relations with the shop floor increasingly turned to new codes and practices of trust. During the late nineteenth century, more and more companies introduced workers' councils that consisted of elected trustees (*Vertrauensmänner*). They were supposed to represent workers' interests and negotiate with the owner or manager of the company. On the employer's invitation, workers' councils held regular meetings voicing complaints and suggesting improvements in social and economic matters. This procedure was widely regarded as bringing about 'essential advantages': it fostered 'mutual understanding' between workers and employers and 'surmounted mutual distrust'.[30]

On all levels, to sum up, trust was seen as a crucial factor enabling communication between people whose economic success and well-being increasingly depended on ever-closer cooperation. Open distrust, in turn, was dismissed as disrupting and obstructing cooperation and hampering the efficiency of economic transactions. Modern industrial society therefore invented all kinds of schemes and procedures to minimize distrust among principals and agents, among producers and consumers, among workers and employers. Some of these schemes were highly formalized and regulated, while others depended on rather weak modes of assurances and promises. In this sense, trademarking and other systems of certification served as much as 'guardians of trust' as the gradual introduction of workers' participation in a company's decision-making processes.[31]

Trust as Work: How to Build Trust

Talking about 'guardians' of trust, though, might obscure the fact that trust has to be produced before it can be guarded and protected. As mentioned earlier, trust does not come about in a carefree way; it is not given generously and unconditionally. Instead, it is widely considered as a scarce resource that has to be nurtured and reproduced at some cost. Even in family relations where it seems to flourish abundantly, it runs the risk of being used up and exhausted by neglect and improper conduct. The same holds true for friendship, another alleged haven of trust. As people in the eighteenth century were well aware, trustful relations among friends did not pop up spontaneously, but had to be carefully prepared and monitored in order to be sustainable. They demanded constant attention, sophisticated effort and verbal intensity. Their performance rested on the never-ending reiteration of trust and affinity that again emphasized trust talk as a major ingredient and stabilizing force in personal relations.[32]

When it came to less intimate relationships, we should consider the increasing presence of voluntary associations since the late eighteenth century. Starting with freemason lodges and patriotic societies, those associations played an important role in the formation of trust as a vital part of social capital. Moving well beyond the close ties of family and friendship, they provided a space where strangers could minimize social distance, engage in face-to-face encounter and gain first-hand knowledge of one another. This knowledge could then be used to start more formal collaborations in business or politics. As the association filtered and carefully selected its members and set up rules of conduct, it not only produced trustful relations, but also served to certify and consolidate them. Although it could never promise ultimate security, it still helped to reduce risks and complexities.

The same held true for more narrowly defined associations like professional organizations and trade unions, sports clubs or choral societies. Structured democratically and guided by principles of free access and exit, they helped strangers to develop what is sometimes called 'thick trust'. This type of trust usually blossoms in social relations that are strong, frequent and long-lasting, as opposed to 'thin trust' that occurs between people who have only randomly and anonymously met. But, as some social scientists argue, thick and thin trust mutually reinforce each other. Instead of closing off against non-members, people who developed 'thick trust' in voluntary associations generally seem to be more capable and willing to display 'social trust' in those whom they do not know from direct experience. 'Thick trust' thus works as a breeding ground for 'thin trust' and helps to bring about patterns of civic behaviour compliant with generalized norms of honesty and respect.[33]

Historical analysis, however, does not always support this rosy picture. In Imperial Germany, to give just one example, social trust and cohesion were far from being omnipresent, although millions of people were active members of voluntary associations. More than a million men had joined the Social Democratic Party, more than two million belonged to socialist trade unions, and hundreds of thousands engaged in the various cultural branches of the workers' movement. Similar degrees of mobilization and commitment could be observed among Catholics. Undoubtedly, this contributed greatly to the level of trust connecting the members of the respective movements. But it obviously did very little to extend trust to other segments of the population. In social encounters and in politics, class differences were observed as meticulously as religious demarcations. Open distrust shaped the relations between working classes and middle classes, as well as between Catholics and Protestants, not to mention Jews.

Another well-known case that does not support the assumption of 'thick' and 'thin' trust being closely linked is the existence of highly organized criminal networks like the Mafia. Here, too, close bonding and trust within the organization goes hand in hand with complete distrust that characterizes relations with the rest of the society.[34] Similar structures can be found among immigrants who tend to socialize among each other and close ranks against majority groups. Vice versa, majority groups under certain conditions tend to exclude newcomers and denounce them as lacking trustworthiness.

In general, trust relations seem to prosper among individuals and groups that share common values, experiences and traditions that speak the same language and agree on its meanings. But this does not imply that trust relations are restricted to societies with a high degree of religious, ethnic and social homogeneity. On the contrary, homogeneity does not in itself guarantee and secure the development of trust. This becomes apparent when turning to countries like Communist Poland or Fascist Germany and Italy. In all of these cases, immense propagandistic effort was undertaken to present them as trust-based societies, trust actually being a major *lemma* in the political lexicon. A closer look, however, instantly reveals the abundance of distrust that characterized social, economic and political life. Denunciations and spying were experienced on a daily basis, free speech confined to inner circles of friends and family.[35]

These examples clarify once more that social trust ('thin trust') does not per se emanate from thick-trust relations that can by and large be found in any society and are most likely to occur in relatively homogeneous social environments. It needs something else for social trust to emerge and spread, which is where democratic institutions come in. Without a protected system of civic rights, without an openly accessible public sphere and without a legal apparatus that sets up general rules of conduct and safeguards individual freedom within this general framework, trust among citizens is highly unlikely to happen. Democratic citizenship thus functions as a major incubator of social trust that is able to extend beyond the narrow limits of small-scale communities and groups.

In this regard, democracy, as it has developed in most Western countries during the nineteenth and twentieth centuries, is all about social and public trust: about trust among citizens – what political scientists call horizontal trust – as well as about trust between citizens and government (vertical trust).[36] While John Locke in his ideas on a 'government by trust' mainly focused on the relations between citizens and parliament, the political discourse in continental Europe with its strong tradition of absolutism first used trust as a weapon and demand waged against monarchical power. Those critical of authoritarian government called upon the latter to trust the people and show trust by sharing power. In turn, rulers would be rewarded by their citizens' trust. 'Trust creates trust' (*Vertrauen schafft Vertrauen*) was the battle cry of early liberal opposition all over Germany. It meant either urging an autocratic ruler to accept a constitutional check on his power or reminding a constitutional monarch to obey the rules, since trust in him and his government could grow and take root only under the protection of the law.[37]

Trust thus had to be gained; it was not given for nothing, and it was not given unconditionally. Trust, in contrast to older concepts of loyalty and allegiance, could be withdrawn if those who were trusted were not found trustworthy anymore. The conditionality of trust found its ultimate expression in parliamentary democracy. Every four or five years trust has to be regained and displayed again: voters being called upon to decide whether politicians are still considered trustworthy or not. Trust is thus only bestowed on its bearers for a limited amount of time. After that, it has to be re-evaluated and renegotiated in a strenuous and sophisticated process. This is where confidence work sets in, expressed in ever-more elaborated and orchestrated election campaigns.

The operations of political trust in domestic and international affairs alert us to a general fact: trust, as it is being defined and advertised since the nineteenth century, is never absolute and unconditional. It always entails a portion, bigger or smaller, of distrust that sends out warning signals, urges for careful checks and calls for continuous proofs of counter-evidence. If distrust (of government, of fellow citizens, of other countries' governments) cannot be openly voiced, trust is nothing more than an empty word. To allow for the co-presence of trust and distrust, institutional arrangements have to be established that accept distrust as given and legitimate, but consensually aim to transform it into trust. Parliamentary democracy and workers' councils are cases in point, and so are international organizations like the International Atomic Energy Agency. They can all be seen as performing confidence work among participants who, despite holding different interests, have come to acknowledge that these interests can best be served by cooperation instead of violent and antagonistic conflict.

Notes

1. Jürgen Kocka, 'Work as a Problem in European History', in this volume.
2. Ute Frevert, 'Vertrauen. Historische Annäherungen an eine Gefühlshaltung', in Claudia Benthien et al. (eds), *Emotionalität: Zur Geschichte der Gefühle* (Cologne: Böhlau Verlag, 2000), pp. 179–84.
3. The Google search engine in January 2005 gave 1,280 results for *Vertrauensarbeit*; the term is used in economic as well as political language. See, for example, the article in *Die*

Welt, 14.1.2005: '*Simonis lobt Vertrauensarbeit ihrer Soldaten*' covering the visit of the state premier of Schleswig-Holstein in Afghanistan. Heide Simonis was quoted praising German soldiers for creating trust among the local population by being accessible and administering medical help. Among the earliest 'hits' was a 1976 document by the SPD treasurer Wilhelm Dröscher in which he talked about the necessary *Vertrauensarbeit* of his party.

4. Quoted in Werner Conze, 'Arbeit', in Werner Conze et al. (eds), *Geschichtliche Grundbegriffe*, vol. 1 (Stuttgart: Klett Verlag, 1979), p. 171f.
5. Philip Rieff, *The Triumph of the Therapeutic* (New York: Harper and Row, 1966); Peter Gay, 'Menschen im therapeutischen Netz', in Ute Frevert and Heinz-Gerhard Haupt (eds), *Der Mensch des 20. Jahrhunderts* (Frankfurt: Campus, 1999), pp. 324–43.
6. This is especially evident in German: Just 'Google' *Trauerarbeit, Liebesarbeit, Beziehungsarbeit, Enttäuschungsarbeit, Angstarbeit* etc. In English, see, for example, the 'work of mourning', the 'work of love' and so forth.
7. Jürgen Gerhards, *Soziologie der Emotionen. Fragestellungen, Systematik und Perspektiven* (Weinheim: Beltz, 1988), p. 174, with a reference to Arlie Russell Hochschild, 'Emotionwork, feeling rules, and social structure', in *American Journal of Sociology* 85 (1979): 551–75.
8. The sociologist Arlie Russell Hochschild has examined different types of emotionwork in contemporary American society, focusing especially on service jobs like that of the stewardess. Here, women are trained meticulously to conform to emotional expectations that are raised by marketing strategies and that they have to meet in order to satisfy their clients; Arlie Russell Hochschild, *The Managed Heart: Commercialization of Human Feelings* (Berkeley: UCP, 1983).
9. William M. Reddy, *The Navigation of Feeling: A Framework for the History of Emotions* (Cambridge: CUP, 2001), Chapter 1, p. 54; Arlie Russell Hochschild, 'Ideology and Emotion Management', in Theodore D. Kemper (ed.), *Research Agendas in the Sociology of Emotions* (Albany: SUNY Press, 1990), pp. 117–42; Steven L. Gordon, 'Social Structural Effects on Emotions', in idem, pp. 145–79.
10. Lila Abu-Lughod, *Veiled Sentiments: Honor and Poetry in a Bedouin Society* (Berkeley: UCP, 1986), p. 258; Catherine A. Lutz and Lila Abu-Lughod (eds), *Language and the Politics of Emotion* (Cambridge, CUP, 1990), pp. 1–23 (introduction, quotation p. 10).
11. Peter N. Stearns and Carol Z. Stearns, 'Emotionology: Clarifying the History of Emotions and Emotional Standards', *AHR* 90 (1985): 813–30; Carol Z. Stearns and Peter N. Stearns, *Anger. The Struggle for Emotional Control in America's History* (Chicago: University of Chicago Press, 1986); idem (eds), *Emotion and Social Change: Toward a New Psychohistory* (New York: Holmes and Meier, 1988); Peter Stearns and Timothy Haggerty, 'The Role of Fear: Transitions in American Emotional Standards for Children, 1850–1950', *AHR* 96 (1991): 63–94; Peter N. Stearns, 'Suppressing Unpleasant Emotions: The Development of a Twentieth-Century American Style', in Andrew E. Barnes and Peter N. Stearns (eds), *Social History and Issues in Human Consciousness* (New York: New York University Press, 1989), pp. 230–61; idem, *American Cool. Constructing a Twentieth-Century Emotional Style* (New York: New York University Press, 1994).
12. Reddy, *Navigation of Feeling*, pp. 321–27.
13. Annette C. Baier, *Moral Prejudices: Essays on Ethics* (Cambridge: Harvard UP, 1994), p. 98ff.
14. Niklas Luhmann, 'Familiarity, Confidence, Trust: Problems and Alternatives', in Diego Gambetta (ed.), *Trust: Making and Breaking Cooperative Relations* (Oxford: Basil Blackwell, 1988), p. 97ff.

15. Georg Simmel, *Soziologie: Untersuchungen über die Formen der Vergesellschaftung* (Frankfurt: Suhrkamp, 1992), p. 383ff.; Niklas Luhmann, *Vertrauen: Ein Mechanismus der Reduktion sozialer Komplexität* (Stuttgart: Enke, 1968). For a discussion of sociological approaches to trust, see Barbara A. Misztal, *Trust in Modern Societies: The Search for the Bases of Social Order* (Cambridge: Polity Press, 1996).
16. Kenneth J. Arrow, *The Limits of Organization* (New York: W.W. Norton and Company, 1974), p. 23.
17. Reddy, *Navigation of Feeling*, pp. 96–111.
18. Dorothea Weltecke, 'Gab es "Vertrauen" im Mittelalter?' in Ute Frevert (ed.), *Vertrauen: Historische Annäherungen* (Göttingen: Vandenhoeck and Ruprecht, 2003), pp. 81–88.
19. Johann Heinrich Zedler, *Grosses vollständiges Universal-Lexicon aller Wissenschafften und Künste*, vol. 48 (Leipzig 1746), pp. 19–33.
20. For further information, see the essays in Frevert (ed.), *Vertrauen*.
21. Quoted in Hartmut Berghoff, 'Die Zähmung des entfesselten Prometheus? Die Generierung von Vertrauenskapital und die Konstruktion des Marktes im Industrialisierungs- und Globalisierungsprozeß', in Hartmut Berghoff and Jakob Vogel (eds), *Wirtschaftsgeschichte als Kulturgeschichte* (Frankfurt: Campus, 2004), p. 143.
22. Jürgen Kocka, *Unternehmer in der deutschen Industrialisierung* (Göttingen: Vandenhoeck and Ruprecht, 1975); Leonore Davidoff and Catherine Hall, *Family Fortunes: Men and Women of the English Middle Class, 1780–1850* (London: Routledge, 1987).
23. Robin Pearson and David Richardson, 'Business Networking in the Industrial Revolution', *Economic History Review* 54 (2001): 657–79, quotations p. 676, 674 (Braidley).
24. Francis Fukuyama, *Trust: The Social Virtues and the Creation of Prosperity* (New York: Simon and Schuster, 1995); Martin Fiedler, 'Vertrauen ist gut, Kontrolle ist teuer: Vertrauen als Schlüsselkategorie wirtschaftlichen Handelns', *Geschichte und Gesellschaft* 27 (2001): 576–92; Tanja Rippberger, *Ökonomik des Vertrauens* (Tübingen: Mohr Siebeck, 1998).
25. James S. Coleman, *Foundations of Social Theory* (Cambridge: Harvard UP, 1990); idem, 'Systems of Trust', *Angewandte Sozialforschung* 10 (1982): 277–99.
26. Timothy W. Guinnane, 'Cooperatives as Information Machines: German Rural Credit Cooperatives, 1883–1914', *Journal of Economic History* 61 (2001): 366–89; Carlos G. Velez-Ibanez, *Bands of Mutual Trust: The Cultural System of Rotating Credit Associations among Urban Mexicans and Chicanos* (New Brunswick: Rutgers UP, 1983). See, from a more general perspective, Robert Putnam, *Making Democracy Work: Civic Traditions in Modern Italy* (Princeton: Princeton UP, 1983).
27. Edward H. Lorenz, 'Neither Friends nor Strangers: Informal Networks of Subcontracting in French Industry', in Gambetta (ed.), *Trust*, pp. 194–210; Bernard Baudry, 'Trust in Inter-Firm Relations', in Nathalie Lazaric and Edward Lorenz (eds), *Trust and Economic Learning* (Cheltenham: Edward Elgar, 1998), pp. 64–77; Bertrand Moingeon and Amy Edmondson, 'Trust and Organisational Learning', in idem, pp. 247–65; Martin Fiedler, 'Netzwerke des Vertrauens', in Dieter Ziegler (ed.), *Großbürger und Unternehmer* (Göttingen: Vandenhoeck and Ruprecht, 2000), pp. 93–115.
28. Berghoff, Zähmung, p. 160f.
29. Alfred Krupp, *Ein Wort an die Angehörigen meiner gewerblichen Anlagen* (Essen 1877).
30. Quotes in Ute Frevert, 'Vertrauen – eine historische Spurensuche', in Frevert (ed.), *Vertrauen*, p. 46f.
31. Susan P. Shapiro, 'The Social Control of Impersonal Trust', in *American Journal of Sociology* 93 (1987): 623–58, quotation p. 635.

32. Wolfram Mauser and Barbara Becker-Cantarino, *Frauenfreundschaft – Männerfreundschaft: Literarische Diskurse im 18. Jahrhundert* (Tübingen: Niemeyer, 1991).
33. Robert D. Putnam, *Bowling Alone: The Collapse and Revival of American Community* (New York: Simon and Schuster, 2000), p. 134ff.
34. Diego Gambetta, 'Mafia: The Price of Distrust', in Gambetta (ed.), *Trust*, pp. 158–75.
35. Piotr Szompka, 'Trust and Emerging Democracy: Lessons from Poland', *International Sociology* 11 (1996): 37–62; Frevert, *Vertrauen – eine historische Spurensuche*, pp. 31–35.
36. Claus Offe, 'How Can We Trust Our Fellow Citizens?' in Mark E. Warren (ed.), *Democracy and Trust* (Cambridge: CUP, 1999), pp. 42–87.
37. Frevert, *Vertrauen – eine historische Spurensuche*, pp. 21–29.

7

Soldiering and Working: Almost the Same? Reviewing Practices in Industry and the Military in Twentieth-Century Contexts

Alf Lüdtke

A Colonial Moment

> The infantry fired steadily and stolidly, without hurry or excitement, for the enemy were far away and the officers careful. Besides, the soldiers were interested in the work and took great pains. But presently the mere physical act became tedious. The tiny figures seen over the slide of the back-sight seemed a little larger but also fewer at each successive volley. The rifles grew hot – so hot that they had to be changed for those of the reserve companies. The Maxim guns exhausted all the water in their jackets, and several had to be refreshed from the water-bottles of the Cameron Highlanders before they could go on with their deadly work. The empty cartridge-cases, tinkling to the ground, formed small but growing heaps beside each man. And all the time out on the plain on the other side bullets were shearing through flesh, smashing and splintering bones; blood spouted from terrible wounds; valiant men were struggling on through a hell of whistling metal, exploding shells, and spurting dust – suffering, despairing, dying.[1]

A young gentleman and trained cavalry officer drafted this report several weeks after having witnessed this action of British troops in Sudan in 1898. The author was Winston S. Churchill, who participated in one of these colonial wars. In his account, Churchill once again makes visible to the wider public what had never vanished from colonial and imperial politics: the physical annihilation of those who did not bend to the various 'civilizing missions' of the agents of the West.

The soldiers Churchill observed at their 'work' were professionally trained 'six-year-old British soldiers'.[2] In his view, they fundamentally differed from those 'boys' or 'conscripts' who would follow 'their officers in blind ignorance' and march 'in a row to their death' as they staffed the armies on the European continent. With these British troops, however, 'every man was an intelligent human being who thought for himself, acted for himself, took pride in himself and knew his own mind'. Thus, 'spontaneity, not mere passive obedience, was the characteristic of their charge'. These soldiers had undergone intensive training on the exercise grounds at home, and most of them had served at various locations in the empire. Churchill therefore saw himself as a witness to the actions of a well-trained body of seasoned experts whose conduct emphasized keeping cool. In this way, the men would stay in control of themselves and of their tools and could continue to cooperate with both comrades and superiors.

Repetitious Action

The regularity of repetitious action was a central feature of industrial division of labour since its beginning in the eighteenth century. The advancement of industrial work processes had been both fervently acclaimed and bitterly contested. Still, whatever position contemporaries took, they agreed that industrial work would dramatically change the role of 'living', or human, labour. In this sense, Karl Marx articulated a commonly held opinion: industry would turn man into the 'mere appendix' of machinery.[3]

The image of machinery resonated with expectations of a well-ordered and steady flow of production. However, more recent case studies of industrial work provide a different view. They reveal fundamentally ambivalent and partly contradictory situations at the very heart of production. Workers permanently faced uncertainty, risk or danger when, for instance, handling open fire at a furnace or operating a small boat in an off-shore fishing operation. Moreover, environmental constraints, such as heat and stench, demanded adaptation of disciplinary regulations and the intricacies of time- and piece-rates. Yet such conditions never seem to constitute what Erving Goffman has called a 'total institution'. These studies also show how workers cope with and appropriate the specific settings of work and, thus, make them their own. Yet workers' efforts to carve out niches for themselves and re-adjust the 'system' do not resonate with heroic attitudes. On the contrary, it is the striving for survival and 'making do' that informs workers' behaviour.[4]

For decades academic studies revolved only on selection of workers and their adaptation to industry. Cases in point are the studies on individual companies designed and supervised by Alfred and Max Weber prior to 1914 (Marie Bernays et al., sponsored by the *Verein für Socialpolitik*). In the mid- and late 1920s the range of research broadened.[5] Concomitantly, German industrial managers began to focus on how women and men actively shape the process of production: they handle tools and materials in their own ways, sometimes in a stubbornly self-willed, or *eigensinnig*, fashion. Such growing awareness of workers' appropriation of work triggered policies of rationalization that were critical of and deviant from Taylorism. In fact, in the 1920s, industrial rationalization movements in Germany relied explicitly on the specific dexterity and skill of the workers, whether trained or untrained. Their hands and heads had to be stimulated and 'put to work' at tools or conveyor belts (few as they were). Only then would an 'optimum [of working and producing] ... be possible'.

Of course, one can dispose of such management-driven analyses just as one can abandon the romanticizing attitudes favoured by many labour historians. Micro-historical explorations of workers' everyday practices show that these people were not 'automatons'. Here, they appear as individual actors, employing their sensual perceptivity, stamina and dexterity. Only occasionally did they join forces – or fight – with workmates.

Room for Manoeuvre versus the Threat of Death

In the battles in Sudan, the British employed Maxim guns (machine guns), shrapnel ammunition and magazine rifles: the three 'weapons of civilization' (as they appeared in Churchill's account).[6] But it was not just such guns or shells that enhanced the firepower of European troops tremendously. The industrialization of warfare since the American Civil War and, in particular, during the First World War has often been described.[7] Rather than going into the details of this process, I want to emphasize here the parallels to industrial production outlined above. Complex apparatuses remained dependent on human performance, ranging from dexterously handling systems of transportation and communication to ever new generations of machines of destruction. Foot soldiers operated guns, flame throwers and tanks; sailors ran battleships and submarines; aviators made airships and airplanes 'work'.

In this context, it is imperative to inspect the logic of command and obedience, which is routinely misunderstood, from the inside. Churchill distinguished between the individual capacities of British professional soldiers, who were recruited as volunteers, from continental armies, which were based on the draft. Both manuals and recollections from the German armies, however, reveal a line similar to the British one. Not only officers, but basically every military person ought to be able to 'act according to the general purpose [of a specific action or of that very war in general], even if orders are lacking'. Textbooks for military training already emphasized this point prior to 1914. This quote, however, stems from the widely popularized version of the regulation for the infantry of the *Wehrmacht* in its 1940 version, the *Reibert*.[8]

Against this background, I want to pursue a twofold thesis. First, room for manoeuvre at the respective point of production was crucial to both industrial work and soldiering. Demands for skilfully moving and using one's body were similar, if not largely identical, in both areas. Only with these demands fulfilled would specific varieties of behaviour combine efficiency with effectiveness. Second, the areas of action and, even more, the specific performances of workers and soldiers still remained fundamentally different. This sense of difference was grounded in, or at least resonated with, the experience and expectation of being killed or – what often was worse in soldiers' recollections – being wounded.

Even more poignant was another sort of soldiers' experience: to encounter the power to kill as something that was not only terrorizing, but also appealing. The extent to which such emotionally heightened responses reflected the dangers and isolation in combat or, instead, distanced participants from these factors must be left open to speculation. The spectrum of soldiers' feelings obviously ranged from disgust and shame to pride, if not pleasure, time and again seemingly combining all of them. But regardless of whether soldiers felt it disturbing or appealing (or both), killing helped transform the meaning of 'doing a good job' into the excitement of an ultimate transgression.

The Army as a 'Steel Mill'?

In 1941 Curzio Malaparte reported for several months on the German invasion into the U.S.S.R. This author had a rather erratic career, moving from staunchly supporting Mussolini and his *Fascisti* in 1922 to a more critical stance, which caused his writing to be temporarily banned in 1929. After some years, however, he had reaffirmed his cooperation with the powers that be. Malaparte's ambition to appear as an autonomous person also reverberated in his reports for the Italian daily *Corriere Della Sera.* Instead of following German war correspondents, who denounced the soldiers of the Red Army as unfit or cowards, Malaparte recognized a similar 'workers' morale' among combatants on either side. He perceived 'two armies at the core formed from specialized workers and "industrialized" peasants'. It would therefore be 'the first time in the history of warfare that two armies fight against each other and the military morale is intricately connected with workers' morale, thus blending military discipline with a technical discipline of work since both armies are manned and run by skilled workers'.[9]

Malaparte took an even closer look: he scrutinized the corpses of Soviet soldiers killed in action. He spotted, for instance, two dead Russians and took notice of their 'stout' bodies and 'long arms'. He saw 'their bright eyes ... wide open'; to him these were 'specialists, two *Stachanov* workers'. And he went on:

> These are new breeds, totally "new" and just delivered; look at their mouths and strong lips. Peasants? Workers? These are specialists, working

> people. Some of those thousands and thousands who work the communal farms – or some of those thousands and thousands who run the factories of the Soviet Union ... All [of these people] are the same, produced in a series. Each of them is like the others are. This is a hard race. These are corpses of workers killed at their workplace.[10]

But Malaparte had started this sequence with an observation that alluded to technology and industrialized work processes. Observing the German troops advancing, he detected:

> not just an army but a huge moving workshop, a colossal steel mill on wheels. It looked as if a thousand chimneys, a thousand cranes, a thousand iron bridges, a thousand steel fortresses, thousands and thousands of ball bearings, of gearings, hundreds of furnaces and steel mills of Westphalia – as if the whole *Ruhrgebiet* was marching on the planes of Bessarabia. As if the huge *Krupp-Werke* ... had started to attack the hills around Zaicani ... I saw not an army but a colossal steel mill with a huge workforce of specialized workers who pursued their tasks according to precise schemes, at first glance hiding the intensity of their work.[11]

Malaparte continued by noting that this 'steel mill on wheels' appeared to move across the fields without inflicting any harm on the villages around it. Only the towns would be attacked. He also observed soldiers whose tank had killed a hog. Some peasants rushed to save the remnants of the animal: still, so the report went on, the German soldiers guaranteed cash compensation to the proprietor. In Malaparte's account, this almost peaceful exchange seemed to spring directly from the reign of modern machinery and industrial work over people's minds and morale. It is particularly this passage that raises serious doubts, though, as internal army reports, letters from the front and recollections of survivors describe a substantially different conduct by victorious troops.[12] They mention destroyed villages and towns in abundance, as well as rather distanced, if not hostile actions of German troops who did not refrain from heavy looting and violence against civilians, without any compensation.

In Malaparte's view, the imagery of the 'steel mill' represented the gist of what armies and soldiers stood for and practised. Such an overarching trope of modernity applied to either side: in Malaparte's account, the troops of Nazi Germany and the armies of the Soviet Union did not differ in this respect, but pursued the same rationale. But what sort of network of meanings did the iconic image of the steel mill invoke? First, the immediate reference is to the mill's gigantic dimensions. Usually a steel mill stretches for several kilometres. Similarly, many of its components and sub-sections are huge and, in any case, larger than man.

Second, a steel mill stands for the professional handling of a large-scale transformation of substances, while controlling any possible dangers for people's lives and bodies. The glow of the furnaces stems from heating up iron and other substances to their respective melting points. This process and its result, fluid steel, not only contain, but display destructive energy ready to consume living people. The effort to securely handle this danger alludes to the third layer of resonances: although the steel mill is a huge complex and employs hundreds, if not thousands, of people, its workers are individuals who complete multiple tasks with tools. They are supposed to employ their minds and hands accordingly. At the same time, they form specific work teams that not only connect and assign different tasks, but also provide support. Thus, the image of the steel mill invokes the concrete practice at the point of production: to keep a complex operation going day and night. Especially while running the furnace, 'necessary cooperation' must be performed in its various, but minute, details. People have to sustain the very ability to cooperate with workmates and colleagues. People's dexterity and individual stamina, but also their courage, remain reliable only if everyone keeps a delicate balance between leaving colleagues their own space and interfering when necessary.[13]

Fourth, the imagery of the dexterous and, at the same time, strong hands and bodies of the operators invokes the experiences and pride of those who tamed the dangers of the system. These are the men who make it possible to exploit this production process. A more concrete inspection shows that during their shift, work teams of about twenty people commonly take steps that range from filling the furnace to handling its products until the steel cools off. During the subsequent steps of production, work teams of a similar size move and roll the slabs and bars. Of course, they fulfil specific tasks, but most of the men are capable of taking over when a colleague from their team is missing or tiring, or commits an error.

This process revolves not only around the furnace. The fifth aspect of this imagery is the interconnectedness that exists beyond the furnace. Molten steel is but the first link in a chain of manufacturing processes, from rolling bars to finishing products ranging from solid tracks to construction bars, armour plates and paper-thin metal foils. In addition, a sixth element comes into play: at least at the furnace, the work is also a process in another sense. For financial and technical reasons it never stops, but runs uninterruptedly day and night, seven days a week. Thus, it is just a small step from – a seventh aspect – connecting the concrete impressions and sensations of those directly involved in production to the actual end. Above all, it evokes the mythical notions of the origin of industry and industrialization: open fire in all its aspects, from lighting the environment to melting and fusing raw materials, transforming them, for instance, from ore and coal to iron and steel. What emerges is the steel mill as both site and symbol of creation. Thus, the steel mill represents man's control of fire for producing usable items: in general, for man's production of human progress.

In contrast to the self-explanatory potential of the steel mill, Malaparte in his journalistic-cum-literary account neither alluded to nor directly addressed what soldiers encounter or, at least, never can neglect: the danger of being wounded, if not killed, but also the likeliness of using their weapon and, possibly, harming if not killing other people or 'the enemy'. Malaparte's presentation of the imagery of the steel mill served as a perfect device to metaphorically transpose the killing fields of destruction onto a totally different plane. In such a light, the grinding mill of warfare would glow only as an icon of productivity and creative power.

Small Teams

Operating in teams of about twenty people can be seen as a characteristic of both military action and manufacturing. This assumption does not ignore the presence of regulations and constraints upon the respective military and industrial fields. Regardless of the concrete forms and their transformation, in either field teams and individuals were tied to chains of command and connected with networks of cooperation and communication.[14]

Different authors have aimed at rewriting the history of industrialization by tracing two profoundly different, but parallel configurations of industrial production. They show that 'mass production' (with its temporary craze for Taylorism and Fordism) was paralleled, if not outdistanced, by branches based on and stimulating 'flexible specialization'.[15] However, this distinction does not affect the micro-level observation that small teams played a crucial role in production, as studies on metallurgical works and steel mills confirm. These studies show that 'mass production' has re-evaluated the pivotal role of individual 'production workers' and small teams.[16] Charles Sabel and Jonathan Zeitlin have argued that dominant notions as, for instance, Taylorism or Fordism (or for this matter: the steel mill) grossly misrepresent both multifaceted historical processes and actual practices of historical actors. In their emphasis on 'one best way', they misrepresent the practices of working people.

A similar investigation of the paths of change in the military since the late eighteenth century would show a comparable width and range of trajectories for the armies of the European and North American powers. For instance, in the Second World War combustion engines powered airplanes and tanks, but also trucks and motorcycles in *Wehrmacht* units. Still, the majority of German soldiers moved and fought on foot or literally relied on horsepower for transport of baggage, food and ammunition.[17] Even artillery or engineering units of the *Wehrmacht* primarily employed horses for transporting and moving canons, guns and other gear, whether bulky or not. Tending to the horses and driving them was a multifaceted job for one group of soldiers. Others drove and repaired trucks, tanks or motorcycles. Tanks had been the symbolic spearheads of the ground forces' military successes between 1939 and late 1941.[18] But it was the newsreels that gave tanks and airplanes (and motorcycles) their ubiquitous presence in people's minds.

Thus, gas, diesel or electric engines, as well as advanced technology in communications, were part of military planning and practice and, hence, of soldiers' tasks. But the actual number of these soldiers remained limited; on the German side, it even shrank considerably in the course of the war. Regardless of the total number of soldiers involved, many German soldiers tended to six or eight horses each. In this capacity, they operated largely on their own, although they were still part of, for instance, the artillery battery that they had been assigned to.[19] In similar ways, the operators of cars, trucks, switchboards or wireless telegraphs were often on their own and had some leeway in fulfilling their tasks. Repair shops, bakeries and many of those rearguard small or medium-sized units that provided calories and ammunition to keep the army going, worked differently. Here, teamwork prevailed to a much larger extent, so the situation was similar to the style of performance in civilian workshops, but also in combat units.

Emotional and Cultural Dynamics

Debates about industry and wage work conventionally assume that those involved direct their behaviours and activities according to rational calculations of their (dis)advantages. Only gradually did observers and those actively working in industry develop a sense for the multifaceted emotional and cultural dynamics that drove people to work or not to work.

Studies of artisan production have pioneered this opening-up by exploring multiple arenas of work. These investigations scrupulously traced the handling of tools and materials. However, their emphasis was on the many folds and trajectories that resonated between working people's strivings for survival and their performances of and at work. This view has revealed in concrete terms (and images) how 'eating, drinking, housing, marrying, bequeathing or inheriting property or rights to property [was part of] work itself'.[20] In his analysis of journeymen's behaviour in eighteenth-century Paris, Michael Sonenscher shows that these reproductive practices 'made up a part of the environment of non-monetary manoeuvre and symbolic negotiation in which masters and journeymen encountered and dealt with one another'. Thus, if researchers ignore this context, they miss, for instance, what 'wage' meant and implied, not to mention the very buying power of cash, as it was not visible in specific amounts demanded, paid or received.

In a similar vein, Robert Darnton has focused on the cultural dimensions of artisan work. In his seminal study of 'the great cat massacre', he analyses an account rendered by a former participant in a demonstrative action of Parisian journeymen against their master and his wife in the 1730s.[21] The historian carefully traces the symbolic and material claims for status and control as acted out by the different inhabitants of the *patron*'s household-cum-workshop. Thus, Darnton reconstructs a field of forces that were produced and employed in the everyday lives of people who, in a very limited physical space, strove for survival and recognition. The journeymen and particularly the apprentices felt themselves treated unjustly: not only did the patron give them orders, but his 'middleman', his wife, did as well. Still more offensive to them was the contempt embodied in the meagre, if not distasteful, food dished out to them. Such daily meals were part of their wage while, at the same time, the cats of the *patronesse* were treated exquisitely. Darnton then emphasizes the potential for revolt in a carnival-like ritual: in a nightly raid several journeymen and apprentices killed those very cats that were fondly cherished and fed by the patron's wife. By taking this action, the workers protested and 'turned things upside down'. Thus, the journeymen stated their claims in violent terms; however, they did not transgress or physically attack the bodies or other properties of the two people whom they wanted to hurt and humiliate.

Historic-ethnographical studies[22] focus on both the simultaneities and the resonances of worker's signs, gestures and material actions. They explore interrelations between people's activities for producing survival and their relating themselves to (or distancing themselves from) others whom they considers as equal to, 'above' or 'below' themselves. A case in point is Gerald Sider's research on the Newfoundland cod fishery, which investigates work and the social interactions that revolved around it both in the present and the past.

Sider traces the behaviour of the men who for generations had formed the boat crews and brought in the catch. He also closely observed the women who processed the catch on the shore, thus 'making' the fish. Sider emphasizes the seasonal occurrence of interactions and experiences: not during, but after the fishing season, people 'acted out' and showed what had occupied them during recent months. They vented the pleasures and anger they had harboured for weeks or months 'inside'. Even in a crew that would 'ideally, consist of patri-kinsmen' the members encountered tensions. In turn, kinfolk tended to 'avoid each other completely' after the summer season was over. However, they came back together in mid-winter when they, for instance, 'jointly beg[a]n to rebuild their equipment'.[23]

A specific form of flexibility seemed present in almost all relationships and (self-) presentations. This intensity was re-informed by ritual activities that revolved around Christmas: carnival-like 'mumming' and a short-lived but boisterous 'turning the world upside down'. This mixture of playfulness and calculated action re-established the possibility of returning to the normalcy of the everyday. Such normalcy involved well-ordered, but not strictly hierarchical cooperation and burden sharing, which remained rigidly gendered.[24]

Similarities between the fisher-folk and military crews are striking. In both instances, the communities not only worked together, but lived together day and night. The permanent presence of workmates and comrades in the barracks, at camp or 'in action', as well as the immediacy of superiors, creates similar situations in each case. There is an analogy in the simultaneous presence of tensions and easygoing cooperation. Rituals and the multitude of performative actions in a military setting are, therefore, of similar importance to those described in the studies undertaken by Gerald Sider.

Killing: A Narrative Void?

Ernst Jünger's accounts of the First World War, written during the 1920s, especially his *Storm of Steel*,[25] have too often been misread as just another loop of the never-ending spiral of officers' attempts at heroic self-presentation. Still, even the hindsight and officer's point of view that are both obviously employed by the author should not blind the reader to the other aspects of the text. Jünger rendered life 'at the front' in superb nuances: especially moments of combat with their intense mixture of fear and joy. Both fear and joy appear in his writings as intricately connected: the recognition of imminent danger with the feeling of utter fulfilment and 'being real' for the first time.[26]

Feelings of insecurity and anxiety are often mentioned – if in abbreviated form – in diaries, letters and accounts written in hindsight; and those looking back on the Second World War are not very different from those describing the First World War. As different as these respective texts may be, perceptions and sensual reactions triggered by the authors' own killing or wounding of people are mostly passed over in silence. It does not matter whether this happens 'face to face' or the other appears only as a barely visible 'dot' in the distance. However, recollections time and again refer to the either/or alternative: 'either he or I' will survive. To invoke an existential urge for survival does more than recall moments of the past; it also sheds some light on moral or cultural codes that might restrict killing actions. At the same time, the emotional intensity of these recollections – so striking with Jünger – becomes even more apparent if the wording in other texts is restrained or clumsy (as in many oral recollections).[27]

Michael Geyer reminded historians some years ago that military and even war history has almost totally neglected 'killing'.[28] A similar point can be made about the neglect of feelings. Analyses ignore the fact that joyful feelings of success and fulfilment were seemingly intertwined with fear and anxiety in war. Perhaps it was this overlap, if not simultaneity, that ran contrary to the various 'normalities' people had encountered in their peacetime settings (of course, also in the military).[29] These dimensions of 'real war' that 'never get in the books'[30] remain preserved in silences or evocative abbreviations: if they are not funnelled to less visible arenas such as the public house or *Stammtisch*, or afternoon tea. On both levels, though, it is not detailed descriptions of specific activities, but short phrases that dominate: the other is *erledigt* ('finished off'), *niedergemacht* or *liquidiert*.[31]

Stories and Practices of 'Comradeship'

Autobiographical and literary accounts of both the First and the Second World War revolve heavily around stories of *Kameradschaft* ('fellowship' or 'comradeship'). This pertains to all combatants, regardless of the side on which they found themselves. Thus, it is not surprising that sociologists Samuel

Marshall and Samuel Stouffer confirmed the pivotal importance of small group relationships for the U.S. military.[32] Thomas Kühne has explored this kind of relationship in regard to the German armies as well, relating it to other forms of trust. He argues that soldiers employ a specific 'faceless' trust, as generated in and reproduced by the small groups they are operating and, in fact, living in. Technically speaking, one is looking into sub-unit relationships: squads (sections) or, at the utmost, platoons; that is, about thirty people.[33]

In this view, reciprocal relationships among comrades were fundamental for coping with physical and mental hardship, especially at the Eastern Front. The relationship of trust also allowed them to outwit the military hierarchy and its harsh disciplinary impositions. It was trust that would muffle the waves of aggressiveness in exchanges not only between superiors and their underlings, but also among rank-and-file soldiers. From this perspective, traditional ideas, as well as those emphasizing the dominance of Nazi ideology in general and Nazi anti-semitism in particular (as stressed by Omer Bartov), seem overstated.[34] To be sure, efforts by military leaders and, especially, the newly introduced NS-*Führungsoffiziere* to fanaticize the troops were not completely meaningless. But evidence such as letters home from the front, diaries, and death announcements in newspapers indicate that people in many ways blended racism with notions of the 'fatherland under siege' that, again, created all sorts of resonances with experiences of companionship among the military work team.

The specific traits that Kühne describes as crucial for military companionship correspond closely to characteristics of industrial work teams. A certain familiarity with the code of conduct, the knowledge of how to treat peers and how to deal with superiors, materials and various constraints and demands (time schedules, wage schemes) was as common on the shop floor as in (or behind) the combat zones. What is missing in Kühne's account, at least partly, applies equally to the small group relationships in industry and the military: the darker side of sociability, namely, social control and social pressure.[35] It is the analysis of such relationships and, particularly, pressures on possible dissenters that has become the main line in Christopher Browning's analyses of the dynamics within the companies of Police Battalion 101. He explores how 'ordinary men' turned into killers in the context of the Holocaust in occupied Poland in 1942 and 1943.

Individual Trajectories I

Individual trajectories are pivotal for this perspective. However, the issue is not to map 'typical', or 'normal' life courses. What matters are the specific details: they allow us to explore the range of potentialities. Dominik Richert was a soldier in the Prussian army from the beginning of the war until the summer of 1918, when he deserted. Born in 1893 in an Alsatian village, the young man was earning his living as a farm labourer when he was drafted in October 1913. Having done his basic training with a *Badische* Infantry regiment, he served first at the Western front. Eventually, his unit was redeployed to the East, only to be later transferred back to the Western front. Only several months after his desertion, he wrote a lengthy text, which survived by chance and was found and edited only a few years ago.[36]

Richert narrates in detail combat situations from the viewpoint of the rank and file. He dwells on the everyday agonizing about one's own and, even more importantly, the enemy's whereabouts 'on the map': or, as it increasingly seemed, the 'troglodytes' in the trenches and underground.[37] He does not exclude eyewitness accounts of people dying; regardless of whether these were close comrades or enemy soldiers. This is never detached from the living conditions and the experiences of unequal treatment of officers and soldiers. He comments bitterly on officers who show no respect for soldiers and treat them brutally while enjoying enormous liberty (and, not to be forgotten, culinary delicacies). Richert also depicts leisure time and, as one of its highlights, a sports festival of his regiment. In many ways the author reconstructs the cosmos of a soldier who suffers from his constant engagement with the cause – if not primarily from his performance 'on the job'.[38]

In early 1918 Richert, who had been promoted to non-commissioned office (NCO), became the leader of a machine-gun squad. The stories he recalls give a concrete picture of his aptness as a military leader, if not his eagerness to be a 'good' soldier. He operated the machine gun and guided his squad, gaining as much room to manoeuvre as possible and thereby effectively keeping the enemy down and his men alive. The German High Command had introduced these specific teams as segments of newly formed assault units in 1915. Close inspection renders similar, if not identical, features of the everyday practices of soldiers and NCOs on the one hand, and workers and industrial masters on the other. In both settings, the actors strove to perform 'German quality work': crucial was the individual handling of tools and materials, as well as of social relationships with both superiors and workmates. Sensitivity for both the material and social features of the task was central; similarly important was the ability to actively shape the handling of the situation.

Let us compare these findings with analyses of industrial work processes. Room to manoeuvre was vital on the shop floor: in the 1910s, as in the 1920s, 1930s and 1940s. The individual operator of a tool had to make decisions about specific performances when manipulating both tools and materials. This included, of course, management of time and energy. It also comprised – and this was no less important – the care for social relationships with comrades and workmates. The latter two were necessary for a job performance ensuring both work safety and a calculable wage.

Therefore, such 'cooperation of necessity' not only framed, but also stimulated individual behaviour. Richert, as NCO, encountered room for manoeuvre especially in his position as leader of a machine gun squad. In these small assault units, the twenty-five to thirty men directly cooperated with or integrated various specialists operating, for example, light cannons (*Infanteriegeschütz*), flame throwers or light mortars. Both training and actual combat demands focused on independent action of these small units and, in the end, of every individual. Finally, the NCOs were no longer those who had 'to push' soldiers from behind; in the new scheme they had to lead from the front, interchangeable with subaltern officers. Thus, the mission-oriented tactics of the German (in particular of the Prussian) army in these new tactics directly affected the 'masses' of NCOs and even rank and file.

The same was true for the industrial work unit. Constant and rigid body drill was, however, special to the military. The aim was to instil a sense of immediate readiness for action into every soldier, so that they would overcome fear and keep cool in actual or imminent combat. It was particular to the German effort to emphasize the importance of coherence in order to ensure the cooperation of units and teams. NCOs and commanding officers were never removed during stints in a reserved position, contrary to British and French practices. In addition, drill never determined mission tactics. In fact, the latter was increasingly highlighted on the German side in war games, not only on the level of the general staff, but also in regular units down to company and even squad level. This regular practice furthered a climate of questioning routines and of experimenting throughout the army, including subaltern officers and NCOs. War gaming became an ever increasing feature of soldiering.[39]

Individual Trajectories II

Children of Richert's age group, born after 1910, filled not only the rank and file, but also the posts of NCOs and subaltern officers in the *Wehrmacht*. One of them was Walter Janka. In the late 1920s this skilled metalworker had become an active Communist who was incarcerated for two years by the Nazis in 1933. Upon his release, he fled into exile and joined the Republican forces fighting the Franco rebels in Spain in 1936.

Janka survived and reached a high-ranking position in the publishing industry in East Germany in the mid-1950s. However, he was ousted from both his job and his position with the ruling Socialist Unity Party in 1957, having been sentenced to jail on account of accusations of treacherous anti-party conspiracy. He started to write an autobiography including episodes of soldiering in the Spanish Civil War. Among others, he recalled an incident where he had served as company commander in a Spanish division (not in the 'International Brigades'). His men had hidden machine guns in the ditches beside the road awaiting busloads of Franco's soldiers:

> Upon first sight of these buses ... I gave a signal ... Within minutes the road became hell: windows burst, oil and gas spread across the road. Most vehicles caught fire. Anyone who had not been gunned down in the buses was killed by the hand grenades of the second company, and those who hoped to escape were killed by gun fire. After twenty minutes there was nothing but fuming wracks, stench and death. We did not take prisoners. We did not have time to spare for prisoners ... The obvious success on the roads heightened the spirits. In fact, this was the second success on this very day.[40]

Calculated and concentrated application of mechanized (and partly automatized) firepower was at the centre of the work processes of these soldiers. They coordinated all their energies and body movements in order to use their tools as swiftly and efficiently as possible to survive themselves and wound or kill the 'others'. Janka, however, at least in hindsight, almost in the same instant started to reflect: 'Killing people is not work. But maybe a soldier sees it that way and most of the soldiers are workers. What they do is just work.' In his account, Janka lets his soldiers speak: they took their action as 'work'. In concrete terms, they had gunned down the enemy soldiers. Their commander recalled this action as both gruesome and tedious, nothing to be fond of. In fact, in hindsight it appeared as hard work, toilsome but also bloody. At least for Janka, the important difference between soldiers' actions and enjoyable activities was, obviously, bloodshed.

Still, what can one make of this remark? The author notifies readers of his unease: is it appropriate, can it be right to render a killing action as work? Janka in the late 1950s was a dissident of the Socialist Unity Party in East Germany. In his account, Janka invoked both the antifascist cause of the Spanish Republic and the socialist and Communist labour movements of Weimar Germany. Central to both was an imagery that presented work as the primordial activity of man. Thus, not only the toil, but also the satisfaction of 'living labour' drove the progress of humankind to produce used values or usable products. Production and productivity had, therefore, broadly framed societal and political vistas as well as the pragmatics of workers' politics on the shop floor. In other words, work drew its aura from its interconnectedness with production. In combat, Janka recalled, worker-soldiers produced destruction. More specifically, with all of their energy, they worked towards killing others.

From Wage-Working to Soldiering in the Second World War

In the Second World War large numbers of both draftees and volunteers of the *Wehrmacht* were wage workers. In their civilian life, they had worked in blue-collar or white-collar jobs, and many had grown up in working class neighbourhoods and milieus. In another context, I have made use of the letters that some soldiers from such backgrounds sent home to their workmates at their respective hometown companies: in this case, Leipzig-based companies.[41] Regardless of whether these letters were mailed in 1940 from France or two or three years later from the Eastern Front, until the spring of 1945 the writers emphasized how much soldiering resembled working in an industrial plant or, for that matter, in a hospital or an administrative office. They stressed tediousness, routine if not boredom, physical toil and exhaustion, and also division of labour and lack of supervision. Comrades are present, too, in these letters, as is 'necessary cooperation' (although 'trust' is less present).[42] A rare find is, however, the letter of a *Luftwaffe* NCO from June 1943. He describes a flight in a plane that had a few days previously circled over Warsaw, immediately after the Jewish ghetto had been destroyed. After referring to this destruction, the NCO finishes with this remark: 'Our troops did a pretty good job [*gute Arbeit*] when destroying the Jewish quarter of that city.'[43]

Such a destruction of this part of the city must have included the killing of inhabitants or other people seeking shelter: soldier's activities that the writer summarily described as 'work'. The lack of more nuanced words is a telling reference to a void. Of course, this void, when submitted to analysis, seems to be totally filled if one considers feelings and their driving power among historical actors themselves. It is that simultaneity of coolness and fulfilment, of terror and fury, and of numbness and activity that is found in documents and traces of small and large battle settings and fighting and killing actions.

Carrying On, 1943 to 1945

Two different but related questions emerge. First, what made these *Wehrmacht* soldiers fight on until the very last instance and even beyond? Second, what caused the ongoing, if not intensified, brutality? This was especially present among many who engaged in what had begun as anti-partisan warfare, at the Eastern Front but increasingly also in the southeast and south.

If one considers, again, the comradeship and cooperation of small-scale military units, the pictures largely overlap with scenarios of industrial work. Accordingly, numerous accounts confirm that the shock reported from first encounters with the killing fields did not last. Soldiers coped through self-willed stubbornness (*Eigen-Sinn*). In fact, the title of the last feature film Nazi propagandists finished and released in 1945 contained the line: 'Life goes on' [*Das Leben geht weiter*].[44] Here, a blend of nonchalance and self-will emerges. It was a sense of cool determination that fuelled people's strivings for every possible relationship, just as it fuelled any material means of survival.

Such images reflected the flexible endurance apparently widespread among seasoned soldiers. However, newly drafted soldiers and volunteering youngsters encountered both the stubborn clinging to old-style rigidity of the military institution (*Kommiss*) and the 'out-of-bounds' of the imminent battle zone. To explore these overlaps, but also their limits, let us embark on the recollections from a semi-military unit of German *Flakhelfer* in the second half of the Second World War.

Like many other young males who were aged sixteen or seventeen, Rolf Schörken and his peers were drafted in 1943 or 1944 for the anti-aircraft batteries (*Flak*) at the home front. Most of them attended high school and all belonged to the 'Hitler Youth', or *Hy*. Training to become gunners, these *Flakhelfer* were concentrated in separate barracks to attend class by day and operate anti-aircraft guns by night. One of the outstanding facets Schörken recalls is what the military hierarchy that the *Hy* had so eagerly adopted meant in their everyday lives: namely that 'someone permanently demanded something from you'.[45] In turn, Schörken and his companions tenaciously strove to preserve as much as possible of their own ways of life. In particular, all of them aimed at keeping a low profile and avoiding situations where superiors 'could reach you'. Their expectation that nobody could 'stem the tide' and defeat the Allied powers generated less relief than gloomy visions of the future. In turn, intensified activity became a means to overcome such visions, if only for a few hours at a time. For these young men, the heightened intensity of action, especially of firing their guns, became a sought-after way out.[46] In the intervals between alarms, these gunners cherished every trace of mutual recognition and respect from family or friends.

On another level, however, individuals at least occasionally voiced their desire, not for identification between working and soldiering, but for their strict separation. Heinrich Böll, a rank-and-file soldier with the infantry, described a 'split' he saw in himself in his letters from the front. In one way, he saw himself as the grudgingly obedient soldier, whereas the other Böll was a 'fanatic individualist'.[47] The 'soldier Böll' would keep his military efforts to a minimum in order to survive threats from enemies and superiors (and, for that matter, from his companions). The 'other Böll' appeared perhaps more often in the dreams and fantasies of the writer. This was the independent spirit who did not care in the least about orders of hierarchy, including superiors. However, the 'other Böll' might not have been content within this bracket of 'fanatic individualism'. Would he not be tempted to seize the opportunity for (re-)producing the simultaneity of coolness and fulfilment, of terror and fury? Perhaps there were too many occasions in which to yield to this temptation, one that not only allowed for, but stimulated brutality in soldiers' actions.[48]

This other or second person may, then, resonate with a peculiar facet of soldiering: the overwhelming, instantaneous pleasure of actively being involved, which contrasts with working: whether it be in industrial, agrarian, or domestic settings. That pleasure might even cut into the field of obedience: working towards a good cause and engaging oneself according to a given blueprint could allow for grand feelings of and for oneself.[49] In order to further understand the interrelationship between rule and self-activity in this setting, one would have to consider Ernst Jünger's tract of 1932 on the worker-soldier, *Der Arbeiter*.

Normal Work: And/or the Fury of the Killing Fields

Ernst Jünger envisioned the worker as a *Gestalt* representing a new era. This idealized (and, hence, stereotyped) industrial worker diverged in principle from the image of an alienated 'appendix of machinery' common among Marxists in particular and intellectuals more generally. The worker Jünger portrayed appeared as 'driven by a will to power' and would blend working with warfare. Hence, Jünger referred to the First World War as a 'comprehensive working process' and to military action as 'battle work' entailing 'work of attack' as well as 'work of the lost post'.[50]

However, the 'heroic realism' Jünger pleaded for did not withstand the actual 'storm of steel' that became imminent in the wars of the late 1930s and 1940s. Walter Janka's sceptical account quoted above poses the question: could one really regard any effective action, killing dozens of enemy fighters, as work? For many German soldiers of the Second World War, whether draftees or volunteers, dexterous performance and effective pursuit of their respective tasks made this 'work'. To many of them, the practices of soldiering that allowed for the active input and cooperation of the rank and file resembled 'German quality work'. In the more distanced view of the observer, similarities between such military teams and fishing crews like those analysed by Gerald Sider emerge. Both involve the harsh conditions of getting by, to the imminent dangers of injury and death, to the formation of intricate relationships. These teams or crews connected one or two dozen males. Most of them had unequal skills and performance levels but, for the time being, they joined forces and acted to survive, at any cost.

Ben Shepherd has recently traced the varieties and intensities of the brutality German troops (and their indigenous helpers) committed in one segment of the Eastern Front. But he also came across occupiers who meandered between ruthlessness and restraint in treating non-combatants (and 'partisans').[51] This account can easily be read as a perfect case in point for the 'split personality' alluded to by Böll.[52] However, the image of the 'split personality' may obscure ongoing relationships or permanent resonances between the two antagonistic poles. The potential simultaneity of both Böll, the fanatic individualist, and Böll, the cooperating soldier, may have emotionally charged the individual before, during and after combat. It could therefore also appeal to the 'fanatic individualist' and, thus, lure him into – possibly collective – military action. In this vein, the 'split', as it were, between the 'fanatic individualist' Heinrich Böll, who withdrew or opposed, and the 'other' Böll, who cooperated and 'did his job', was oftentimes blurred. One can sense an undercurrent that differed from the joy of workers: to re-produce an 'order of things'. This was a longing for fulfilment born out of the fears of uncertainties and ruptures, but also the pleasures, of entering – and of exiting – the killing fields alive.[53]

Allusions to 'work' allowed soldiers to normalize their actions and behaviour. At the same time, however, the intensity of terror and fury on the killing fields enticed these soldiers to move beyond the very normality they longed for, but also despised. It was this attraction of terror and fury that unsettled the claims soldiers (and bystanders) made that their actions were 'nothing but work'.

Notes

1. Winston Churchill, *The River War: An Historical Account of the Reconquest of the Soudan,* [vol. 3 of *The Collected Works of Sir Winston Churchill*] (1974; 1st edn, London: Longmans, Green and Co, 1899), pp. 247–48.
2. Frederick Woods (ed.), *Winston S. Churchill: War Correspondent, 1895–1900* (London: Leo Cooper, 1992), pp. 150–51; dispatch of 11 September 1898, two days after the battle of Omdurman and the cavalry charge that Churchill referred to.
3. Karl Marx, *Das Kapital,* 3 vols (1965; 1st edn Berlin: Dietz, 1865), vol.1, pp. 445, 674.
4. Michael Burawoy, *Manufacturing Consent: Changes in the Labor Process under Monopoly Capitalism* (Chicago: Chicago University Press, 1979); Horst Kern and Michael Schumann, *Das Ende der Arbeitsteilung: Rationalisierung in der industriellen Produktion* (4th edn, Munich: Beck, 1990).
5. See Alf Lüdtke, '"Deutsche Qualitätsarbeit", "Spielereien" am Arbeitsplatz und "Fliehen" aus der Fabrik: Industrielle Arbeitsprozesse und Arbeiterverhalten in den 1920er Jahren', in Friedhelm Boll (ed.), *Arbeiterkulturen zwischen Alltag und Politik* (Vienna: Europa Verlag, 1986), pp. 155–97, esp. p. 155–67, 173–77; Mary Nolan, *Visions of Modernity: American Business and the Modernization of Germany* (Oxford: Oxford University Press, 1994).
6. Churchill in Woods, *War Correspondent,* p. 133; dispatch 8 September 1898.
7. Bruno Thoß and Hans-Erich Volkmann (eds), *Erster Weltkrieg – Zweiter Weltkrieg: ein Vergleich* (Paderborn: Schöningh, 2002); Gerhard Hirschfeld (ed.), *Enzyklopädie Erster Weltkrieg* (Paderborn: Schöningh, 2003).
8. Wilhelm Reibert, *Der Dienstunterricht im Heere: Ausgabe der Schützenkompanie* (12th edn, Berlin: E.S. Mittler, 1940), p. 237. See also my article, '"Fehlgreifen in der Wahl der Mittel". Optionen im Alltag militärischen Handelns', *Mittelweg* 36 (2003): 61–73, esp. 64–65.
9. Curzio Malaparte, *Die Wolga entspringt in Europa* (Köln: Kiepenheuer and Witsch, 1989), p. 44; earlier edns, (Paris, 1948), (Rome 1952); transl. from the German here and in the subsequent quotations by A.L.
10. Malaparte, *Wolga,* p. 45.
11. Malaparte, *Wolga,* p. 32.
12. See Martin Humburg, *Das Gesicht des Krieges: Feldpostbriefe von Wehrmachtssoldaten aus der Sowjetunion 1941–1944* (Opladen: Westdeutscher Verlag, 1998); Hannes Heer (ed.), *"Stets zu erschießen sind Frauen, die in der Roten Armee dienen": Geständnisse deutscher Kriegsgefangener über ihren Einsatz an der Ostfront,* (2nd edn, Hamburg: Hamburger

Edition, 1996); Klaus Latzel, *Deutsche Soldaten – nationalsozialistischer Krieg?: Kriegserlebnis – Kriegserfahrung; 1939–1945*, (2nd edn, Paderborn: Schöningh, 2000); Peter Jahn and Ulrike Schmiegelt (eds), *Foto-Feldpost: geknipste Kriegserlebnisse 1939–1945* (Berlin: Elefantenpress, 2000).

13. Heinrich Popitz, *Technik und Industriearbeit: Soziologische Untersuchungen in der Hüttenindustrie*, (3rd. edn, 1976; 1st edn, Tübingen: Mohr Siebeck, 1957), passim; cf., for other industrial branches and tasks, Alf Lüdtke, 'Deutsche Qualitätsarbeit' in Boll, *Arbeiterkulturen*, pp. 155–97; Lüdtke, 'Polymorphous Synchrony' in *International Review of Social History*, Supplement (1993): 39–84.
14. Small teams (of about twenty or fewer people) are mostly located in the branches of metal processing and machine construction. However, the pivots of the putting-out system and cottage industry in textiles had also been small teams and family units. Here, however, mechanization in factory production allowed for a rapid intensification of the division of labour. Oftentimes, this meant the separation of single women (and men) at their specific workplaces, but also an effort to degrade the knowledge of their craft. Still, recent interpretations underline that even in textiles, one cannot observe 'a trend towards any single structure', see Maxine Berg, *The Age of Manufactures, 1700–1820* (London: Fontana Press, 1985), p. 228; Berg, *The Age of Manufactures* (2nd edn, London: Routledge, 1994), pp. 257–79.
15. Charles Sabel and Jonathan Zeitlin, 'Historical Alternatives to Mass Production: Politics, Markets and Technology in 19th Century Industrialization', in *Past and Present* 108 (Aug. 1985): 133–76.
16. Kern Schumann, *Das Ende der Arbeitsteilung?*
17. Militärgeschichtliches Forschungsamt, *Das Deutsche Reich und der Zweite Weltkrieg*, vol. 4: *Der Angriff auf die Sowjetunion* (Stuttgart: Deutsche Verlagsanstalt, 1983), pp. 1138f. and vol. 5, part 2: *Organisation und Mobilisierung des deutschen Machtbereichs* (Munich: Deutsche Verlagsanstalt, 1999), pp. 636f., 648ff.
18. Cf. Karl-Heinz Frieser, *The Blitzkrieg Legend: The 1940 Campaign in the West* (Annapolis: Naval Institute Press, 2005; 1st edn, Munich: Oldenbourg, 1995); Evan Mawdsley, *Thunder in the East: The Nazi-Soviet War 1941–1945* (London: Hodder Arnold, 2005).
19. See the case discussed in detail by Magnus Koch, '"... wenn der Tod mit seinen furchtbaren Arten seine Ernte holt". Deutungen physischer Gewalt am Beispiel des Wehrmachtsgefreiten Hermann Rombach', in *Historische Anthropologie* 12 (2004): 179–98.
20. Michael Sonenscher, 'Work and Wages in Paris in the Eighteenth Century', in Maxine Berg, Pat Hudson and Michael Sonenscher (eds), *Manufacturer in Town and Country Before the Factory* (Cambridge: Cambridge University Press, 1983), pp. 147–72, esp. p. 171; in more traditional parlance: of the inter-relations between production and reproduction, ibid.
21. Robert Darnton, 'Workers Revolt: The Great Cat Massacre of the Rue Saint-Séverin', in Darnton (ed.), *The Great Cat Massacre and Other Episodes in French Cultural History* (London: Vintage, 1984), pp. 75–104, 270–72.
22. See Gerald Sider, 'Christmas Mumming and the New Year in Outport Newfoundland', in *Past and Present* 71 (1976): 102–25, esp. 108f. As to industry, cf. Burawoy, *Manufacturing Consent*; Tamara Hareven, *Family Time and Industrial Time: The Relationship between the Family and Work in a New England Industrial Community* (Cambridge: University Press of America, 1982). In their efforts of finding and deciphering traces, historians have renewed scrutiny *modo ethnographico*, see Joan Scott, *The Glassworkers of Carmaux* (Cambridge,

Mass.: Harvard University Press, 1974); Patrick Joyce, *Work, Society and Politics: The Culture of the Factory in Later Victorian England* (Brighton: Harvester, 1980); Franz-J. Brüggemeier, *Leben vor Ort: Ruhrbergleute und Ruhrbergbau 1889–1919* (Munich: Beck, 1983); Dorothee Wierling, *Mädchen für alles: Arbeitsalltag und Lebensgeschichte städtischer Dienstmädchen um die Jahrhundertwende* (Berlin: Dietz, 1987).

23. Sider, 'Christmas Mumming', p. 108f.
24. Husbands and sons, brothers and fathers (also nephews and uncles) operated the boats. While at port, the female half of the families and households devoted, in turn, their time and energy to the task of processing the catch and 'making' fish, Sider, 'Christmas Mumming', p. 109.
25. Ernst Jünger, *Storm of Steel* (first published 1920, *In Stahlgewittern* (London 1928); see Bernd Weisbrod, 'Military Violence and Male Fundamentalism: Ernst Jünger's Contribution to the Conservative Revolution', *History Workshop Journal* 49 (2000): 69–94.
26. See Eric J. Leed, *No Man's Land: Combat and Identity in World War I* (Cambridge: Cambridge University Press, 1979), pp. 150–62; also Paul Fussel, *The Great War and Modern Memory* (Oxford: Oxford University Press, 1975).
27. Hans Joachim Schröder, *Die gestohlenen Jahre. Erzählgeschichten und Geschichtserzählung im Interview: Der Zweite Weltkrieg aus der Sicht ehemaliger Mannschaftssoldaten* (Tübingen: Niemeyer, 1992).
28. Michael Geyer, 'Von einer Kriegsgeschichte, die vom Töten spricht', in Thomas Lindenberger and Alf Lüdtke (eds), *Physische Gewalt* (Frankfurt am Main: Suhrkamp, 1995), pp. 136–61.
29. On this very level an otherwise most insightful study on the 'military culture' and its 'habitual practices' in Imperial Germany falls short: Isabel Hull, *Absolute Destruction: Military Culture and the Practices of War in Imperial Germany* (Ithaca/London: Cornell University Press, 2005), p. 92, 98ff.
30. Joanna Bourke, *An Intimate History of Killing: Face-to-face Killing in Twentieth-Century Wars* (London: Basic Books, 1998), pp. 267ff.
31. Schröder, *Die gestohlenen Jahre*, p. 565.
32. Samuel L.A. Marshall, *Men Against Fire: The Problem of Battle Command in Future War* (New York: University of Oklahoma Press, 1947); Samuel Stouffer, *The American Soldier: Combat and Its Aftermath* (Princeton: Princeton University Press, 1949), pp. 130–37.
33. Thomas Kühne, 'Vertrauen und Kameradschaft. Soziales Kapital im "Endkampf" der Wehrmacht', in Ute Frevert (ed.), *Vertrauen* (Göttingen: Vandenhoeck and Ruprecht, 2003), pp. 245–78, esp. pp. 256–57, 263–64; see also his comprehensive account *Kameradschaft: die Soldaten des nationalsozialistischen Krieges und das 20. Jahrhundert* (Göttingen: Vandenhoeck and Ruprecht, 2006).
34. Omer Bartov, *The Eastern Front 1941–1945: German Troops and the Barbarisation of Warfare* (Basingstoke: Macmillan, 1985).
35. See Lüdtke, '"Deutsche Qualitätsarbeit"' in Boll, *Arbeiterkulturen*, pp. 155–97; for military units see Christopher Browning, *Ordinary Men: Reserve Police Battalion 101 and the Final Solution in Poland* (New York: Harper Perennial, 1992). Cf. a recollection relating a specific kind of fear with one's desire for recognition: 'It was the fear of not performing as expected, making the wrong decision at a critical time, and letting my crew down.' This particular recollection stems from the memory of an American bomber pilot, James M. Davis; Davis, *In Hostile Skies: An American B-24 Pilot in WW II*, ed. by David L. Snead (Denton: Texas A and M University Press, 2006), p. 92.

36. Dominik Richert, *Beste Gelegenheit zum Sterben: Meine Erlebnisse im Kriege 1914–1918*, ed. by Angelika Tramitz and Bernd Ulrich (Munich: Knesebeck, 1989).
37. Cf. Leed, *No Men's Land*, quoting Henri Barbusse, p. 139.
38. The rift between officers and ordinary soldiers was not experienced by Richert alone. Investigations of the German military after the war emphasized this particular trait as decisive for the final collapse in 1918. See more generally Wilhelm Deist, 'Verdeckter Militärstreik im Kriegsjahr 1918?', in Wolfram Wette (ed.), *Der Krieg des kleinen Mannes. Eine Militärgeschichte von unten* (Munich/Zurich: Piper, 1992), pp. 146–67.
39. Bruce I. Gudmundsson, *Storm Troop Tactics: Innovation in the German army, 1914–1918* (New York/London: Praeger Press, 1989), pp. 50–53, 173–77.
40. Walter Janka, *Spuren eines Lebens* (Reinbek: Rowohlt, 1992), pp. 109–10; the author could only publish his text, however, after the implosion of the GDR.
41. See Alf Lüdtke, 'Arbeit, Arbeitserfahrungen und Arbeiterpolitik', in Lüdtke, *Eigen-Sinn. Arbeiter, Arbeitserfahrungen und Politik vom Kaiserreich bis in den Faschismus* (Hamburg: Ergebnisse Verlag, 1993), pp. 351–440, 406–09.
42. Cf. letters of a medical doctor and officer, born 1907, from the Eastern Front: Ingo Stander (ed.), '*Ihr daheim und wir hier draußen*'. *Ein Briefwechsel zwischen Ostfront und Heimat, Juni 1941–März 1943* (Cologne: Böhlau, 2006).
43. Cf. Lüdtke, 'Arbeit, Arbeitserfahrungen und Arbeiterpolitik', p. 408.
44. Werner Blumenberg, *Das Leben geht weiter. Der letzte Film des Dritten Reiches* (Berlin: Rowohlt, 1993).
45. Rolf Schörken, *Luftwaffenhelfer und Drittes Reich: Die Entstehung eines politischen Bewusstseins* (Stuttgart: Klett-Cotta, 1984), p. 141.
46. Cf. also the biographical reconstruction of a soldier from a rural background, who was born in 1924 and eagerly expected the draft in 1942,aiming to join the navy or the *panzers*: Bernhard Haupert and Franz Josef Schäfer, *Jugend zwischen Kreuz und Hakenkreuz* (Frankfurt am Main: Suhrkamp, 1991), pp. 191–209, 135–237. See the remark of a communications officer, born in 1917, in a letter from occupied France to his girlfriend in June of 1940: he wanted to volunteer for the paratroopers and noted that, 'if there is war I cannot survive it in the rear'. In 1943 he courageously stood against the persecution of the family of Sophie Scholl: Sophie Scholl and Fritz Hartnagel, *Damit wir uns nicht verlieren. Briefwechsel 1937–1943*, ed. by Thomas Hartnagel, (Frankfurt am Main: Fischer, 2005), p. 180.
47. Heinrich Böll, *Briefe aus dem Krieg*, ed. by. Jochen Schubert, vols. 1 and 2 (Cologne: Kiepenheuer & Witsch, 2001), p. 343. This remark from Summer 1940 finds no direct resonance in his writings of the years at the front that followed. For instance, in several notes of November 1943 he distinguishes strictly between the horrors and terrors of war and their concreteness in 'the East' on the one hand and on the feeling of undeserved luck of surviving and enjoying, yet again, the little pleasures of relief after 'another' round of combat on the other, see pp. 948–61.
48. See Benjamin Ziemann, 'Die Eskalation des Tötens in zwei Weltkriegen', in Richard van Dülmen (ed.), *Erfindung des Menschen: Schöpfungsträume und Körperbilder 1500–2000* (Vienna: Böhlau, 1998), pp. 411–29, 424–28; Hamburger Institut für Sozialforschung, *Verbrechen der Wehrmacht: Dimensionen des Vernichtungskrieges 1941–1944* (Hamburg: Hamburger Edition, 2001); especially insightful, and relating brutality primarily to rear-guard troops and less to front-line units, is Christoph Rass, *'Menschenmaterial': Deutsche Soldaten an der Ostfront. Innenansichten einer Infanteriedivision, 1939–1945* (Paderborn: Schöningh, 2003).

49. See the praise of the automaton in eighteenth-century theories of individualization: Barbara Stollberg-Rilinger, *Der Staat als Maschine: Zur politischen Metaphorik des absoluten Fürstenstaats* (Berlin: Duncker and Humblot, 1986).
50. Ernst Jünger, *Der Arbeiter: Herrschaft und Gestalt* (Stuttgart: Klett Cotta, 1982; 1st edn, 1932), p. 66; the three subsequent quotations pp. 153, 82, 113.
51. Ben Shepherd, 'The Continuum of Brutality: Wehrmacht Security Divisions in Central Russia, 1942', in *German History* 21 (2003): 49–81; for a similar line, see Theo Schulte, *The German Army and Nazi Policies in Occupied Russia* (New York: Berg, 1989).
52. Böll in one of his letters admiringly describes what appeared to him to be a scene of radiant beauty: his lieutenant approaching the unit on horseback from afar. Obviously, the impression this image made on the private Böll also affected the 'other' Böll, the 'individualist'; see Böll, *Briefe aus dem Krieg*, vol. 1, p. 343–344, letter of 22 May 1942 ('From the West').
53. See also the notes of a U.S. combatant in Vietnam who in his literary account refers to soldiers' fear of the 'blush of dishonour' and, thus, fighting and also killing. He concomitantly depicts scenes where 'war wasn't all terror and violence. Sometimes things could get almost sweet', Tim O'Brien, *The Things They Carried* (New York: Broadway, 1998; 1st edn 1990), pp. 21, 31.

8

Forced Labour in the Second World War: The German Case and Responsibility

Klaus Tenfelde

I. Perceptions of Work and Definitions of Forced Labour

In 1912 Adolf Levenstein published the results of an opinion poll among German workers that, to my knowledge, must be considered the first systematic survey of the perception of work among workers themselves.[1] This survey relied on questionnaires sent to miners and textile and metal workers living in different regions of the Reich and utilized some five thousand responses, solely from male workers of different age groups. The survey was undertaken between 1907 and 1911, and the author clearly relates the difficulties he faced during the procedure. It must be mentioned that, first, he made use of trade union contacts, so the responses show an inclination towards the social democratic labour movement. Second, during the procedure, attention was gradually shifted from trade union contacts to those established on a private level. Furthermore, it should be mentioned that the publication itself does not indicate any connections to what was going on within the major social reform organization called Verein für Socialpolitik since the turn of the century.[2] This association, under guidance of the Weber brothers and others, launched a major investigation into 'selection and adjustment of the modern industrial worker' ('Auslese und Anpassung der modernen Industriearbeiterschaft') during those years. It resulted in a couple of important studies on recruitment, composition and the social mobility of workers of different branches during the pre-war years. Levenstein was connected to such efforts, but he obviously relied on experiences he had made on his own during a time of no less than eight years when he had held so-called 'workers' evenings' in his Berlin apartment each week on Wednesdays.

Levenstein asked a number of questions that were aimed at discovering the workers' perception of their economic condition, their relations within the social and political community and their position towards culture, religion and nature.

The most important chapter dealt with working conditions and asked for workers' attitudes towards piecework, machine work, work grievances such as fatigue, the ideas of work and during work and, finally, whether workers would feel exploited by low wages or workplace dependencies. Levenstein categorized the responses and constructed tables by which we are told that, despite differences according to age group, wage level and region, more than 60 per cent of the miners who had responded documented their aversion to wage work, and an additional 18 per cent claimed indifference. The respective percentages for textile workers are 75 per cent and 14 per cent, and for metal workers the numbers are at 57 per cent and 17 per cent. Another question about the perception of dependency on low wages or, alternatively, workplace dependencies may have been asked and evaluated on doubtful grounds. Levenstein weighted the perception of dependency and found out that 40 per cent of the miners, 37 per cent of the textile workers and 31 per cent of the metal workers considered themselves in strongly dependant work situations, whereas between 32 per cent and 53 per cent considered income dependencies to be more important.

Thus, in many cases, income shortages played a more important role than workplace dependency. It may be even more interesting to consider verbal responses that Levenstein had asked for, which were presented in the volume in a sort of concrete workers' language. When asked if they enjoyed work, one of the miners responded that he 'went to work as if I went to my death'. Another miner maintained that it was impossible to enjoy mine work: 'Finally, I haven't met anyone who enjoyed mine work. One is working simply mechanically, under force.' 'My work is almost no work but, rather, hell,' a third one said, 'so that there can be no talk about pleasure, nor about interest'. A textile worker believed that it was work that made a man a human being, 'but nowadays, work has become a curse to mankind'. Quite a few workers made it clear that they simply hated work, and some of them added that they could not enjoy work because of the nature of the present society: 'It is private capitalism that fundamentally exorcized my interest in work', a Berlin metal worker said. A lathe operator simply believed himself to be 'a slave', and one of the workers stated that if he wanted to feed his family on honest grounds, he would have to work with pleasure, because in that case he achieved better results. Another worker believed that 'only voluntary work would be a pleasure'.

There were no statements that talked unconditionally about pleasure at work, but many that reasoned about the causes of the lack of pleasure. Some of these, such as a Silesian miner, clarified what had shaped their opinion: 'I surely have interest in my work, but this is dried out by the capitalist system and its henchmen, who make me feel all day long more like a work machine that has to obey.' When asked whether he felt low wages or work dependencies to be more oppressive, a miner from Silesia responded that he suppressed workplace dependency with proletarian pride, and another Silesian claimed that children were born as work slaves.[3]

There was a sort of hidden Protestantism underlying the question whether work could produce pleasure: beginning with Luther himself, especially the educated classes in Protestant Germany had internalized the opinion that perfection in life is to be reached by work.[4] Keeping this in mind, we may learn from statements like the ones quoted here that the capacity to make judgements about work can be gained from different sources, and that such judgements do not tell us sufficiently about the real harshness of work. Work grievances may be found everywhere, but their interpretations in each case strongly depend upon communications and are thus determined culturally. This explains why it is difficult to talk about forced labour, or compulsory work. It is by the values prevailing within a given culture and by the dominant tendencies and contradictions of the cultural mainstream that opinions about work are shaped, almost regardless of the factual nature of such work.

In contrast to the Lutheran work ethic that, of course, was spread from the pulpits for centuries, there was quite another perception of work, especially widespread within continental rural societies. At the end of the nineteenth century in Germany, work under feudal conditions was not a matter of the past. Formally, feudal exploitation had been overcome at the beginning of the nineteenth century, but it was well into the 1860s before its remnants were removed, and such mental remnants usually last for generations. As one of many examples, one could take the Prussian farm and house servants' law (*Gesindeordnung*), decreed in 1810. Introduced to grant big land-owners compensation for the loss of cheap feudal labour, this law in fact continued the legal practice of compulsory service that had been introduced in the fifteenth century. This practice had entitled the lords to choose personal servants for their manors from among their subjects' children every year. The Prussian law of 1810 was in force until 1918. It held that home and farm servants, who for the time of service had to render their complete work capacity to the employer, were rented on a yearly basis, either in spring or in autumn. They could be asked to work all day and night without additional payment. If they escaped, they could be returned by police. They even had to tolerate corporal punishment. Until 1914 some 1.6 million young people, primarily women, were subject to this Prussian law (and analogous legal provisions elsewhere in Germany) in the big cities; this does not include the many farmhands and maids subject to the same law in the countryside.[5]

These arrangements implied 'educational' purposes as well. To raise fully fledged members of society (or, more appropriately, of the respective estates within society), it seemed advisable to educate them through work. Indeed, this is why Frederick the Great in the eighteenth century had introduced orphanages, and 'work houses' for those who apparently needed improvement. Friedrich August Ludwig von der Marwitz, a Prussian conservative of the first half of the nineteenth century, fiercely criticized the agrarian reforms because of the removal of the kind of education that had been provided by feudal dependency and compulsory service ('Untertänigkeit und Zwangsdienst').[6] To a degree, it is this sense of education that also accompanied British moves to introduce forced labour in the colonies well into the twentieth century,[7] although it was primarily by British diplomatic initiatives that compulsory labour was outlawed by the 1930 Forced Labour Convention of the Geneva International Labour Office (ILO).[8]

Thus, for several reasons, it cannot be clear at all what is meant by 'forced labour'. By looking back from a position held by labour historians in the 1970s and thereafter, an ideal type of 'free wage labour' has been constructed that tends to conceal the manifold varieties that have been the result of legal, political, social and cultural, and therefore even regional, restrictions to 'free wage labour'. First of all, even at the beginning of the twentieth century, the principle of free wage labour was not accepted everywhere: neither within more developed countries, nor in the colonized world. Even within the most advanced industrial societies, forms of compulsion to work played a partially important role. Second, work, especially manual work, can easily be understood to exert compulsion: a living is made only by work so that, under conditions of scarcity, the definition of work comprises a sense of compulsion. Third, it is precisely this basic fact that opens the field for many different constructions of the meaning of work that are influenced by mainstream thought and therefore change over time.

The Forced Labour Convention mentioned previously defined 'forced or compulsory labour' as 'all work or service which is exacted from any person under the menace of any penalty and for which the said person has not offered himself voluntarily'.[9] In order to escape from an endless relativism of definition, recent historians of forced labour during the Second World War mainly turned to descriptive definitions of forced labour. According to them, forced labour is made possible and enforced by government measures that aim at compulsory labour market regulation and compel people to work for an unlimited period of time, whereby these people are removed from their homes. Thus, some authors maintain that the existence of work camps serves as a clear indication of compulsory work. Furthermore, workplace discrimination is considered a criterion of definition, and in war, 'work for the enemy', as well as social deprivation, are considered to be important. Finally, forced labourers are seen as having no or little chances of improving their work and living conditions; in cases of abuse, their complaints would not be taken into consideration.

We shall see that even such concrete attempts at definition lack clarity under certain circumstances. I shall now turn first to one part of that definition: physical removal from home. In this way, the dimensions of forced labour throughout the twentieth century should become clearer. After discussing these dimensions in some detail, I will turn to a description of the dimensions and forms of forced labour in different mining districts under German occupation. In my conclusion, I will again bring up the question of perception.

II. A Century of Compulsory Migration

It should be remembered that the twentieth century as a whole was a century of compulsory migration, in contrast to the forms of mobility well-known in Europe before the age of industrialization. Such compulsory migration was not in all cases connected to compulsory work, but in most cases it was, and therefore it needs consideration. Looking at European experiences, there seem to have been six different causes of such migration.[10] First, millions of Europeans were clearly forced to escape from wars. This, of course, was not limited to the great wars of the twentieth century, but also took place, to a very large extent, for instance, in south-eastern Europe during the 1990s. Second, one may broadly identify political coercion as a cause of compulsory migration. This becomes clear in the case of the one to two million Russians who escaped from the consequences of the Bolshevik revolution in 1917 and thereafter, or of those people who fled from Nazi Germany before the Second World War, or those who fled from Spain after the Civil War. Third, compulsory migration can be enforced by violence in the case of expulsion. The Germans, of course, are prone to emphasize their own post-1945 experiences, but it must be kept in mind that expulsion had already been a legalized consequence of the peace treaties after the First World War. It was again provided for by the Teheran and Yalta agreements of the Allied powers during the Second World War, not to mention the Soviet coercive displacement of ethnic minorities, which was by no means limited to Russo-Germans, well before the war. One may distinguish another form of physical violence resulting in compulsory migration: deportation. The Soviet Gulag and the Nazi concentration camps come to mind, but millions of prisoners of war must also be counted within this category.

Fifth, forced labour forms just one part of this large framework of compulsory migration, but an important one. In the German case, there were three major categories of compulsory labour: the prisoners of war mentioned previously, inmates of concentration camps (sometimes, German and European Jews were considered to form a separate group when they were forced to work outside concentration camps, in or outside the ghettos),[11] and civil labour recruited from occupied territories to work within such territories or within the borders of the German Reich. I shall turn to this immediately. Finally, for the sake of completeness, another form of compulsory migration in the twentieth century should at least be mentioned, and that is repatriation.

Such forceful migrations concerned millions of individuals. A peak was reached during the Second World War when, according to recent estimates, 50 to 60 million people – that is, more than 10 per cent of the entire European population – had to move as a result of coercion. It is also estimated that already in 1925 the number of those being displaced as a consequence of the First World War was some 10 million people. During the First World War the French government hired 700,000 foreign workers, and the British government recruited 100,000 Chinese labourers to work behind the front lines in northern France; the forms of recruitment by the military and camp accommodations resemble at least some features of compulsory work. Indeed, the Chinese in northern France were considered to be prisoners by the indigenous population. Germany during the First World War held at least 2.5 million foreigners as workers within the borders of the Reich, among them 1.5 million POWs, which amounts to one-seventh of the whole work force.[12] Among the one million civil workers, there were at least 500,000 Polish workers whose work conditions came very close to compulsory labour as defined above. Under pressure by leading industrialists, the Reich government in late 1916 agreed to deport Belgian workers, primarily miners and foundry workers, to work especially in the Ruhr area, but this move had to be stopped because of worldwide protest that involved even the Pope. This case indicates that, to a certain degree, the judicial system in Germany, as well as public opinion, remained influential during the First World War, contrary to what happened after 1939. If we look at the Armenian deportation and genocide or at the consequences of the 1923 Treaty of Lausanne that ended the war between Greece and Turkey, the indifference or toleration of European governments towards compulsory resettlement and deportation becomes obvious. It is an important question, still to be answered, as to why such indifference gradually ceased in the second half of the twentieth century. I tend to believe that a worldwide response to Nazi cruelties and especially the rise of human rights issues played an important role.

Time and again, historians have attempted to estimate the number of victims of such compulsory migration, especially the number of victims of deportation and genocide.[13] Among other problems, the controversy about the singularity of National Socialist mass murder and German responsibility influences such estimates, although it will be clear that this controversy can by no means be based on the count of victims. I also hesitate to compare a long tradition of Soviet banishment that was reinforced in 1930 in order to complete collectivization with the Nazi system of compulsory labour: to which I shall now turn.

III. Forced Labour in Germany during the Second World War

In what follows, figures will be introduced to indicate the extent of forced labour in Germany during the war. It must be mentioned at the beginning that already before the outbreak of war, work conditions in Germany had become harsh, especially under the rule of the Four Year Programme introduced in 1936. It is important to remember that as a consequence of the world economic crisis, several 'Western' governments had conceived of compulsory work schemes, at least for young male adults.

Some further developments should be mentioned.[14] In 1935 compulsory service was introduced for male workers, and workers were forced to document their occupational conditions in so-called work-books (*Arbeitsbuchpflicht*). In June 1938 and February 1939 decrees concerning the obligation to serve

(*Dienstpflichtverordnungen*) entitled the labour market authorities to forcibly recruit workers regardless of existing work contracts in order to use them for work that was considered to be of basic political necessity (*staatspolitische Notwendigkeit*). The principle of private contract was thereby abolished. Since February 1938 women had to face a so-called *Pflichtjahr*, which meant obligatory work for one year. In March and July 1939 job turnover in certain branches of industry was made subject to agreement with the labour bureaucracy, and a decree on work hours issued by Göring introduced a forty-five-minute increase of mining shifts, compensated by a certain increase of wages. Since about 1937 the labour market was exhausted, and attempts were made to attract foreign labour, though this occurred on a seemingly voluntary basis until the war began. Thus, agreements were signed with Poland, Italy, Yugoslavia, Hungary, Bulgaria and the Low Countries to provide a workforce especially for farm work. Such efforts, however, remained limited because of a severe lack of foreign currency in the Reich. Overall, it seems that 'free wage labour' within the Reich had become considerably limited long before the war began.

Conditions changed fundamentally beginning in September 1939. Prisoners of war became available immediately, but during the Blitzkrieg phase German industries widely resisted the employment of POWs. Arguments differed, but generally it was maintained that POWs lacked skill, that they were badly motivated and that their employment would induce a danger of sabotage. Before the raid on Poland, some 300,000 foreigners had been employed in Germany primarily in farm and construction work. Until the end of May 1940 that number had risen to some 800,000, of whom 350,000 were prisoners of war.

As Table 8.1 shows, the general dimensions of employment did not change that much during the war years: employment decreased from almost 40 million employees to almost 36 million. First, the Deutsche Faven, Deutsche Männer and In die Wehrmacht Einberufene columns are of interest here. The deutsche männer columns show that the number of male workers of German citizenship strongly decreased from about 25 million to about 14 million, and this decrease, of course, was caused by army recruitment represented by the green columns. The number of active soldiers was raised from 4.5 million early in 1940 to 10.6 million in May 1944; figures for the last war year are difficult to interpret, so I leave them aside. Incidentally, the UK Crestellte columns refer to the numbers of those who had been recruited to the army already, but were released for work because of the urgent need of skilled workers in different branches. The Deutsche Fraven columns show the numbers of women in German employment, and it is no surprise that these numbers remained fairly stable throughout the war. National Socialist perceptions of sex roles and their family policies did not allow for a complete extension of German female labour, even during the war. Conditions changed in this respect during the last year of war.

Finally, the figures presented in the Kriegsgetangene sections represent the numbers of POWs employed during the war, whereas the black columns include foreign labourers. Taken together, the figure rose from 1.2 million people early in

Table 8.1: The German Labour Market (Pre-war Territory) during the Second World War, 1939–1944

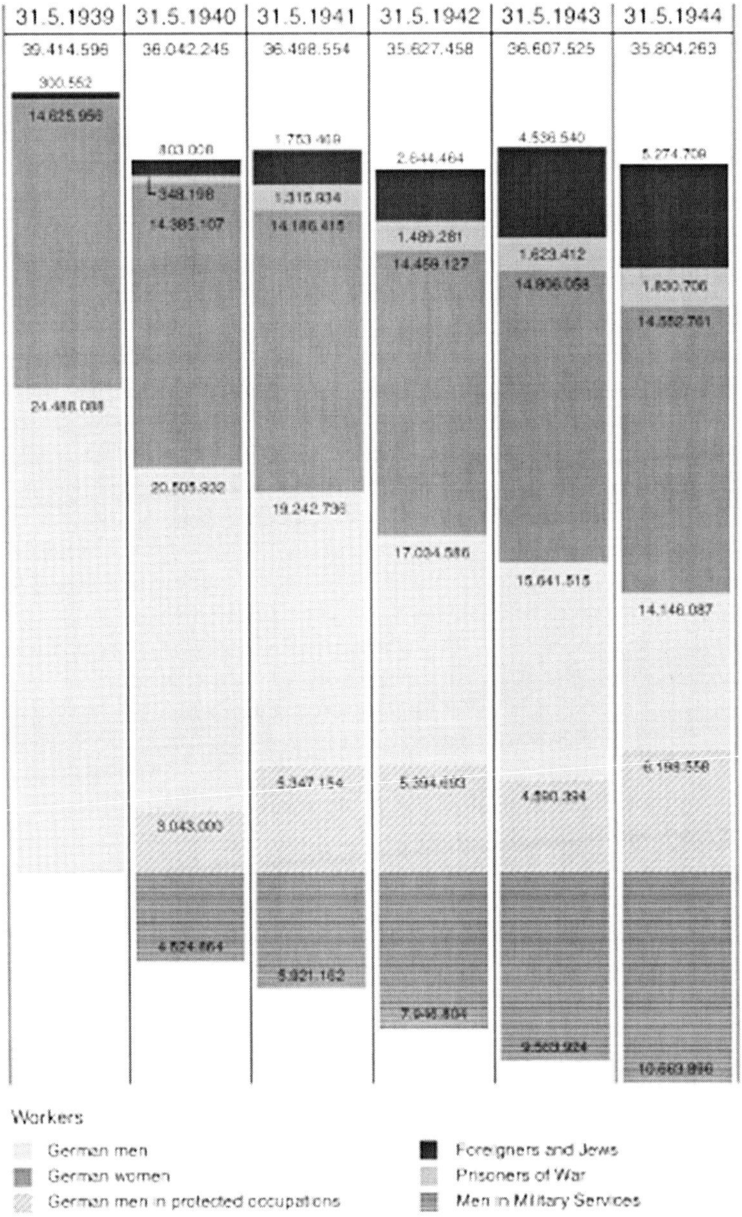

Source: Bernhard R. Kroener et al., *Das Deutsche Reich und der Zweite Weltkrieg*, vol. 5: *Organisation und Mobilisierung des Deutschen Machtbereichs*, part 1: *Kriegsverwaltung, Wirtschaft und personelle Ressourcen 1939–1941* (Stuttgart: DVA, 1988), p. 810.

1942 to 7.1 million in May 1944. These figures are generally accepted among historians.[15] Interestingly enough, growing numbers of forced labourers roughly compensated for the workforce losses caused by army recruitment. Because of the importance of ammunition industries, a certain shift within the occupational structure from services to industries may be noted. It is quite clear that, overall, the German labour market somehow remained stable during the war years, with the exception of the last year, and, to the degree that army recruitment was replaced by forced labour, to an approximately equalizing extent.

Table 8.2: Prisoners of War by National Origin

	15.2.1942	15.8.1943	15.11.1943	1.1.1945
French	971,000	736,324	664,736	637,564
Soviet Russian	154,000	496,106	564,692	972,388
Belgian	58,000	53,311	53,858	57,392
British	41,000	44,087	66,586	101,564
Serbian	105,000	93,872	92,103	100,830
Polish	31,000	29,128	30,548	34,691
Dutch	–	–	–	6,174
Others*	10,000	9,270	382,906	280,012
Total	*1,370,000*	*1,462,098*	*1,855,429*	*2,190,615*

* Includes Italian military internees.

Source: Bernhard R. Kroener et al., *Das Deutsche Reich und der Zweite Weltkrieg*, vol. 5: Organisation und Mobilisierung des Deutschen Machtbereichs, part 2: Kriegsverwaltung, Wirtschaft und personelle Ressourcen 1942–1944/45 (Stuttgart:DVA, 1999), p. 212.

Turning to the national origins of POWs, the most important groups are easily identified (Table 8.2). The whole number went up to 2.2 million soldiers early in 1945, and French and Soviet POWs formed the main labour force. The French slightly decreased, whereas the Soviets strongly increased, even after the fate of war had changed at the beginning of 1943. It will be shown later that a change of maintenance strategies played a role in this increase.

Understandably, the composition of civil workers recruited for service within the Reich territory was quite different. As shown above, the number strongly increased since 1942, up to almost 6 million foreign civil workers in summer 1944. Among those, the biggest group consisted of the so-called 'Eastern workers' (*Ostarbeiter*) who had been recruited in the Soviet Union. The second most numerous group came from Poland; both nations accounted for two-thirds of the forced labour employed in Germany. The next important groups were the French, the Dutch and workers recruited from the Bohemian Protectorate, including Slovakia. The column called *Schutzangehörige* contains Polish workers from regions that had been annexed in 1939. Thus, forced labour mainly consisted of forcefully recruited workers from Russia and Poland, but a considerable number of French workers were forcefully recruited from the occupied zones.

Table 8.3: Workers Recruited from the Occupied Territories for Employment within the Reich Borders

	20.1.42	**31.12.42**	**31.12.42**	**15.2.44**	**Late summer 1944**[c]
Belgium	131,470	144,974	222,851	209,976	199,437
France	62,589	191,463	660,610	650,230	646,421
Italy	188,122	165,885	124,939	126,411	287,347
Former Yugoslavia (without Croatia)	78,107	50,686	43,242	42,608	97,760[d]
Croatia	56,318	67,068	68,224	66,592	–
Netherlands	96,151	161,862	274,368	226,827	254,544
Hungary	30,521	27,945	25,893	24,863	24,263
Soviet Territories	55,081[a]	1,263,312	1,812,091	1,872,516	2,174,644[a]
Baltic Regions	–	29,681	33,687	35,460	–
Generalgouvernement and Bialystok	1,032,196	918,117	1,054,537	1,028,816	1,662,336[e]
Schutzangehörige[b]	unknown	494,069	558,675	590,581	–
Protectorate	140,693	209,278	280,313	279,290	313,890[f]
Employed foreigners in total	*2,138,360*	*3,724,340*	*5,438,178*	*5,454,628*	*5,770,340*

[a] Including the Baltic regions.
[b] Polish workers from the annexed Polish territories.
[c] This column according to Herbert, *Zwangsarbeit* p. 8.
[d] Including Croatia.
[e] Including the "Schutzangehörigen".
[f] And Slovakia.

Source: Kroener et al., p. 218.

The distribution of foreign workers by branches of occupation indicates the overwhelming role farm work played for both foreign workers and POWs. Within industries in general, the percentage of foreign workers and POWs rose from 15 per cent in 1942 to about 29 per cent in 1944, but there were strong differences among branches of industries. In construction industries, more than half of the workforce consisted of foreigners and POWs, and this percentage was high from the very beginning. In metal industries, steel production and mining, in contrast, the percentages and real numbers doubled from 1942 to 1944.

Table 8.4: Proportions of Foreign Workers and POWs According to Industrial Branches

	1942	1943	1944
Construction	47.0	50.0	52.1
Metal Industries	17.4	31.0	37.6
Iron and steel	15.4	28.7	33.0
Mining	14.0	25.0	32.8
Mechanical engineering	15.1	29.4	32.0
Chemistry	15.4	26.3	30.2
Electrical industries	13.9	19.3	23.5
Textile	7.1	12.3	13.0
Total industries	*14.8*	*25.0*	*28.8*
Agriculture	*53.0*	*58.1*	*51.4*

Source: Ulrich Herbert, *Fremdarbeiter. Politik und Praxis des 'Ausländer-Einsatzes' in der Kriegswirtschaft des Dritten Reiches* (2nd edn, Essen: Klartext-Verlag, 1999), p. 266.

The total number of foreign workers employed in Germany, including the annexed territories, from 1939 to 1945 is now estimated at 13.5 million. This includes prisoners of war (4.6 million), civil workers from occupied territories (8.4 million), inmates of concentration camps, and Jews (*Arbeitsjuden*) compelled to work (1.7 million).[16] The numbers for civil workers also include 'voluntary civil workers', so that the total number of forced labour in Germany may be estimated at some 12 million people.

IV. Europe under German Occupation: Forced Labour in Different Mining Districts

The figures presented here seem to indicate rather clear-cut developments and to provide a clear impression about the dimensions of forced labour during the Second World War. Yet this is by no means a correct impression. First of all, it is not always completely clear to which territories such figures refer. Thus, the so-called Polish eastern strip – that is, the territory annexed in Upper Silesia after the raid into Poland – may have been left out from the figures given for the Reich as a whole. Second, the figures do not take into account that forced labour had started before the war began; there were cases of forced labour following the imprisonment of many Jewish males as a consequence of the November pogrom of 1938. Territories annexed prior to 1939 are also not included. Thus, in Vienna the employment offices formally compelled Jews to carry out work since October 1938. In July 1939 an obligation to work was introduced within the Protectorate for Czechs aged sixteen to twenty-five years, so that the door was opened to extend such regulations during wartime. Inhabitants of the Protectorate who were formally counted as Reich citizens (*Inländer*) were usually not housed in camps, but both sexes of the age group between eighteen and fifty were compelled to work. Already before the war, unskilled workers that came from the Polish part of former Czechoslovakia were brought together in camps to be delegated to seasonal and public work.

Third, and much more importantly, the figures presented so far do not include compulsory work within those territories that were occupied by the German army during the war. At the present state of research, it seems impossible to introduce any reliable estimate of their numbers, though in many individual cases, historians do have some knowledge about the numbers, recruitment, work conditions and even mortality. After all, sources covering this most important field of forced labour are clearly available, but in most cases, local archives would have to be consulted to consider additional materials. This has been done within a research project carried out at the Institute for Social Movements at the University of Bochum in recent years, and it is from this background that I am presenting selected material.[17] Cases that will be considered would by no means cover the problem of compulsory work in occupied territories as a whole, but are meant to illustrate the extent to which German authorities exploited the respective labour markets. It seems appropriate to roughly follow the course of war and thereby include the respective territories where German officials gained power.

Almost everywhere within the occupied territories German authorities issued decrees to compel the population of the respective regions to work (*Arbeitspflichtverordnungen*). These decrees usually followed the scheme of the German decrees of 1938. They differed as to the time of enforcement, the people concerned and the extent of compulsion. In Poland – that is, within the territory called *Generalgouvernement* – such a decree was released in October 1939, compelling unemployed urban male workers from eighteen to sixty years to work. This was soon extended to youngsters above the age of fourteen and to the people from the countryside. From the annexed Polish territories, half a million Poles were moved into the *Generalgouvernement* to live in camps and serve in the construction and armament industries. Polish Jews of both sexes were compelled to work above the age of twelve. Many of them – at least 700,000 at the end of 1940 – worked in the urban ghettos and in special camps erected for compulsory work. It seems that at least 200,000 inmates of concentration camps situated in Polish territories had to carry out compulsory work under mostly indescribable conditions. When the German military forces invaded Soviet Russia, so-called Eastern workers who were to become a major part of the work force within the Reich were recruited for the Polish industrial sites such as Upper Silesia, along with Soviet prisoners of war. Clearly, the freedom given to forcefully recruit a workforce from the indigenous population was used especially within the mining districts.

In France the German occupational forces compelled unemployed French construction workers to serve with the Organization Todt. This concerned about two million workers, the majority of whom could live at their homes, not in camps. The Vichy regime had introduced a general obligation to work for men aged between eighteen and fifty and women between twenty-one and thirty-five since September 1942. Within the Service du Travail Obligatoire (STO), male workers had to serve for two years beginning in February 1943. In one programme of the STO, 30,000 workers were to be recruited for mine work in Nord-Pas de Calais, but this programme partially failed. Instead, some 16,000 Soviet Russian and Serbian prisoners of war, as well as many Soviet civil workers, were recruited for the mining districts.

In Belgium early in 1942, 190,000 Belgian workers were compelled to work either in their home country or in Nord-Pas de Calais for the German army and military construction. Those who refused were driven into work camps, and the conditions for obligatory work were tightened several times. Also, in the Netherlands workers could be compelled to serve and could be sent to work inside German borders. Because of military developments, late plans for a programme to employ Soviet prisoners of war in the Dutch mining district of Limburg could not be realized.

In occupied Yugoslavia a decree on work compulsion was introduced, but could not be realized, so the German authorities erected work camps for dissidents. Early in 1943 some 176,000 Serbians worked for the German occupational forces, many of them in mining; in the Bor copper district, only one third of about 30,000 workers worked voluntarily. Later during the war Hungarian Jews, as well as Italian military internees, were employed here. In Greece early in 1942, 100,000 Greeks worked for the German army, and, beginning in January 1942, a general work obligation was applied to Greeks between the ages of 16 and 45.

Work compulsion in the Soviet Union was tightened several times. Since the spring of 1942 violent compulsory recruitment to work either at local workplaces or somewhere else began. Within the Soviet Union the German military forces, the Organization Todt and the Eastern Railways (Reichsbahn Ost) were the most important employers. The railway company alone employed 643,000 workers. For the construction of Road No. 4 (Durchgangsstraße 4),[18] Jews were recruited from ghettos and forced labour camps; in addition, four concentration camps were erected. In all, it is estimated that between 25 and 26 million Soviet citizens worked under German occupation. It is not clear how many of them were housed in work camps. To take only the Ukrainian territory under occupation, 7.5 million workers were employed under compulsory conditions, most of them in farm work, but compulsory recruitment took place from the very beginnings of occupation, so that seventy-eight camps for forced labour for Jews have been counted, and 50,000 Jews and POWs had to construct Road No. 4.

To the best of my knowledge, an estimate of the numbers of male and female workers being employed under coercive conditions in the occupied territories does not exist. Wherever German forces had occupied the territories, labour market authorities were among the first to be established to satisfy the hunger for workers in farming and industries, on construction sites and with civil and military authorities. The Soviet Union is the only exception from this general development. The means of compulsion differed greatly, a point still to be addressed. Among the big employers in the occupied territories, the German mining and foundry authorities (Berg- und Hüttenwerksgesellschaft Ost, BHO) developed an arsenal of compulsory measures to recruit thousands of workers, including women, for mine work from local citizens, the POW camps and from other regions which seemed to be able to provide workers. Whereas the coal production of the traditional German mining districts could be held at the pre-war level until 1944, with the support of forced labour that counted for up to one-third of the work force, the coal production of the Reich as a whole was more than doubled by running coal mines in the occupied zones. A sort of permanent mutual migration exchange came into being: German mining specialists, primarily from the Ruhr, went into the occupied mines to reconstruct them as soon as possible where they had been destroyed by warfare – as was the case in the Ukraine – or to keep them running on the highest possible level. In the Donez basin results were poor, because it took so much time to reconstruct the pits: which was done, incidentally, with the help of local mine authorities. The other direction of compulsory migration led from the European mine districts to those of the Reich where large parts of the local work force had been recruited for the army and were to be replaced by forced labour.

V. Experiences and Perceptions of Compulsory Work

Recent research has informed us about the many different variants of compulsory work and especially about the work and living conditions within the many thousands of work camps.[19] Within the Reich borders and within the occupied territories such conditions ranged from a quasi-normal occupation – where coercion was not felt at all but, objectively, the definition of forced labour would apply – to destruction by work as it was executed, for instance, among the estimated 20,000 mine workers provided by the Auschwitz concentration camp for the surrounding pits.[20] Apart from such destruction by work exercised by SS authorities in the concentration camps, a legal difference has to be made between the treatment of prisoners of war and forced civil workers. Whereas the latter were usually housed in work camps under control of company officials and local police authorities, POWs remained under military control, which meant that their camps were guarded by military forces and that military officials could interfere if work and living conditions deteriorated to an extent that came close to destruction. This happened time and time again. Originally, Ruhr mining officials refused to employ POWs, and Polish POWs in particular, partially in the light of experiences derived from the First World War and also because of problems that might arise from the existence of a considerable number of Polish workers who had migrated into the region prior to 1914. In addition, the mining authorities expected a high job turnover among Polish civil workers if they were employed within a scheme of time-limited work contracts. Such contracts were thus extended to an unlimited time period ending only with the end of warfare, a legal background that completed the definition of forced labour. Initially, the authorities also resorted to the employment of 'Eastern' POWs. Later, when productivity of such POWs strongly declined and mortality rates in the camps increased, the authorities started to consider improvements. For instance, they established so-called 'Russian seams' to increase work efficiency and introduced a system of work stimulation that favoured more efficient workers with more and better food and other preferential treatment.[21] Such newly exerted care for workers' health and well-being must also be seen in the light of decreasing availability of Soviet POWs in the course of war.

'Eastern workers' from civilian backgrounds also suffered from bad conditions concerning camp hygiene, nutrition, compulsory additional work and typical camp infections. In legal terms, German work conditions did not apply to Poles and 'Eastern workers'; they were subject to a discriminating judicial system regulated by the so-called Poles' and Eastern workers' decrees. Their work relations were understood to be based not on private agreement, but as a 'special occupation' legalized by special work regulations (*Polenerlasse*, *Ostarbeitererlasse*). Thus, as early as summer 1940 the Poles and – later, in 1942 – civil workers from the Soviet Union did not receive any kind of work document anymore. In practical terms, all forced civil workers from occupied Eastern territories received much lower wages, justified by an apparently lower work capacity and further reduced by expenditures for accommodation. Parts of their wages automatically went to their families. Their freedom to move was limited by local and employers' regulations, and contact with German workers was inhibited, but unavoidable, at least at the work places. Vacations were conceded only rarely, usually in case of sickness. The work contracts were unlimited. Among the criteria defining compulsory work, this legal clause, together with the camp existence, seems to be decisive.

When complaints by the military about bad conditions and increasing mortality among POWs accumulated, conditions were improved, starting in late 1943. It seems that mortality rates were coming under a certain amount of control. Table 8.5 shows the total numbers of foreign civil workers employed in the Reich during the war and the estimated proportions of those who survived. Of some 8.5 million foreign workers, almost 500,000 died during the time of employment. Thus, the overall mortality rate was at 5.8 per cent, which certainly is very much above of what may be expected to be a normal death toll in a workforce of comparatively young age groups. There was a telling difference among nations of origin. Soviet civil workers suffered most, with a mortality rate at 9 per cent, followed by the Poles, who died at 8.1 per cent. The racial hierarchies established within the foreign work force in terms of nutrition, work loads and general treatment clearly account for such mortality differences. Conditions in work camps established within the occupied territories were much worse, but figures differ greatly, with a

Table 8.5: Employment and Survival of Foreign Civil Workers in Germany 1939–1945

	Total No. 30.9.44	Female workers in %	Total No. 1939–45	Survivors May 1945	Mortality in %
Baltic	44,799	36. 5	75,000	75,000	0
Belgian	199,437	14.7	375,000	365,000	2.7
Bulgarian	16,257	12.6	30,000	30,000	0
Danish	15,970	23.7	80,000	80,000	0
French	646,421	6.6	1,050,000	1,015,000	3.3
Greek	15,658	20.0	35,000	35,000	0
Italian	287,347	7.8	960,000	940,000	2.1
Croatian	60,153	28.4	100,000	100,000	0
Dutch	254,544	8.2	475,000	465,000	2.1
Polish	1,375,817	34.4	1,600,000	1,470,000	8.1
Swiss	17,014	30.4	30,000	30,000	0
Serbian	37,607	22.4	100,000	100,000	0
Slovakian	37,550	44.5	100,000	100,000	0
Soviet citizens	2,461,163	49.3	2,775,000	2,525,000	9.0
Czech	276,340	16.1	355,000	330,00s0	7.0
Hungarian	24,263	29.1	45,000	45,000	0
Others	206,633	31.5	250,000	240,000	4
Foreigners in total	*5,976,673*	*16.5*	*8,435,000*	*7,945,000*	*5.8*

Source: Mark Spoerer, *Zwangsarbeit unter dem Hakenkreuz. Ausländische Zivilarbeiter, Kriegsgefangene und Häftlinge im Deutschen Reich und im besetzten Europa 1939–1945* (Stuttgart: Deutsche Verlagsanstalt, 2001), p. 222.

strong increase in all of Eastern Europe.[22] Finally, an attempt should be made at systematizing at least some of the major influences that shaped the course of compulsory labour during the war. First of all, there was the legal difference between prisoners of war and foreign civil workers compelled to work in the Reich or abroad. Among prisoners of war, the degree of coercion reached a peak among Polish and especially Soviet POWs: the worst maltreatment probably occurred within POW camps in the occupied Eastern zones when the German army had to retreat and partisan fights occurred. There are estimates that in certain places the mortality of Soviet POWs amounted to 30 and even 50 per cent. Most cases of death happened during the first weeks and months after capture, when prisoners were kept in provisional camps, selected for work and sometimes deliberately worked to death or murdered. French, British and American POWs were widely, but not entirely, held according to international law.[23]

Second, this mirrors the fundamental category of difference of treatment that applied to all forms of compulsory work, but especially to civil workers: that is, racism. Upper Silesia may serve as a telling example. Here, when the Nazi authorities came in, a 'list of ethnicities' (*Volkstumsliste*) was introduced, which distinguished between four categories.[24] There were those people of German origin, those who confessed to be German-minded and showed appropriate behaviour, the Poles who were expected to become Germanized, and, finally, national Poles. The latter were expelled from their home territories and sent into the *Generalgouvernement* to be housed in work camps and forcefully employed. A continuous ethnic cleansing began, using ethnic differences that had shaped the region for centuries.

Third, by looking at the occupied zones, the distinctive political conditions prevailing before the German seizure must be considered. In Croatia and other parts of the Balkan countries the Germans were welcomed for historical reasons. In Eastern Poland, which had been under Soviet rule according to the Hitler-Stalin pact, Germans were accepted as liberators and, to a degree, this is also true for the educated classes in the Ukraine, where large parts of the population considered Soviet rule to be a sort of occupation. Very probably, the degree to which work coercion was perceived as such depended on traditional loyalties, cultural attitudes and the anticipation of improvement of personal conditions.

Fourth, as already mentioned, certain political and cultural traditions and personal experiences within given populations played a major role. For example, Ukrainian work experiences had been determined largely by feudal traditions and, more recently, by Stalinist industrialization. For people coming from such traditions and living within village structures, there existed few experiences of free wage labour and citizens' rights. Having been previously employed by the Soviet mining bureaucracy, not many things would change if they managed to stay at their homes: the food supply remained scarce, and they were already familiar with the coercive prolongation of work hours. Things were different for those who had been recruited elsewhere and were housed in the work camps under bad conditions. These workers also experienced a highly competent German mining bureaucracy that reconstructed the mining sites which had been destroyed by the Soviet troops within a few months. It was the Germans who reconstructed what had made their living. Yet the same Germans increasingly recruited local Ukrainian workers to be sent to the Reich, and they did so increasingly by brutal coercion. Thus, it seems that the Ukrainian miners changed their minds from initial appreciation to distrust and rejection. Overall, the occupation lasted only for about two years, and since the beginning of 1943 the war had changed.[25] In contrast, the mining workforce in Nord-Pas de Calais had developed a leftist tradition long before the events of 1936, and the trade unions were dominated by Communist influence. To a considerable degree, mine owners remained in charge under occupation, and thus, a major strike could be waged against them, with the German occupational forces to bring them back to work by force. The strike was seemingly fought over work and wage issues, but the events also included a sense of national unity and resistance against occupation. 'Eastern workers' in particular had been recruited by the Germans in addition to the indigenous work force, but these newcomers were already familiar with Polish traditions in the coalfields.[26] Things worked out differently again in mining sites in Yugoslavia.[27] Here, it seems that the workforce had to be restructured almost weekly, because guarding the workers was difficult: workers escaped, not so much because of German coercion, but rather because of ethnic diversity and conflict.

Finally, it seems appropriate to come back to the introductory remarks presented above. Escape from POW camps was rather difficult, but escape from camps for forced labour happened frequently and may have taken an almost legal shape when workers tried to obtain a release by all means possible.[28] Among the many Eastern workers in the countryside, an escape could mean that a worker had become fed up with his farmer because of brutal treatment and wanted to move; there are indications that such changes were allowed. In any case, if we rely on the camp criterion of definition, we should not include farmhands of this or another origin. Escape had also been one of the possible reactions to feudal oppression; another one was to withhold work capacity, a practice that is difficult to prove, but happened frequently.

Keeping in mind the German debate on compensation, which evolved especially after German reunification in the 1990s,[29] research into the dimensions and conditions of compulsory wartime work has gained public interest. It has fostered a sense of victimization that aims at reconstructing the victims' experiences to enforce legal claims. So far, many research projects began to make clear the responsibilities of different institutions and companies: these included large cities, as employers of forced labour, the German Bundesländer such as Schleswig-Holstein or Rhineland-Palatinate, even the churches:[30] but especially big business. Business history has therefore recently undergone an important revival.[31] The debate remains highly charged but filled with commitment. The great variety of coercive work conditions makes it difficult to distinguish between what should be seen as coercive labour under quasi-normal but oppressive workplace conditions, and what resulted from direct coercion during conditions of wartime occupation and forcible recruitment.

Notes

1. This is a revised version of a lecture presented at the European Studies Centre of St. Antony's College, 18 February 2005. I am most grateful to Dr. Hans-Christoph Seidel and his colleagues at the Institute for Social Movements of the Ruhr University Bochum for advice, given on the ground of research results from a project that dealt with the history of forced labour in European mining (Germany and Occupied Territories 1939–1945) and was funded by the RAG Aktiengesellschaft: Zwangsarbeiterforschung als gesellschaftlicher Auftrag, Bochum 2001; for further information, see below, note 17. The notion of 'forced' or 'compulsory' labour as a translation of the German term *Zwangsarbeit* may be contested; 'slave labour' has been suggested instead occasionally. Yet forced labourers were not subject to bargaining, and, more importantly, a slaveholder society would not consider the destruction of lives by work. Adolf Levenstein, *Die Arbeiterfrage. Mit besonderer Berücksichtigung der sozialpsychologischen Seite des modernen Großbetriebes und der psycho-physischen Einwirkungen auf die Arbeiter* (Munich: Ernst Reinhardt, 1912).

Among other references, see Gerhard A. Ritter and Klaus Tenfelde, *Arbeiter im Deutschen Kaiserreich 1871–1914* (Bonn: Dietz, 1994), p. 774 and *passim*.

2. See Rüdiger vom Bruch, 'Bürgerliche Sozialreform im deutschen Kaiserreich', in idem (ed.), *Bürgerliche Sozialreform in Deutschland vom Vormärz bis zur Ära Adenauer* (Munich: Beck, 1985), pp. 61–179.
3. Quotations from Levenstein, pp. 54–72, 134, my translations. For comparisons to the 1950s/1960s, see Burkart Lutz, 'Integration durch Aufstieg. Überlegungen zur Verbürgerlichung der deutschen Facharbeiter in den Jahrzehnten nach dem Zweiten Weltkrieg', in Manfred Hettling and Bernd Ulrich (eds), *Bürgertum nach 1945* (Hamburg: Hamburger Edition, 2005), pp. 284–309.
4. The notion and perception of work since early modern times has been discussed frequently: Werner Conze, 'Arbeit', in Otto Brunner et al. (eds), *Geschichtliche Grundbegriffe. Historisches Lexikon zur politisch-sozialen Sprache in Deutschland*, vol. 1 (Stuttgart: Klett, 1972), pp. 154–209; as a comparison, see, for example, Josef Ehmer, 'Die Geschichte der Arbeit als Spannungsfeld von Begriff, Form und Praxis', in Gerda Dohle (ed.), *Bericht über den 23. österreichischen Historikertag in Salzburg* (Salzburg: Verb. Österr. Historiker und Geschichtsvereine, Österr. Staatsarchiv, 2003), pp. 25–44. See also: Jürgen Kocka, 'Arbeit früher, heute, morgen: Zur Neuartigkeit der Gegenwart', in Kocka and Claus Offe (eds), *Geschichte und Zukunft der Arbeit* (Frankfurt am Main: Campus, 2000), pp. 476–92; Manfred Bierwisch, *Die Rolle der Arbeit in verschiedenen Epochen und Kulturen* (Berlin: Akademie Verlag, 2003) (includes another article by Kocka); more recently Michael S. Aßländer, *Von der vita activa zur industriellen Wertschöpfung. Eine Sozial- und Wirtschaftsgeschichte menschlicher Arbeit* (Marburg: Metropolis, 2005); for comparison, see Arthur McIvor, *A History of Work in Britain, 1880–1950* (Basingstoke/New York: Palgrave, 2001).
5. On details presented in this paragraph, see Klaus Tenfelde, 'Ländliches Gesinde in Preußen. Gesinderecht und Gesindestatistik 1810 bis 1861', in *Archiv für Sozialgeschichte* 19 (1979): 189–229; ibid., 'Dienstmädchengeschichte. Strukturelle Aspekte im 19. und 20. Jahrhundert', in Hans Pohl and Beate Brüninghaus (eds), *Die Frau in der deutschen Wirtschaft* (Stuttgart: Steiner, 1985), pp. 105–19; basically: Reinhart Koselleck, *Preußen zwischen Reform und Revolution. Allgemeines Landrecht, Verwaltung und soziale Bewegung von 1791 bis 1848* (Stuttgart: Klett Cotta, 1967); as a recent revision of rather well-established views on primarily Eastern Prussian post-feudal conditions, see Patrick Wagner, *Bauern, Junker und Beamte. Lokale Herrschaft und Partizipation im Ostelbien des 19. Jahrhunderts* (Göttingen: Wallstein, 2005).
6. Friedrich August Ludwig von der Marwitz, 'Von der Schrankenlosigkeit', 1836, reprint in Carl Jantke and Dietrich Hilger (eds), *Die Eigentumslosen. Der deutscher Pauperismus und die Emanzipationskrise in Darstellungen und Deutungen der zeitgenössischen Literatur* (Freiburg/München: Alber, 1965), pp. 134–48, 138.
7. See Oliver von Mengersen, 'Zwangsarbeit im kolonialen Kontext. Ideologie und Praxis britischer Arbeitspolitik in Nigeria 1900–1930', in von Mengersen et al. (eds), *Personen. Soziale Bewegungen. Parteien. Beiträge zur neuesten Geschichte. Festschrift für Hartmut Soell* (Heidelberg: Manutius, 2004), pp. 177–201; cf. Herwart Sieberg, *Colonial Development. Die Grundlegung moderner Entwicklungspolitik durch Großbritannien 1919–1949* (Stuttgart: Steiner, 1985).
8. See Max Kern and Carmen Sottas, 'The Abolition of Forced or Compulsory Labour', in International Labour Office (ed.), *Fundamental Rights at Work and International Labour Standards* (Geneva: International Labour Office, 2003), pp. 33–55.

9. Quoted in Kern and Sottas, p. 34. Problems of definition come up everywhere in the growing field of research literature on the topic. Also as a guide to this literature, see Klaus Tenfelde and Hans-Christoph Seidel (eds), *Zwangsarbeit im Bergwerk, Der Arbeitseinsatz im Kohlenbergbau des Deutschen Reiches und der besetzten Gebiete im Ersten und Zweiten Weltkrieg*, vol. 1: *Forschungen*, vol. 2: *Dokumente* (Essen: Klartext Verlag, 2005); most recent research has mainly departed from Ulrich Herbert, *Fremdarbeiter. Politik und Praxis des 'Ausländer-Einsatzes' in der Kriegswirtschaft des Dritten Reiches* (2nd edn, Essen: Klartext-Verlag, 1999); Mark Spoerer, *Zwangsarbeit unter dem Hakenkreuz. Ausländische Zivilarbeiter, Kriegsgefangene und Häftlinge im Deutschen Reich und im besetzten Europa 1939–1945* (Stuttgart: Deutsche Verlagsanstalt, 2001). Before research on the topic increased in the 1990s, the field had not been neglected completely, see, for example, Edward L. Homze, *Foreign Labor in Nazi Germany* (Princeton: Princeton University Press, 1967).
10. In what follows, I rely heavily on the systematization and the figures presented in Jochen Oltmer, 'Migration, Integration und Krieg im Europa des "Jahrhunderts der Flüchtlinge"', in *Geschichte, Politik und ihre Didaktik. Zeitschrift für historisch-politische Bildung* 32 (2004): 90–100; see also ibid. (ed.), *Migrationsforschung und interkulturelle Studien: 10 Jahre IMIS* (Osnabrück: Rasch, 2002); more recently: ibid., *Migration und Politik in der Weimarer Republik* (Göttingen: Vandenhoeck and Ruprecht, 2005); also Klaus J. Bade, *Europa in Bewegung. Migration vom späten 18. Jahrhundert bis zur Gegenwart* (München: Beck, 2000), pp. 233 ff.; Jochen Oltmer, 'Flucht, Vertreibung und Asyl im 19. und 20. Jahrhundert', in Klaus J. Bade (ed.), *Migration in der europäischen Geschichte seit dem späten Mittelalter*, IMIS-Beiträge 20 (Osnabrück: IMIS, 2002). For a comparison of the dimensions of compulsory migration caused by the Nazi and Soviet regimes, see Dittmar Dahlmann and Gerhard Hirschfeld (eds), *Lager, Zwangsarbeit, Vertreibung und Deportation. Dimensionen der Massenverbrechen in der Sowjetunion und in Deutschland 1933–1945* (Essen: Klartext-Verlag, 1999).
11. See Ulrich Herbert, 'Zwangsarbeit im "Dritten Reich". Kenntnisstand, offene Fragen, Forschungsprobleme', in Norbert Reimann (ed.), *Zwangsarbeit in Deutschland 1939–1945. Archiv- und Sammlungsgut, Topographie und Erschließungsstrategien* (Bielefeld: Verlag für Regionalgeschichte, 2001), pp. 16–37.
12. See Friedrich Zunkel, 'Die ausländischen Arbeiter in der deutschen Kriegswirtschaft des 1. Weltkrieges', in Gerhard A. Ritter (ed.), *Entstehung und Wandel der modernen Gesellschaft* (Berlin: de Gruyter, 1970), pp. 280–311, and recently Kai Rawe, *'... Wir werden sie schon zur Arbeit bringen!' Ausländerbeschäftigung und Zwangsarbeit im Ruhrkohlenbergbau während des Ersten Weltkrieges* (Essen: Klartext Verlag, 2005).
13. See especially Steven G. Wheatcroft, 'Ausmaß und Wesen der deutschen und sowjetischen Repressionen und Massentötungen 1930–1945', in Dahlmann and Hirschfeld (eds), pp. 67–109.
14. See Timothy W. Mason, *Sozialpolitik im Dritten Reich. Arbeiterklasse und Volksgemeinschaft* (2nd edn, Opladen: Westdeutscher Verlag, 1978); Rüdiger Hachtmann, *Industriearbeit im 'Dritten Reich'. Untersuchungen zu den Lohn- und Arbeitsbedingungen in Deutschland 1933–1945* (Göttingen: Vandenhoeck and Ruprecht, 1989); Andreas Kranig, *Lockung und Zwang. Zur Arbeitsverfassung im Dritten Reich* (Stuttgart: Deutsche Verlagsanstalt, 1983). On the development of ideas for compulsory service, see Henning Köhler, *Arbeitsdienst in Deutschland. Pläne und Verwirklichungsformen bis zur Einführung der Arbeitsdienstpflicht im Jahre 1935* (Berlin: Duncker and Humblot, 1967); Angela Vogel, *Das Pflichtjahr für Mädchen. Nationalsozialistische Arbeitseinsatzpolitik im Zeichen der Kriegswirtschaft* (Frankfurt am Main: Lang, 1997); Kiran Klaus Patel, *'Soldaten der Arbeit'.*

Arbeitsdienste in Deutschland und den USA 1933–1945 (Göttingen: Vandenhoeck and Ruprecht, 2003), esp. chapters 1 and 2.

15. As a most reliable source, the data provided by the Central Labour Office ('Reichsarbeitsverwaltung'; 'Der Arbeitseinsatz im Großdeutschen Reich') concerning forced labour are generally accepted within historical research. The last figures shown on these grounds refer to September 1944, a time phase that seems to coincide with the peak of foreign workers' occupation in the Reich: 7,906,760 foreign workers, of whom 1,930,087 were POWs; of the civil workers, 3.986,308 were male and 1,990,367 female. See Herbert, *Zwangsarbeit*; also Spoerer, *Zwangsarbeit*, pp. 219–29, and ibid., 'NS-Zwangsarbeiter im Deutschen Reich. Eine Statistik vom 30. September 1944 nach Arbeitsamtsbezirken', in *Vierteljahreshefte für Zeitgeschichte* 49 (2001): 665–84; Spoerer and Jochen Fleischhacker, 'Forced Laborers in Nazi Germany. Categories, Numbers, and Survivors', in *Journal of Interdisciplinary History* 23 (2002): 169–204.
16. See reference note 15.
17. From this project, some thirty research articles have been published; see *Geschichte und Gesellschaft* 31,1 (2005), and, for example, Hans-Christoph Seidel, 'Arbeitseinsatz und Zwangsarbeit im europäischen Steinkohlenbergbau unter deutscher Herrschaft', in Johannes Bähr and Ralf Banken (eds), *Das Europa des 'Dritten Reiches'. Recht, Wirtschaft, Besatzung* (Frankfurt: Klostermann, 2005), pp. 259–86. As a comprehensive edition of articles and documents, see 'Zwangsarbeit im Bergwerk'. The most extensive overview on forced labour in the occupied territories can be obtained from Ulrich Herbert (ed.), *Europa und der 'Reichseinsatz'. Ausländische Zivilarbeiter, Kriegsgefangene und KZ-Häftlinge in Deutschland 1938–1945* (Essen: Klartext, 1991).
18. See Hermann Kaienburg, 'Jüdische Arbeitslager an der "Straße der SS"', in *1999. Zeitschrift für Sozialgeschichte* 11 (1996): 13–39.
19. See for farm workers: Stefan Karner and Peter Ruggenthaler, *Zwangsarbeit in der Land- und Forstwirtschaft auf dem Gebiet Österreichs 1939 bis 1945* (Vienna: Oldenbourg 2004); Ela Hornung et al., *Zwangsarbeit in der Landwirtschaft in Niederösterreich und dem nördlichen Burgenland* (Munich: Oldenbourg, 2004); industries: Gabriella Hauch et al. (eds), *Industrie und Zwangsarbeit im Nationalsozalismus. Mercedes – VW – Reichswerke Hermann Göring in Linz und Salzgitter* (Innsbruck: Studien-Verlag, 2003); Manfred Grieger and Hans Mommsen, *Das Volkswagenwerk und seine Arbeiter im Dritten Reich* (Düsseldorf: Econ, 1996); Oliver Rathkolb (ed.), *NS-Zwangsarbeit. Der Standort Linz der Reichswerke Hermann Göring AG Berlin 1938–1945*, 2 vols. (Vienna: Böhlau, 2001); Christian Ruch et al., *Geschäfte und Zwangsarbeit. Schweizer Industrieunternehmen im 'Dritten Reich'* (Zürich: Chronos, 2001); Florian Freund et al., *Zwangsarbeiter und Zwangsarbeiterinnen auf dem Gebiet der Republik Österreich 1939–1945* (Munich: Oldenbourg, 2004) (mostly statistics); regional: Uwe Danker et al. (eds), *'Ausländereinsatz in der Nordmark'. Zwangsarbeitende in Schleswig-Holstein 1939–1945* (Bielefeld: Verlag für Regionalgeschichte, 2001); Michael A. Kanther, *Zwangsarbeit in Duisburg 1940–1945* (Duisburg: Mercator Verlag, 2004); selected groups of forced labourers: Annette Schäfer, *Zwangsarbeiter und NS-Rassenpolitik. Russische und polnische Arbeitskräfte in Württemberg 1939–1945* (Stuttgart: Kohlhammer, 2000); Gabriele Hammermann, *Zwangsarbeit für den 'Verbündeten'. Die Arbeits- und Lebensbedingungen der italienischen Militär-Internierten in Deutschland 1943–1945* (Tübingen: Max Niemeyer, 2002).
20. See Adrianna Harazim, 'Bergbau nahe Auschwitz. Der Einsatz von Konzentrationslagerhäftlingen auf oberschlesischen Zechen', in Tenfelde and Seidel (eds), vol. 1, pp. 411–32.

21. See Hans-Christoph Seidel, 'Der "Russenstreb". Die betriebliche Organisation des Ausländer- und Zwangsrbeitereinsatzes im Ruhrbergbau während des Zweiten Weltkrieges', in *Geschichte und Gesellschaft* 31 (2005): 8–37.
22. See, for example, document no. 309 in Seidel and Tenfelde (eds), *Zwangsarbeit im Bergwerk*, vol. 2. Within our Bochum research project, we had the good fortune to find that the general manager of the German administration of one of the mining districts in the Donez basin was still alive; he died recently. We organized a public discussion with him. During that discussion, he felt inclined to maintain that in the work camps under his supervision, no deaths had occurred. We already knew from different sources that his work camp had shown the highest mortality rate of the Ukraine. See Tanja Penter, 'Zwischen Hunger, Terror und einer "glücklichen Zukunft". Der Arbeitseinsatz im Steinkohlenbergbau des Donezbeckens unter deutscher Besatzung 1941 bis 1943', in Tenfelde and Seidel (eds), vol. 1, pp. 433–66, 449.
23. See Rolf Walter and Reinhard Otto, 'Das Massensterben der sowjetischen Kriegsgefangenen und die Wehrmachtsbürokratie. Unterlagen zur Registrierung der sowjetischen Kriegsgefangenen 1941–1945 in deutschen und russischen Archiven', in *Militärgeschichtliche Mitteilungen* 57 (1998): 149–80; on treatment of POWs: Rüdiger Overmanns, 'Die Kriegsgefangenenpolitik des Deutschen Reiches 1939–1945', in Jörg Echternkamp (ed.), *Die deutsche Kriegsgesellschaft*, vol. 9: *Deutschland im Zweiten Weltkrieg* (Stuttgart: DVA, 2005), pp. 729–875; Reinhard Otto, *Wehrmacht, Gestapo und sowjetische Kriegsgefangene im deutschen Reichsgebiet 1941/42* (Munich: Oldenbourg, 1998).
24. See Valentina Maria Stefanski, 'Nationalsozialistische Volkstums- und Arbeitseinsatzpolitik im Regierungsbezirk Kattowitz 1939–1945', in *Geschichte und Gesellschaft* 31 (2005): 38–67.
25. See Tanja Penter, 'Zwangsarbeit – Arbeit für den Feind. Der Donbass unter deutscher Okkopation (1941–1943)', in *Geschichte und Gesellschaft* 31 (2005): 68–100; ibid., 'Arbeitseinsatz', pp. 464–66.
26. See Natalie Piquet, '"Privilegierte" Zwangsarbeiter. Sowjetische und serbische Arbeitskräfte im nordfranzösischen und belgischen Steinkohlenbergbau während der deutschen Besatzung', in Tenfelde and Seidel (eds), vol. 1, pp. 467–93.
27. See Sabine Rutar, 'Arbeit und Überleben in Serbien. Das Kupfererzbergwerk Bor im Zweiten Weltkrieg', in *Geschichte und Gesellschaft* 31 (2005): 101–34.
28. An example is documented in Klaus Tenfelde (ed.), *Suche nach Wahrheit. Aufarbeitung von Zwangsarbeit und Unrecht im 20. Jahrhundert* (Bochum, Klartext 2006), pp. 21–30.
29. See Susanne-Sophia Spiliotis, *Verantwortung und Rechtsfrieden. Die Stiftungsinitiative der deutschen Wirtschaft* (Frankfurt am Main: Fischer, 2003); Klaus Tenfelde and Hans-Christoph Seidel (eds), *Zwangsarbeit im Europa des 20. Jahrhunderts* (Essen: Klartext, 2007).
30. As examples, see Peter Pfister (ed.), *Katholische Kirche und Zwangsarbeit. Stand und Perspektiven der Forschung* (Regensburg: Schnell and Steiner, 2001), and Jochen-Christoph Kaiser (ed.), *Zwangsarbeit in Diakonie und Kirche 1939–1945* (Stuttgart: Kohlhammer, 2005).
31. See, for example, Hartmut Berghoff, 'Wozu Unternehmensgeschichte? Erkenntnisinteressen, Forschungsansätze und Perspektiven des Faches', in *Zeitschrift für Unternehmensgeschichte* 49 (2004): 131–48; also, Paul Erker, '"A New Business History?" Neuere Ansätze und Entwicklungen in der Unternehmensgeschichte', in *Archiv für Sozialgeschichte* 42 (2002): 557–604, and several articles in *Geschichte in Wissenschaft und Unterricht* 3 (2005). As an example for views held among German industrialists shortly after the war towards the problem of forced labour, see Tilo Freiherr von Wilmowsky, *Warum wurde Krupp verurteilt? Legende und Justizirrtum* (Stuttgart: F. Vorwerk, 1950), pp. 128–96.

9

Work, Max Weber, Confucianism: The Confucian Ethic and the Spirit of Japanese Capitalism

Sebastian Conrad

> The Japanese are conquering world markets through unfair competition – they're working during working hours! (Ephraim Kishon)

Of the numerous volumes on world history produced in the last few years, David Landes's account is surely both the best-known, as well as the most economically successful. In his *The Wealth and Poverty of Nations*, he portrays the last thousand years of history from a decidedly Eurocentric perspective. This he not only openly acknowledges but propagates offensively: 'Over the thousand and more years of this process that most people look upon as progress, the key factor – the driving force – has been Western civilization and its dissemination.'[1] Landes explicitly rejects all forms of political correctness and sees only one way for non-European nations to modernize successfully. They must learn from and imitate Europe. In evoking this apotheosis of the ascent of Europe, whose achievements are then imported by the rest of the world, Landes acknowledges a single exception: Japan. He expresses his belief that 'even without a European industrial revolution, the Japanese would sooner or later have made their own'. He identifies the reason for this in Japanese culture or, more precisely, in the Japanese morality of work, which he believes to be rooted in the country's religious traditions. Landes thus explains the fact that Japan is the only nation outside of Europe that would have been capable of active, independent modernization by pointing to the Japanese 'national character'. He adds: 'If we learn anything from the history of economic development, it is that culture makes all the difference.'[2]

This perspective is anchored in a thesis that has been widely discussed, not only in Japan. The connection between Confucianism, work ethic and economic modernization in Japan was vigorously debated in the 1980s and 1990s and continues to this day. While this was a thoroughly political (and economic policy) debate, its claims were also subject to intense academic scrutiny. The 'Confucianism thesis', as I shall call it, assumes that Japan's economic success can be pinned down to its cultural peculiarity. Here, the dynamism of Japanese capitalism is traced back to a culturally specific economic style. What follows is a brief discussion of this argument that is divided into three sections. The first section reconstructs the Confucianism thesis and briefly outlines its components and overall logic. Sections two and three subject this thesis to critical examination. My criticisms relate to the malleability of this line of argument and the fiction of cultural autonomy upon which it rests. I round off the discussion by arguing that the thesis of Confucian industrial relations can only arise (and be maintained) if one continues to regard Japan as a country sealed off from the rest of the world and fails to take account of its manifold interactions with other societies.

The Confucianism Thesis

In the 1980s the thesis of an interrelatedness of what could be called, in Weberian fashion, the 'Confucian ethic and the spirit of Japanese capitalism' was highly popular. The fundamental assumption here was that the dynamics of Japanese modernization and particularly the rapid economic growth (*kôdô seichô*) from the 1960s onward were due to Japan's specific industrial relations and the attitudes to work prevalent there. The alleged uniqueness of Japanese industrial relations is usually defined through three dimensions: the principle of life-long employment (*shûshin koyô*), the principle of seniority in relation to wages (*nenkô joretsu*) and the organization of employees in company unions (*kigyô kumiai*). These organizational features are understood as an expression of a specifically Japanese work mentality and work ethic, which are in turn traced back to indigenous cultural traditions. A this-worldly, active attitude to work seemed built in to Confucian ethics in particular. This attitude, the thesis claims, made Japanese industrialization and the post-war 'economic miracle' possible in the first place.[3] In the mid-1950s American sociologist Robert Bellah was one of the first to attempt to explain Japanese modernization with reference to the connection between Confucianism and a modern work ethic.[4] He transposed Max Weber's famous attempt to identify the causes of European capitalism – and to understand the historical uniqueness of this process – to the Japanese context. He found what Max Weber, in vain, had sought in the Confucian tradition, particularly teachings encouraging religiously motivated inner-worldly asceticism (which taught the individual that he would be rewarded in the afterlife if he worked hard, thus laying the groundwork for the development of an active business class and diligent work force). In Confucianism – above all, in the thought of the philosopher and merchant Ishida Baigan writing in the early eighteenth century – Bellah discovered an organic conception of society based on the division of labour and a tendency towards the rationalization of economic thought. Finally,

Bellah was convinced that Confucian ethics were linked with the dynamics and rigidity of *bushidô*, the ethical code of the Samurai class.[5]

This thesis, which initially inspired much criticism, particularly in Japan, has enjoyed a second career since the 1980s, when the Japanese economy was peaking. The best-known book in this vein was probably *Why Has Japan Succeeded?*, by economist Morishima Michio, which was widely received and translated into numerous languages. Morishima also views Confucianism and its work ethic as the key to Japan's success. Compared to Bellah, however, he lays more emphasis on political factors: while he sees a passive-apolitical Confucianism prevailing in China, he claims that the Japanese adoption of this religious tradition led to a worldview supportive of the ruling class. On this view, loyalty was therefore a basic feature of Confucian-influenced Japanese culture: a loyalty that might be given to the state or the firm.[6]

Morishima's explanation of Japan's economic development resonated widely and was eagerly taken up by economic historians and management scholars. The notion that there is a connection between Confucianism and the modern work ethic has found general acceptance, although some authors have also placed emphasis on other worldviews: those of Buddhism, Shintôism, or Samurai ethics. The economic rise of the 'little tigers' – South Korea, Taiwan, Singapore and Hong Kong – lent additional support to the Confucianism thesis, their development making the link between Confucian tradition and capitalist-economic performance appear yet more plausible.[7]

The discussion was not confined to the Japanese (or Asian) case, but in its subtext always included propositions about the 'West': Japan's swift economic ascent and potential to become the greatest economic power in the world seemed to threaten the future and well-established certainties in the 'West' (symbolic transactions such as the purchase of little castles on the Rhine or the takeover of CBS and half of Hollywood played a special role here). Consequently, Western managers were sometimes encouraged to study *bushidô*, the Samurai ethical code from the seventeenth century, in order to prepare themselves for the realities of the Japanese business world. To be sure, the Japanese form of work was not merely viewed as a threat: in Europe and the United States many attempts were made to adopt Japanese ways of organizing work and management practices. Discussions of the Japanese work ethic, in other words, were thus not only about Japan, but always about the 'West' as well.[8]

Genealogy of a Discourse

In what follows, I wish to subject this explanatory approach to critical examination and argue that the deduction of the modern work ethic from the spirit of Confucianism is at bottom a retrospective construction. This does not mean that the thesis and the issues underpinning it lack all validity. The general issue, the question of continuities of culture and mentality across what is usually seen as the divide between pre-modern and modern Japan, is both important and relevant to an understanding of the dynamics of Japanese modernity. My critique, however, concerns the image of Japan that the thesis conveys, which I believe to be problematic.

A closer look at the logic of the Confucianism thesis reveals a number of difficulties that are already present in the original Weberian formulation and which are therefore outlined here only briefly.[9] The starting point itself is paradoxical: the more the impact of religious traditions wanes, these analyses imply, the greater their long-term cultural impact seems to be. The full impact of Calvinist and Confucian ethics thus appears to be felt only in secular society.[10] There is another problem. While the rapid economic growth of the nineteenth and twentieth centuries is causally related to religious texts from the sixteenth and seventeenth centuries, these cultural traditions are rarely mentioned to explain the decline of the hard-working mentality in the post-war period (in Japan, this decline has been proven statistically and debated intensively since the 1990s).[11] In any case, equating a society's cultural practices and mentality with its religious canon is prone to essentialisms of all kinds.[12] Beyond these general points of critique, two objections will be raised specifically related to the Japanese case.

The first objection relates to the malleability of the argument. In its most general form, the Confucianism thesis suggests that Japan's economic success rests upon its special industrial relations – a familial structure within the firm (*kazoku shugi*) and a fundamental harmony (*wa*) between employers and employees – which are understood as the legacy of Confucianism. This has been the prevailing view since the 1980s and is highly popular in both Japan and beyond.[13] However, a closer look at Japanese history shows that this thesis itself has to be grasped in its social and historical context.[14] The evaluation of the Confucian heritage has changed radically over the last few decades. In the early post-war period, for example, surviving cultural traditions and social customs were still primarily viewed as obstacles on the path of modernization. In fact, the familial structure of Japanese firms was mentioned as evidence that the Japanese economy was still feudal in nature. Paternalistic industrial relations were by no means viewed as the key to economic success, but rather as cause and symptom of Japanese backwardness.[15]

In the 1950s peculiarly Japanese working conditions were therefore regarded as a problem and were criticized heavily. The fact that these existed was not, however, seriously disputed.[16] Yet if we trace the genealogy of this debate and turn to the interwar period, we discover that the notion of the uniqueness of Japanese working conditions played only a little role (although this discourse was by no means monolithic and other notions sometimes competed with it). After the First World War, trade unions emerged in Japan, and Communist and socialist parties were founded.[17] The 1920s saw frequent pay negotiations and conflicts over the passing of legislation on health and safety standards at work. The general consensus – not only among reformers, but also most businessmen – was that Japan's economy faced problems no different from those in the West: a large working class, the rise of trade unions and conflicts over wages and working conditions.[18]

Only when we turn to the Meiji era (1868–1912), the period following the foundation of the modern nation state on the Western model, do we once again encounter the rhetoric of the special character of Japanese industrial relations, although only from the 1880s onward. In the first few years after the Meiji Restoration, influenced by the import of European economic theory, a broad consensus still prevailed that Confucian concepts of business were a hindrance to successful modernization.[19] Only when the euphoric phase of 'Westernization' came to an end around 1880 does Confucianism again appear as a tradition worth preserving. One now begins to encounter the topos of 'beautiful customs' (*bifû*), which characterize the sphere of production and the world of work at every turn. In the exemplary words of a representative of the Mitsubishi shipyard: 'Since ancient times, Japan has possessed the beautiful custom of master-servant relations based firmly on a spirit of sacrifice and compassion, a custom not seen in the many other countries of the world. ... Because of this relationship, the employer loves the employee, and the employee respects his master.'[20] It would, however, be short-sighted to view Confucianist discourse merely as an instrumental ideology in the hands of the employers. So-called 'pre-modern' values were appropriated and could be instrumentalized in workers' protests. Reference to 'traditional' conceptions was not only an instrument of repression, but also of resistance.[21]

This brief sketch illustrates how the trope of unique, Confucianist industrial relations could lead to quite different assessments. Depending on the political and economic context, cultural traditions (if they were considered decisive in the first place) could either appear as catalyst of or obstacle to modernization *à la japonaise*. A glance back at the Meiji era, moreover, has already intimated that the notion of specifically Japanese industrial relations, which in turn alluded to indigenous social traditions, arose at a time when industrial production was taking off in Japan. We are dealing here, in the words of Eric Hobsbawm, with an 'invented tradition' which was not simply 'natural', but also constructed. This is apparent in the very neologisms, such as *kazoku shugi* (familism) and *onjô shugi* (paternalism), coined during this period to express the development of new social practices and to manage them.[22]

The History of Interconnections and the 'Invention of a Tradition'

This invention of traditions, and this is my second point of critique, was not only the result of attempts to ensure the survival of a cultural heritage, but equally the product of a history of interconnections and interaction. The discourse on Confucian industrial relations not only linked a modern (or at least modernizing) present with the national past (temporally), but was just as much a reaction to changes in the transnational relations of exchange (spatially). The modern work ethic and industrial relations in businesses and factories arose in Japan during a period of intensive contact with the West. As a 'latecomer', Japan took Europe as its model for industrial development. Regardless of the fiction of cultural autonomy that the Confucianism thesis implies, the modern conception and practice of work also arose in the context of these interactions and interconnections.

A good example of this predicament is the history of the silk spinning mill in Tomioka, founded by the Japanese government in 1872. In the first few years of the Meiji state, economic liberalization had led to palpable trade deficits and strains on the national budget. The foreign trade deficit was largely the result of the import of English cotton. At the same time, there was demand for Japanese silk on the European market. The government thus decided to improve the quality and promote the production of Japanese silk. A model factory was set up in Tomioka, and eighteen French technicians were employed to familiarize the newly trained Japanese workers with European technology. Over the next few years, the now more experienced workers were transferred to newly-founded silk spinning mills to train new employees in the know-how they had acquired in Tomioka. Most of these new factories were built in the countryside far from the cities, and the workers had to be recruited from far and wide. Factory work thus meant a new experience that entailed changes in social relations (including, for instance, new work hierarchies, separation from one's family and living in a workers' hostel).[23]

The inculcation of modern work discipline in Tomioka and subsequently in other factories throughout the country can thus hardly be separated from the simultaneous introduction of European technology, from the knowledge of experts and conceptions of work. This is not to say that the modern conception of work and modern industrial relations in Japan are merely imports from Europe. What can be said, however, is that social practices and notions of work were transformed decisively and enduringly in a context whose dynamics were shaped significantly by the process of coming to terms with the 'West'. Economic historian Taira Kôji, for example, has shown that 'lifelong employment' and the 'seniority principle' applied to wages were by no means expressions of Confucian traditions; these forms of Japanese workplace organization, in fact, arose only when the world market was gripped by crisis and when employers (initially in heavy industry) wished to tie skilled workers to the firm by means of annual wage increases. Japanese industrial relations were thus more than a mere import from the 'West'. Yet it would be equally false to portray them as a tradition, rooted in the pre-modern era, of tying workers to one company only and of lifelong commitment to a firm understood as a replacement family.[24]

The political and intellectual transmission of knowledge about 'work' also took place in a context characterized by appropriation and blurred boundaries. The Association for Social Policy (*shakai seisaku gakkai*), for example, which was founded in 1896 and had a huge influence on government policies, clearly drew heavily on its German forebear, which a number of students and economists had got to know during their travels in Europe. At the same time, however, the concept of harmony between labour and capital also tallied with notions characteristic of the Confucianist economic policies of the Tokugawa period. Kanai Noboru, a key figure in the Association for Social Policy and well-acquainted with the German debate after studies in Halle, Heidelberg and Berlin, made particularly important contributions to this fusion of 'traditional' and 'modern' concepts of industrial relations and political economy.[25]

The government made a concerted effort to encourage diligence among workers as the country industrialized, a policy intended to inculcate modern work discipline. This included, as just one example, banning the after-lunch rest in public. The manuals produced for young women textile workers were intended to meet the demands made on an emerging industrial workforce in more concrete fashion. Here, one learned, for example, that 'if you all work to the utmost of your abilities from morning to night, there can be no loyalty to the country greater than this. If you do not work thus and stay idly at home, the country of Japan will become poorer and poorer. Therefore, work with all your might for the country's sake, enabling Japan to become the greatest country in the world.'[26]

This policy of encouraging diligence seemed necessary in order to create a workforce accustomed to modern work discipline. Once again, though, 'promoting diligence' was not just a disciplining strategy 'from above', but was also one of the 'technologies of the self' through which individuals demonstrated their 'modernity'. These technologies were also related to expectations that had entered Japan through interaction with the 'West'. In fact, to many European observers who came to Japan in the 1870s, the Japanese by no means seemed the diligent and hard-working people familiar from modern clichés. Economist Karl Rathgen, for example, told his German readership of a lack of enthusiasm for work among the Japanese: 'What is as yet little known in Japan is continuous work. This seems to me a large part of the explanation for the fact, confirmed by every foreigner, that Japanese workers work relatively little and that all work progresses only slowly.'[27] Max Nitzsche agreed: 'Continual, intensive work is nothing less than detestable to the average Japanese. He has no interest in working long hours if he can work slowly. He constantly stops and takes a break, to sing, smoke, chat or sip his tea.'[28] The so-called 'Confucian' work ethic, supposedly anchored in traditions hundreds of years old, apparently required lots of practice: this at least is what many Japanese and European observers believed. A few decades later this impression had already changed profoundly. The Japanese were increasingly thought of as industrious and disciplined workers, and the term 'Yellow Peril' was doing the rounds in Europe. The term did not evoke a purely military and cultural threat, but also fears of 'competition between White and Yellow labour'.[29]

The sense of a break with earlier types of working practices reflected in these observations corresponded to the gradual taking hold of industrial forms of production. Nonetheless, Meiji Japan was to remain a primarily agrarian country for some decades to come. The discourse of work was thus more than simply the effect of changed industrial relations in the wake of industrialization. It was at the same time a reaction to the profound social upheavals of the time. A key component of changed industrial relations was the slackening of social ties as a result of the dissolution of the feudal order. One of the first steps taken by the Meiji government was the abolition of all regulations restricting the freedom of labour, which had dominated the social structure of Japanese society during the Tokugawa period. From 1869 all legal obstacles to finding a new job and taking up an occupation out of sync with one's inherited social position were abolished. At the same time, the discourse on work was now closely related to the new nation state. The notion of work that took shape in the debates of the time was thus loaded with connotations rooted in quite different contexts: the dissolution of feudal labour relations, the new capitalist order, theories of political economy transposed from Europe, the demands of industrial production and the ideologies of the nation state.

The reorganization of social practices was a departure from accustomed paradigms, and this unsettling experience translated into problems of terminology. The common terms for 'work' no longer seemed to go along with the changed realities. All of these expressed the social context within which the work was carried out. *Suke*, for example, was the work done by the personally dependent as compensation and thanks for borrowed land, for animals or a house. *Yui* referred to an exchange of labour between two individuals on the same social level, such as mutual neighbourly assistance in planting rice. *Hôkô* was the service owed by family servants, who were quasi-members of the family. A number of other words for work existed independently of social relations, but they related exclusively to the physical aspect of work (*shigoto*, *hataraki*, *kasegi*). It proved extremely difficult to find a term for work within a social context, but free of the notion of obligation to others. None of the existing terms could be applied to factory work, which was based on a contract freely entered into by autonomous and equal partners. It was only around the turn of the century that the term commonly used to this day (*rôdô*) gained general acceptance.[30]

These terminological difficulties illustrate the contemporary impression of a profound turning point in the practice of work and its place in society in the first decades of the Meiji era. From now on, work was at the centre of a wider and more comprehensive discourse that linked individual and society in new and complex ways. Not only did the conception of 'work' change, but the modern nation and the individual (as subject of the nation state) were simultaneously reconstituted with the help of 'work'.

This complex situation is well illustrated by the way young working women came to symbolically represent the nation. Industrialization, which the government did much to stimulate, was an important component of the 'self-strengthening movement' (*fukoku kyôhei*) of the Meiji period and thus helped produce conceptions of masculinity, both in terms of collective ideals of national strength and in terms of individual concepts of male work. At the same time, however, the large number of young, single women in the workforce was one of the special features of Japanese economic development (in international comparison). The cotton and silk spinning mills were among the first branches of production to be industrialized and were thus a key component of the early phase of Japanese industrialization. In line with the textile industry's importance to the Japanese economy, women made up more than 60 per cent of the entire industrial workforce as late as 1909. Their huge contribution to the work of the nation made national subjects of these women, while their work was represented as essentially Japanese. This nationalization of work was a universal feature of Meiji-era discourse, transcending differences in social background and political leanings. A socialist such as Hirasawa Keiichi could thus assert: 'Observing the almost magician-like dexterity of the hands of factory women, I thought that only women could undertake this kind of work. I also intuitively felt that only Japanese women (*Nippon no onna*), not Western women, could. The Japanese woman (*Nippon no fujin*), who identifies sewing with the female vocation, is already destined to develop the dexterity of her hands from the time she is in her mother's womb.'[31]

Women, especially from agricultural regions, were thus turned into national subjects through their labour. In the first years of the Meiji era, the Samurai daughter was still viewed as the incarnation of the Japanese character. This changed around the turn of the century. One of the invented traditions of modern Japan is the notion that the true, authentic 'Japan' can be found in the villages and countryside. Folklore was among the disciplines that institutionalized this idea. However, the new role that rural women took on in the country's economic modernization also played a part here. In the early 1870s, even factory work was dominated by the higher social classes. In the early days, it was mainly the daughters of samurai and big landowners who were recruited to work in the newly established textile factories (in Tomioka among other places); they saw this as a task of national importance entirely suited to their social standing. From the 1880s onward, they were replaced by young girls from peasant households, sold to the factories by their impoverished parents. This change affecting the actors of industrialization – expressed symbolically in the subtle adjustment of the terminology (the term for 'woman factory worker' was now *jokô* rather than *kôjo*) – also facilitated a shift in how women from peasant regions and social classes were represented.

The fact that the overwhelming majority of the workers were female also inspired a Meiji-era debate dealing specifically with the risks involved in factory work. Proposals for a law on health and safety at work (introduced only in 1911), for example, provided for prohibition of strenuous night work by women, not only because it conflicted with specific rights enjoyed by employees, but also because it threatened to impair women's reproductive potential. Workplace hygiene was also subject to discussion, the desire to protect Japanese mothers again playing a central role. Japanese women workers' status as subjects was thus linked to conceptions of the gender-specific nature of work. At the same time, women were integrated into a national discourse; their status was related to their contribution to the national cause, in the sphere of both production and reproduction.[32]

The individual's self-conception and social status were linked with work and his or her place in the labour market; the nation state was also increasingly judged in terms of its economic policy achievements and the results of 'national work' (GNP in modern parlance). Work was measured, its product exhibited, counted, compared; work became a national project.[33] Enforcing a modern work ethic was a part of Japan's modernization through which it wished to establish itself as an equal member of the family of nations. In this context, work was nothing less than synonymous with distance from the pre-modern past, with the non-traditional.

The concepts of work, modernity and nation were thus interwoven and partially identified with one another, as is well illustrated in the incorporation of Okinawa into the Japanese state. The transnational framework of interconnections, within which the modern conception and practice of work developed in Japan, not only linked the country with Europe and the 'West', but also with neighbouring regions in Asia. Okinawa had been subject to dual suzerainty up to the nineteenth century and paid tribute to both Japan and China. In 1879, the island group was annexed by Japan and subjected to a strict policy of assimilation during the subsequent decades, intended to make reliable 'Japanese' of its inhabitants. Alongside political integration and language policy, work and work discipline played a key role in this process.[34]

The development of a work ethic and 'Japanization' followed the logic of progress: the inhabitants of the southern island chain were to be freed from their backwardness and introduced to modernity by means of work. As late as 1903, people from Okinawa – alongside Ainu, Koreans and Taiwanese – were presented as members of backward tribal communities at the great industrial exhibition in Osaka; Okinawa was still Japan's 'Other', and in public consciousness its inhabitants as yet scarcely figured as part of the nation. This changed in the wake of labour migration on a massive scale, which brought a large number of Okinawans to the industrial areas of Osaka. They attempted to counter the discrimination they initially encountered by assimilating everyday and working practices. Over the course of the 1920s, a reform movement emerged that aimed to organize and manage the process of self-disciplining. Toyokawa Tadayuki, one of its leading activists, put the reformers' central concern in a nutshell: 'What makes me wring my hands in despair – each time I go abroad or leave Osaka – is our people's frivolous attitude … We have to work day and night to cultivate an attitude of diligence.' To acquire diligence and modern work discipline, cast aside Okinawa's traditions and become 'Japanese': for him, these were all part of a single process.[35]

Transnational History, not the 'Clash of Civilizations'

The Confucianism thesis, which has become highly popular since the 1980s, postulates a connection between the Confucian heritage and the specific characteristics of Japanese capitalism. More generally, it relates Japan's successful economic modernization to the country's cultural traditions. Here, Japanese history is not interpreted primarily as 'Westernization'. The emphasis is instead on continuities with the 'pre-modern' era.

This thesis presents two general problems. First, its popularity in the academic literature and beyond can be understood only against the background of Japan's economic growth in the 1980s. Yet as recently as the 1950s, during the post-war recession, the Confucian legacy was considered a veritable obstacle to economic development (while it was regarded as utterly irrelevant in the interwar period). We are thus dealing with a malleable, adaptable argument. Second, this approach is anchored in the fiction of cultural autonomy. It thus overlooks the interconnections and interdependencies that played such a crucial role in the development of the modern work ethic and labour relations. In late-nineteenth-century Japan, notions of work changed fundamentally, as the country came to terms with the 'West' and its Asian neighbours (within a colonial framework).

This is not to suggest that the issue of differing economic cultures is entirely irrelevant. It is apparent that enduring social traditions influence the specific form of economic processes or find expression in them. Against claims frequently made within sociological literature, the regulation of the modern working world did not simply develop in line with the functional demands of industrial society.[36] The specific combination of actors, but also different cultural practices (of law for example), contributed to the particular historical development of institutional systems. From time to time, specific national 'styles' formed in this process. These should, however, be viewed not merely as the natural product of a 'national culture', but also as a result of comparison, differentiation and transfer.[37]

For the most part, however, the concept of 'economic cultures' is used in a quite a different way and is understood as an expression of autonomous cultural spheres. This concept of culture is sometimes seen as a reaction to the impositions of a form of modernity apparently levelling everything in its path and the fear that cultural peculiarities will be subsumed in universal processes. In most cases, the attempt to hold on to the significance of cultural specifics is no longer the expression of an anti-modern essentialism, but part of efforts to pluralize theories of modernity. Thus, when the authors of the so-called 'Japan discourse' (*Nihonjinron*) discuss the possibility of a specifically Japanese modernity (and the Confucianism thesis is part and parcel of these attempts), the underlying motivation is not a desire to 'overcome modernity', as was the case in the 1930s, but to explain it differently.[38] The debate on the role of 'Asian values' in relation to Chinese modernization is a similar case. It should not primarily be seen as the quest for an alternative to capitalist modernity, but rather as an attempt to anchor it in Chinese traditions.[39]

This emphasis on unique cultural paths is part of the project (in the current era of globalization) by many intellectuals in the (former) Third World to emancipate themselves from Eurocentric notions of modernity.[40] Here, as a rule, modernity is no longer understood as a foreign body or European imposition; such thinkers, in fact, seek to correlate it to local traditions. The risk here, however, is one of cultivating an 'anti-Eurocentric Eurocentrism', as Immanuel Wallerstein has put it.[41] Here, capitalism is derived from the cultural resources of non-European societies and thus indigenized. In this way, according to Wallerstein, a specific European development and product of historical processes is stylized as a universalism, as one bestows upon it whatever cultural roots apply in the individual country's case. Capitalism is thus turned into an unexamined, universal process without actors, a force of nature. This derivation of capitalism from autochthonous traditions, he asserts, fails to acknowledge the central role played by Europe and America and the central role of power, as it were, in the historical process of globalization, instead projecting the results of this process back into the national pasts.[42]

The Confucianism thesis, to return to our main theme, can also be understood as a reaction against the assumption of a universal, unidirectional process of modernization, which continues to hold sway over much of the writing of history.[43] In contrast, the Confucianism thesis operates with a notion of cultural uniqueness and autochthonous development. Universalism is thus confronted by a form of nativism (if not cultural fundamentalism). In both cases, however, the actual interactions and (mostly asymmetrical) exchange relations, which have characterized the world since at least the mid-nineteenth century, are ignored. Rather than giving up a universal model only to embrace the notion of islands of particularity, we should focus on exchange and (by no means equal, often colonial) interaction. We cannot, of course, assume that everything under the sun was linked and entangled to the same degree, in the same way and at all times. Nonetheless, scrutinizing transnational contexts provides an important corrective to notions of cultural particularity, which continue to saturate most meta-narratives of modernization.[44]

Discussions of how capitalism arose in the context of transnational interconnections point in this direction, the debate on Eric Williams's thesis being a good example. According to Williams, capitalism was not developed in Europe alone, but can be traced back to economic exchanges between European colonial powers and the great island plantations of the Caribbean.[45] In his study of the 'sweet power' of sugar, Sidney Mintz has described how the specific methods of production on the Caribbean sugar plantations pre-empted forms of capitalist and industrial production in Europe.[46] In his important book, Kenneth Pomeranz has shown that the key turning point in European economic history, the taking hold of industrial capitalism from around 1800, is comprehensible 'only when Europe's complex and often violent relations with other parts of the globe' are taken into account.[47] Rather than projecting internal and culturally autonomous temporal axes and searching traditions for the 'origins' of an indigenous capitalism, synchronous interactions should take centre stage in a relational history of modernity. Against the logic of the Confucianism thesis, therefore, my point has been to read the past as the history of transnational interconnections. Against the logic of the Confucianism thesis, therefore, my point has been to read the past as the history of transnational interconnections.[48]

Notes

1. David Landes, *The Wealth and Poverty of Nations: Why Some Are So Rich and Some So Poor* (New York: W.W. Norton, 1998), p. 513.
2. Landes, *Wealth*, p. 368, 516.
3. See Günther Distelrath, *Die japanische Produktionsweise. Zur wissenschaftlichen Genese einer stereotypen Sicht der japanischen Wirtschaft* (Munich: iudicum Verlag, 1996).
4. On the Japanese reception of Weber's study of Protestantism: this commenced before the First World War, particularly in the 1920s, see Wolfgang Schwentker, 'Der "Geist" des japanischen Kapitalismus. Die Geschichte einer Debatte', in Wolfgang J. Mommsen and Wolfgang Schwentker (eds), *Max Weber und das moderne Japan* (Göttingen: Vandenhoeck and Ruprecht, 1999), pp. 270–98.
5. See Robert Bellah, *Tokugawa Religion. The Cultural Roots of Modern Japan* (1st edn 1957, New York: Free Press, 1985). On reception, see also the critical review by Maruyama Masao, 'Shôkai. Berâ "Tokugawa jidai no shûkyô"', in *Kokka gakkai zasshi* 72 (1958): 437–58. Also cf. Wolfgang Schwentker, *Max Weber in Japan. Eine Untersuchung zur Wirkungsgeschichte 1905–1995* (Tübingen: Mohr-Siebeck, 1998), esp. p. 272–82.
6. Morishima Michio, *Why Has Japan Succeeded? Western Technology and the Japanese Ethos* (Cambridge: Cambridge University Press, 1982).
7. See, for example, Christoph Deutschmann, 'Der "Betriebsclan". Der japanische Organisationstypus als Herausforderung an die soziologische Modernisierungstheorie', in *Soziale Welt* 39 (1987): 133–48.
8. Typical contributions to this debate are collected in Peter Hanau et al. (eds), *Die Arbeitswelt in Japan und in der Bundesrepublik Deutschland – ein Vergleich* (Neuwied: Luchterhand Verlag, 1985). See also James R. Lincoln and Arne L. Kalleberg, *Culture, Control, and Commitment. A Study of Work Organization and Work Attitudes in the United States and Japan* (Cambridge: Cambridge University Press, 1990); William G. Ouchi, *Theory Z. How American Business Can Meet the Japanese Challenge* (New York: Avon Books, 1981); Jon P. Alston, *The American Samurai. Blending American and Japanese Practices* (New York: de Gruyter, 1986). See also Christian Kleinschmidt, *Der produktive Blick. Wahrnehmung amerikanischer und japanischer Management- und Produktionsmethoden durch deutsche Unternehmer 1950–1985* (Berlin: Akademie Verlag, 2002).
9. The literature dealing with Weber's thesis is vast. A good starting point is the collection of classic texts in Constans Seyfarth and Walter M. Sprondel (eds), *Seminar: Religion und gesellschaftliche Entwicklung. Studien zur Protestantismus-Kapitalismus-These Max Webers* (Frankfurt: Suhrkamp, 1973). Useful recent contributions include: Gordon Marshall, *In Search of the Spirit of Capitalism. An Essay on Max Weber's Protestant Ethic Thesis* (London: Blackwell Publishing, 1982); Annette Disselkamp, *L'éthique protestante de Max Weber* (Paris: Presses universitaires de France, 1994); Wolfgang Schluchter, 'Religion, politische Herrschaft, Wirtschaft und bürgerliche Lebensführung. Die okzidentale Sonderentwicklung', in idem

(ed.), *Max Webers Sicht des okzidentalen Christentums. Interpretation und Kritik* (Frankfurt: Suhrkamp, 1988), pp. 11–128; Richard van Dülmen, 'Protestantismus und Kapitalismus. Max Webers These im Licht der neueren Sozialgeschichte', in Christian Gneuss and Jürgen Kocka (eds), *Max Weber. Ein Symposion* (Munich: Deutscher Taschenbuch Verlag, 1988), pp. 88–101; Shirô Takebayashi, *Die Entstehung der Kapitalismustheorie in der Gründungsphase der deutschen Soziologie. Von der historischen Nationalökonomie zur historischen Soziologie Werner Sombarts und Max Webers* (Berlin: Duncker and Humblot, 2003).

10. See Hans-Christoph Schröder, 'Max Weber und der Puritanismus', in *Geschichte und Gesellschaft* 21 (1995): 459–78, especially p. 463.
11. See Sepp Linhart and Wolfram Manzenreiter, 'Japan: Von der Arbeitsgesellschaft zur Freizeitgesellschaft', in *Minikomi. Informationen des Akademischen Arbeitskreis Japan*, 1 (1999): pp. 5–11. See also Sepp Linhart, 'From Industrial to Postindustrial Society. Changes in Japanese Leisure-Related Values and Behavior', in *Journal of Japanese Studies* 14 (1988): 271–307.
12. On the history of the debate on Weber's thesis, see Malcolm H. MacKinnon, 'The Longevity of the Thesis. A Critique of the Critics', in Hartmut Lehmann, Guenther Roth (eds), *Weber's Protestant Ethic. Origins, Evidence, Contexts* (Cambridge: Cambridge University Press, 1993), pp. 211–43; Hartmut Lehmann, 'Asketischer Protestantismus und ökonomischer Rationalismus. Die Weber-These nach zwei Generationen', in Wolfgang Schluchter (ed.), *Max Webers Sicht des okzidentalen Christentums. Interpretation und Kritik* (Frankfurt: Suhrkamp, 1988), pp. 529–53.
13. See Francis Hsu, *Iemoto. The Heart of Japan* (New York: John Wiley and Sons, 1975); Yasuke Murakami, 'Ie Society as a Pattern of Civilisation', in *Journal of Japanese Studies* 10 (1984): 281–363.
14. On what follows, see Andrew Gordon, 'The Invention of Japanese-Style Labor Management', in Stephen Vlastos (ed.), *Mirror of Modernity. Invented Traditions of Modern Japan* (Berkeley: University of California Press, 1998), pp. 19–36.
15. The most important and hugely influential representative of this view was Ôtsuka Hisao. See, for instance, his 'Kyôdôtai no kiso riron', in *Ôtsuka Hisao chosakushû*, vol. 7 (Tokyo: Iwanami Shoten, 1969), pp. 1–104. For a detailed examination, see Distelrath, *Produktionsweise*, pp. 39–62; Horst Arnold-Kanamori, *Der Menschentyp als Produktivkraft. Max-Weber-Studies des japanischen Wirtschaftshistorikers Ôtsuka Hisao* (1907–1996) (Hamburg: Kovac, 1998).
16. This is evident in the central role ascribed to Confucian traditions in explaining Japanese backwardness. See, for example, Kawashima Takeyoshi's particularly influential *Nihon shakai no kazokuteki kôzô* (Tokyo: Nihon Hyôron Shinsha, 1950). Another representative example is the labour economist Okôchi Kazuo, see, for instance, his *Nihon no rôdôsha kaikyû* (Tokyo: Tÿyô Keizai Shinpôsha, 1955).
17. See George M. Beckmann, *Genji Okubo. The Japanese Communist Party 1922?1945* (Stanford: Stanford University Press, 1969).
18. For a general examination, see Andrew Gordon, *Labor and Imperial Democracy in Prewar Japan* (Berkeley: University of California Press, 1991); Sheldon Garon, *The State and Labor in Modern Japan* (Berkeley: University of California Press, 1987); see also William M. Tsutsui, *Manufacturing Ideology. Scientific Management in Twentieth-Century Japan* (Princeton: Princeton University Press, 1998). This attitude was reinforced by the intensive reception of Marxism in the 1920s; see Germaine Hoston, *Marxism and the Crisis of Development in Prewar Japan* (Princeton: Princeton University Press, 1992).
19. See Distelrath, *Produktionsweise*, p. 62. See also Johannes Hirschmeier and Tsunehiko Yui, *The Development of Japanese Business 1600–1973* (London: Harper Collins, 1975).

On economic thought at the time, see Tessa Morris-Suzuki, *A History of Japanese Economic Thought* (London: Routledge, 1989), esp. Chapter 2; Sugiyama Chuhei, *Origins of Economic Thought in Modern Japan* (London: Routledge, 1994).

20. Quoted in Gordon, 'Invention', p. 21.
21. See Gordon, *Labor*, p. 73.
22. On this 'invented tradition', see Dean W. Kinzley, *Industrial Harmony in Modern Japan. The Invention of a Tradition* (London: Routledge, 1991).
23. See E. Patricia Tsurumi, *Factory Girls. Women in the Thread Mills of Meiji Japan* (Princeton: Princeton University Press, 1990). See also the autobiography by one of the women workers in Tomioka: Wada Ei, *Teihon Tomioka nikki* (Tokyo: Sôjusha, 1976).
24. Taira Kôji, *Economic Development and the Labor Market in Japan* (New York 1970).
25. See Morris-Suzuki, *A History of Japanese Economic Thought*, Chapter 2; Shakai seisaku gakkai shiryô shûsei hensan iinkai (ed.), *Shakai seisaku gakkai shiryô shûsei* (Tokyo: Ochanomizu Shobô, 1978). Cf. also Erik Grimmer-Solem, 'German Social Science, Meiji Conservatism, and the Peculiarities of Japanese History', in *Journal of World History* 16 (2005): 187–222.
26. Quotation from the *Factory Girls Reader*, a 1911 manual, quoted in Tsurumi, *Factory Girls*, p. 94.
27. Karl Rathgen, *Japans Volkswirtschaft und Staatshaushalt* (Leipzig: Duncker and Humblot, 1891), p. 422.
28. Max Nitzsche, 'Die japanische Konkurrenz', in *Preußische Jahrbücher* 117 (1904): 225–43, esp. p. 232.
29. Alexander Tille, *Der Wettbewerb weisser und gelber Arbeit in der industriellen Produktion* (Berlin: Elsner, 1904). See also Heinz Gollwitzer, *Die Gelbe Gefahr. Geschichte eines Schlagworts. Studien zum imperialistischen Denken* (Göttingen: Vandenhoeck and Ruprecht, 1962); Ute Mehnert, *Deutschland, Amerika und die 'Gelbe Gefahr'. Zur Karriere eines Schlagworts in der Großen Politik, 1905–1917* (Stuttgart: Steiner, 1995).
30. Thomas C. Smith, 'Peasant Time and Factory Time in Japan', in idem, *Native Sources of Japanese Industrialization, 1750–1920* (Berkeley: University of California Press, 1988), pp. 199–235. See also Sogo Masaaki (ed.), *Meiji no kotoba jiten* (Tokyo: Tôkyôdô, 1989), pp. 603–05; Wolfgang Lippert, *Entstehung und Funktion einiger chinesischer marxistischer Termini. Der lexikalisch-begriffliche Aspekt der Rezeption des Marxismus in Japan und China* (Wiesbaden: Steiner, 1979), pp. 183–86.
31. Quoted in Mariko Asano Tamanoi, *Under the Shadow of Nationalism. Politics and Poetics of Rural Japanese Women* (Honolulu: University of Hawaii Press, 1998), p. 96.
32. See Tamanoi, *Shadow*, esp. Chapter 4.
33. See Byron K. Marshall, *Capitalism and Nationalism in Prewar Japan. The Ideology of the Business Elite, 1868–1941* (Stanford: Stanford University Press, 1967).
34. On what follows, see Tomiyama Ichirô, *Kindai Nihon shakai to 'Okinawajin'* (Tokyo: Nihon Keizai Hyôronsha, 1990).
35. Quoted in Tomiyama Ichirô, 'Nashonarizumu – Modanizumu – Koroniarizumu. Okinawa kara no shiten', in Iyotani Toshio/Sugihara Tôru (eds), *Nihon shakai to imin. Kôza gaikokujin teijû mondai*, vol. 1 (Tokyo: Akashi Shoten, 1996), pp. 129–64 (quotation on p. 142).
36. See Marshall Sahlins, 'Cosmologies of Capitalism. The Trans-Pacific Sector of "The World System"', in Nicholas B. Dirks et al. (eds), *Culture/Power/History. A Reader in Contemporary Social Theory* (Princeton: Princeton University Press, 1994), pp. 412–56: although Sahlins is open to the criticism that he risks constructing essentialisms.
37. See, for example, Peter Wagner et al. (eds), *Arbeit und Nationalstaat. Frankreich und Deutschland in europäischer Perspektive* (Frankfurt am Main: Campus, 2000).

38. For an introduction to *Nihonjinron*, see Aoki Tamotsu, *Nihon bunkaron no henyô* (Tokyo: Chûô Kôron Shinsha, 1990).
39. Tu Wei-ming, 'The Confucian Dimension in the East Asian Development Model', in Josef Kreiner (ed.), *The Impact of Traditional Thought on Present-Day Japan* (Munich: Iudicium, 1996), pp. 31–48; Ronald Dore, 'Confucianism, Economic Growth and Social Development', in ibid., pp. 17–30; Gordon Redding, *The Spirit of Chinese Capitalism* (New York: de Gruyter, 1993).
40. In the Japanese context, see, for example, the work of economic historian Kawakatsu Heita, such as his monograph *Nihon bunmei to kindai seiyô* (Tokyo: NHK Books, 1991), and *Fukoku yûtokuron* (Tokyo: Chûô Kôronsha, 2000). See also Ueyama Shumpei, *Nihon bunmeishi no kôsô. Juyô to sôzô no kiseki* (Tokyo: Kadokawa Shoten, 1990). For an overview of these approaches, see Sebastian Conrad, 'The Opened and the Closed Country. Conflicting Views of Japan's Position in the World', in Benedikt Stuchtey and Eckhardt Fuchs (eds), *Writing World History 1800–2000* (Oxford: Oxford University Press, 2003), pp. 327–51.
41. Immanuel Wallerstein, 'Eurocentrism and Its Avatars. The Dilemmas of Social Science', in idem, *The End of the World as We Know It. Social Science for the 21st Century* (Minnesota: University of Minnesota Press, 1999).
42. For a similar approach, see also Arif Dirlik, 'Modernity as History. Post-revolutionary China, Globalization and the Question of Modernity', in *Social History* 27 (2002): 16–39.
43. Cf. Prasenjit Duara, *Rescuing History from the Nation: Questioning Narratives of Modern China* (Chicago: University of Chicago Press, 1995).
44. On this form of methodological nationalism, see Shalini Randeria, 'Geteilte Geschichte und verwobene Moderne', in Jörn Rüsen et al. (eds), *Zukunftsentwürfe. Ideen für eine Kultur der Veränderung* (Frankfurt: Campus, 1999), pp. 87–96; Shalini Randeria, 'Jenseits von Soziologie und soziokultureller Anthropologie. Zur Ortsbestimmung der nichtwestlichen Welt in einer zukünftigen Sozialtheorie', in *Soziale Welt* 50 (1999): 373–82.
45. Eric Williams, *Capitalism and Slavery* (Chapel Hill: University of North Carolina Press, 1944). For an assessment and critique, see Barbara Solow and Stanley Engerman (eds), *British Capitalism and Caribbean Slavery. The Legacy of Eric Williams* (Cambridge: Cambridge University Press, 1987); Seymour Drescher, 'Capitalism and Slavery after Fifty Years', in *Slavery and Abolition* 18 (1997): 212–27; Joseph E. Inikori, *Africans and the Industrial Revolution in England: A Study in International Trade and Economic Development* (Cambridge: Cambridge University Press, 2004).
46. Sidney W. Mintz, *Sweetness and Power: The Place of Sugar in Modern History* (New York: Viking, 1985). Robin Blackburn has also pointed to the central role of transnational processes, particularly the slave trade, in the development of capitalism and the Industrial Revolution. See Robin Blackburn, *The Making of New World Slavery. From the Baroque to the Modern, 1492–1800* (London: Verso, 1997).
47. Kenneth Pomeranz, *The Great Divergence. Europe, China, and the Making of the Modern World Economy* (Princeton: Princeton University Press, 2000), p. 24.
48. Cf. Sebastian Conrad and Shalini Randeria, 'Geteilte Geschichten. Europa in einer postkolonialen Welt', in idem (eds), *Jenseits des Eurozentrismus. Postkoloniale Perspektiven in den Geschichts- und Kulturwissenschaften* (Frankfurt: Campus, 2002), pp. 9–49; Sanjay Subrahmanyam, *Explorations in Connected History*, 2 vols (Oxford: Oxford University Press, 2005); Anthony G. Hopkins (ed.), *Globalization in World History* (London: W.W. Norton, 2002).

10
What is Global Labour History Good For?

Andreas Eckert

I.

World history and global history have recently become very popular fields of historiography. Although there is a lively and multifaceted debate about these fields, it is still far from clear what 'global history' exactly means. There is a common consensus that global history is not the history of everything everywhere. The field's approach does not attempt to engage in an additive-encyclopaedic claim, nor does it represent a simple extension of national history. In general, global history is concerned with relationships and transactions in a spatial dimension. These relationships can be between regions or nations. Yet these regions, as migration history shows, are not necessarily directly connected.[1]

The global perspective has the potential to assign a new significance to local and regional perspectives, as it considers the permeability and alteration of state borders and promises an alternative approach to the traditional focus on nation states. However, a global perspective on history does not imply that the nation state is not important: quite the contrary. Sebastian Conrad's groundbreaking study on globalization and the nation in Germany between 1880 and the First World War, for instance, aptly demonstrates that the stabilization and the fixed territory of the nation state were important aspects of globalization processes before the First Word War.[2] Moreover, the concept of global history implies that on the one hand, different cultures and societies share certain experiences because of their interdependence, but that on the other hand, new particularities and fragmentations emerge. Thus, global history must take into consideration the asymmetries between the 'West and the rest', as well as hierarchies, inequalities and violence.[3]

One still gets the impression, however, that debates in global history are mainly about the question 'what ought to be done', and that there are, up to now, comparatively few studies that 'do' global history. It apparently does not make sense to reconstruct entanglements and global connections as such; such a reconstruction has to put its subjects in a concrete framework. This article does not 'do' global history either, but attempts to evaluate – in a still rather sketchy and fairly programmatic way – the potential of a global approach to the history of labour and work.[4] It will be argued that a focus on labour and work provides a good approach to analysing processes transcending the nation state and interaction over great distances.[5]

II.

Only very few terms summarize such manifold and at the same time fundamental issues as the concept linked with the word 'work'. What is widely understood by this term today is still very much determined by the conditions that industrial development and the labour movement imprinted on modern societies. Work is regarded as one of the key issues in the political discourses of most industrialized countries. It is sometimes even suggested that once the problem of work is solved, all other problems could be solved much more easily. Thus, this term is linked to political expectations of salvation and seems to touch upon the core of many people's mentalities today. Success and failure, both personally and professionally, are closely linked to the concept of work. Work defines status. The supposed unambiguity of the term easily leads one to ignore the fact that 'work' covers an enormous range of activities and meanings that are linked to very different horizons of experience in time and space. In current debates in industrialized countries, there is the tendency to equate work with market-related work or gainful employment (*Erwerbsarbeit*), which is more or less clearly separated from the domestic sphere. This distinction, though, no longer corresponds to the experiences of many people: just think of the debates about workplaces at home or payments for childrearing.

One of the reasons that work is currently widely discussed has to do with the observations of Jürgen Kocka and Claus Offe, made a few years ago.[6] According to them, in industrialized countries gainful employment is in a state of double crisis, characterized by the two problems of mass unemployment and a new fluidity of work relations. On the one hand, for some time now the volume of labour offered exceeds the amount of labour that is in demand on the labour market. In the industrialized world, a considerable number of people able and ready for gainful employment no longer have access to it, and consequently no access to what, according to current standards, is necessary for leading a 'meaningful life'. From this perspective, work is more than an activity that secures monetary income to support those who work and members of their households. Work is also an institution that provides meaning and, in doing so, meets virtually religious functions. The second factor of crisis mentioned by Kocka and Offe is the 'rise of fluidity', the changing character of gainful employment. According to them, lifelong occupation in one and the same job is no longer the rule. 'Normal work relations' are eroding. Flexibility is the new magic word. Workplaces, working hours, types of work, employers, and qualifications needed and incomes are all in a state of flux. This has many consequences for life security and, above all, for other central spheres of life such as family or social environment. Someone who constantly has to adapt to new places and kinds of work will inevitably develop social behaviours and strategies different from someone who assumes his work to be continuous throughout his life. It should be stressed that, historically, continuity in work has always been an exception and mainly applies to the *trentes glorieuses* or thirty glorious years experienced in Europe following the Second World War. However, it is crucial to note that longing for such continuities and the idea that they are 'normal' very much shape current debates about work in industrial societies.

These perspectives equate work with labour and gainful employment. Thus, what is in crisis (or perceived as being in crisis) is above all a specific experience of work that could be contrasted with very different experiences in other parts of the world and in other time periods. The huge variety of conceptions of work and the manifold ways in which work is embedded in societies is widely ignored in debates about the state and future of work in the present. Looking at work and labour from a global perspective will enable us to better capture the scope of possibilities (*Möglichkeitsräume*) in which the factors determining the relations between work and other expressions of life have shifted. This perspective will also show how the current narrow understanding of work is far from self-evident, and how arduously and circuitously this understanding has developed. In other words, a global perspective on the history of work and labour is crucial in order to reconstruct the process in which the current, largely unquestioned and apparently 'natural' idea of work came out ahead.

In this context, two assumptions seem to be important. First, there was a fundamental change in the mid-nineteenth century linked with industrialization, when new ideas and practices of work emerged. Work was legally codified and from then on established the link between the individual and broader social groups, and especially the nation state: labour became the basis of the social and political order.[7] In the context of the nation state and the emerging welfare state, the difference between work or labour (in the sense of gainful employment, largely performed by men) and non-work (including other activities, e.g., at the household level and largely performed by women) developed. Moreover, the difference between having work in the sense of gainful employment and being unemployed was reflected in the language and the statistics of the time and also became part of social policy.[8] Until this period *Arbeit*, *travail*, 'work' and 'labour' had been defined in different ways, but had never been limited to marketable work. But from the nineteenth century onwards in the industrialized world, work came to be defined more or less exclusively as gainful occupation, with wage labour as its most important and most widespread form.[9]

Second, this form of codified work was soon spread not only across Europe, but also in non-European societies. This was, however, not only a one-way process, but at least partly an entangled one: experiences in the non-European, to a large extent colonial world also shaped conceptions and practices of work in Europe. Work was always part of transnational exchange processes. Before the latter assumption will be discussed in some further detail, it is useful to look briefly at the state of research in labour studies and the history of work.

III.

Work has always been an important category in social theory, considered by thinkers such as John Locke, Karl Marx and Max Weber. In contemporary theories, work has become almost irrelevant and has been replaced by, for instance, the category of communication, as in Niklas Luhmann's work.[10] At the same time, many critics have diagnosed 'the end of the labour society'.[11] This unresolved tension is based on the traditional understanding of 'labour' as 'gainful occupation' or *Erwerbsarbeit*, which is no longer fully appropriate to describe realities in the globalized world following the Cold War. It is becoming more and more evident that received understandings of labour closely associated with capitalism and the developed nation state have to be reconsidered.

The state of the historical research on labour currently reflects a certain degree of helplessness. On the one hand, labour certainly belongs to the better researched aspects of modern history.[12] On the other hand, as Jürgen Kocka has rightly emphasized, 'the history of work as a field of research still appears oddly unstructured. It is not the case that we do not know anything about the history of work and especially of labour in Europe. Quite the contrary, we know a lot or at least could know much. It is doubtful, however, if and, if yes, how work could be picked out as central theme, because it was always closely linked with other aspects of life.'[13]

This uncertainty is linked with a widespread disillusionment about the possibilities and the intellectual excitement of labour history. 'Ever since', Marcel van der Linden argues, 'many labour historians have viewed the state of their discipline as a protracted crisis. First, the emerging paradigms of women's and ethnic history showed that there had been giant blank spots on labour history's maps, and that filling in these blanks made a complete rewriting of the old narratives unavoidable. Second, the unilinear conception of class-consciousness that had long been dominant came into question.'[14] Following growing uncertainty about its organizing categories, labour history began to lose its character as a 'discipline'. The distinction between labour history and historiographies such as women's history, ethnic history, anthropological or sociological histories, was dissolving. Conceptual difficulties and political disappointments further fuelled the impression of a state of crisis.[15] In anthropology, not many ethnographies focus on the subject of work, nor are there many theoretical monographs and articles.[16] Social scientists researching labour more or less exclusively focus on industrialized societies. They usually concentrate on national labour markets and discuss questions of current labour market policies, new employment risks and the relationship between the labour market and the welfare state.[17] In legal studies, the development of research on questions of labour is closely linked with the set-up of labour relations in a nation state (contract and status). In the context of globalization, this limited perspective becomes increasingly problematic, for instance, in the efforts to do justice to 'globalized labour relations' on the level of the European Union.[18]

On the other hand, in many non-European areas the interest in labour history is rapidly rising. This is especially the case in South Asia.[19] In Latin America, too, a real boom in labour studies has taken place in recent years.[20] As far as the historiography of Africa is concerned, it would be an exaggeration to talk about a boom in labour history. However, there is a steady flow of related studies, and many of the more influential syntheses of African history analyse wage labour as one of, if not the most important factor for societal changes in sub-Saharan Africa.[21] At the same time there is a growing consciousness among historians of labour and work of the necessity of transcending the limits of the nation state, because 'borders are not very relevant to the object of study. Working-class formation and restructuring are not neatly contained within particular national borders; they are processes on which voluntary and forced immigration and emigration have a great deal of influence. Dramatic developments in one country may cause turbulence in other countries; strike waves often have a transnational character; new forms of campaigning are imitated elsewhere; national labour movements communicate with each other, learn from each other and create international organizations.'[22] From a global history perspective, it is important to note that while there is no doubt that Western ideas and practices profoundly shaped developments in the non-European world, there is some evidence, too, that developments in Africa, Asia and Latin America exerted some influence in the West. The concept of 'entangled' or 'shared histories' is useful here.[23] This concept implies, on the one hand, the idea that the creation and development of the modern world can be conceptualized as a 'shared history', in which different cultures and societies shared a number of central experiences and through their interactions and interdependence commonly created the modern world. On the other hand, the growing circulation of goods, people and ideas not only produced common ground, but at the same time created disassociations and differences, the need for particularities and the hypostatization of dichotomous structures. Moreover, the reference to 'interaction' must not divert attention away from inequality, power and violence. Relations between Europe and the non-European world were often hierarchical or even repressive. 'Europe was made by its imperial projects, as much as colonial encounters were shaped by conflicts within Europe itself.'[24] It is impossible to conceptualize European modernity and leave out colonialism and imperialism. Europe realized itself in the world by arguing and disputing with other societies beyond its own boundaries. European expansion changed the world, and it changed Europe. European expansion not only affected the conquered and colonized territories overseas, it also affected the metropolitan states. This also applies to issues of work and labour.

IV.

The links between Europe and the rest of the world in terms of work and labour was already apparent in the early modern period through slavery and the slave trade.[25] In the long history of relations between Europe and Africa, labour always played a central role. The creation of a world economy by European capitalism and the reordering of economic relations in nearly every part of the world were followed by a huge need for human labour, which could only be satisfied by various forms of force and coercion.[26] The slave trade completely transformed labour regimes in most parts of the 'New World', but also in Africa, where in many regions slaves now became not only a crucial commodity, but also the main resource for labour.[27] On the other hand, some authors have labelled the slave plantations in the Caribbean as 'factories in the field'. They argued that on these estates industrial production methods and capitalist labour relations anticipated and then influenced production methods in industrialized Europe.[28]

In South Asian history, Ravi Ahuja has argued that the development of labour relations and cultures in India and European labour history have been linked and influenced each other for at least two centuries.[29] This entanglement and mutual influence emerged against the backdrop of a general political and economic context that was characterized by the project of colonialism. This common historical context implied common development trends, but not necessarily the levelling of difference and inequality. Quite the contrary: the uneven development of capitalist labour markets not only preserved differences, but deepened and continuously recreated them. But what did these entanglements look like? South Asia became part of the social history of capitalism before the region became part of the British Empire.[30] During the seventeenth and eighteenth centuries various trades and the agrarian sector gradually commercialized, and labour relations were at least partly based on contracts. Thus, wage labour entered the scene already before the establishment of colonial rule. Moreover, there was no need to import European terms in order to express the phenomenon of wage labour. In the Tamil language, a wage labourer was (and is) called a *Kuliyal* or *Kuli*. Indian workers were also conscious about the difference between free and unfree labour: a *Kuli* was regarded as nobody's servant. On the other hand, this term had a negative connotation and was linked to subordination and lower caste background. During the nineteenth century the British used *Kuli* to describe an 'unfree' labourer, and from this colonial context, the term entered European languages. It was used by them, however, not as a synonym for wage labourer, but as a symbol for the unlimited subordination of the labour force.[31]

Another interesting aspect of entanglement, although still not systematically researched, is the way in which the practices embedded within colonial labour regulations in the British Empire affected the situation within England and the rest of the U.K. Acts of Parliament regulating masters and servants, the cornerstone of English employment law for more than four hundred years, gave largely unsupervised, low-ranking magistrates wide discretion over employment relations, including the power to whip, fine and imprison men, women, and children for breach of private contracts with their employers. The English model was adopted, modified and reinvented in more than a thousand colonial statutes and ordinances regulating the recruitment, retention and discipline of workers in shops, mines and factories; on farms; in forests; on plantations and at sea.[32] The claim that the British colonies were used as laboratories for institutional reforms still needs further evaluation. It is evident, however, that the 'globalization' of the English employment law did not lead to the levelling of difference. The most repressive and unequal elements of this law and related legal practices survived much longer in the colonies than in England. In the colonies, they were even tighter and more developed. The system of indentured labour is a case in point. Indenture (apprentice contract or contract of employment) stands for a specifically colonial legal form that was not restricted to South Asia. For the period of the contract (which the worker could not terminate) the plantation owner had nearly unlimited right of disposal of 'his' workers. This practice went beyond 'free wage labour' and was justified with the argument that indenture was 'a school for Indian workers' to teach them how to finish a job and keep to a contract.[33]

In the colonial world in general, 'work' was assigned the task of overcoming the supposed 'backwardness' of the colonized people. 'Work' promised to open the access to civilization, while colonial ideology claimed that it would take a long time to distil a sufficient amount of capitalist work ethics into Asians and especially Africans. The 'lazy native' soon became a classic stereotype of colonial literature.[34] This very persistent stereotype also reflects the fact that European rule in the colonies was far from being omnipotent. For instance, the characterization of African workers as 'lazy' implied in the end that colonizers had to accept the limits of colonial rule, that Africans were partially successful in struggles over work: even in the harsh system of South African gold mining. Even in this context, Africans shaped the limits of their own exploitation: they generated pressure for systems of day labour or workers' guilds in cities, or various forms of labour tenancy on farms, all of which allowed them to allocate family labour and shape work rhythms to a significant extent.[35] On the other hand, the way work was supposedly performed in Africa and other non-European regions was contrasted with the 'high quality' and 'standard' of 'national types of work'.[36]

Nevertheless, 'education for work' was a crucial element of colonial policies. Sebastian Conrad has argued that efforts to discipline the homeless in Germany in the late nineteenth and early twentieth centuries shaped the parallel project of 'civilizing' the Africans in the German colonies.[37] Moreover, he claims that the 'colonial mission' had effects on the debates and practices back in Germany. However, in the end there are very few clues that could justify the idea that there was a mutual linking-up of experiences, discourses and practices in 'East Africa and East Westphalia'. To be sure, the parallel structure of educational projects in Germany and East Africa are apparent, and the effects of the practice in the Reich upon practices in the colony of East Africa are quite evident. However, it is far from clear whether the radicalization of the labour discourse in Germany has anything to do with colonial experiences and practices.

Especially after the Second World War, labour movements in Europe clearly influenced their counterparts in the colonies. For instance, in francophone Africa, members of the (Communist) French trade union *Conféderation Génerale du Travail* (CGT) acted as advisors for West African politicians and trade unionists.[38] It should be noted, however, that African labour movements also influenced colonial policies in the metropole. The fact that African politicians successfully made claims on social welfare standards led colonial officials to rethink their ideas about reforming and 'modernizing' the colonies. The decision by Europeans to accept unionist demands that African labourers be treated on the same basis as their European counterparts can be seen as a mutual failure to comprehend African social reality. It was a very consequential failure, since the cost of providing European-scale wages and benefits under African economic conditions could not be borne by either colonial or postcolonial regimes. European governments were thus encouraged to withdraw from Africa, while their local successors co-opted some of the labour leadership, but rather quickly suppressed the unions as an autonomous force.[39]

Finally, a global perspective on labour helps to 'provincialize' European concepts that more or less exclusively focus on work as 'gainful employment' or even 'wage labour'. This becomes especially apparent when we look at aspects such as 'age' and 'youth'. While in Western societies, the model of a lifelong occupation is still prevalent, some African societies practise another system. In parts of Benin work is structured in accordance with age. People do wage labour for a time, then work as independent businessmen. What is striking about this model is the adaptation to age-specific physical and intellectual capacities.[40] Child labour is ideologically a highly charged issue and is usually seen by the Western world as a continuation of slavery. Studies on Africa differentiate this picture without neglecting the violence and exploitation that often goes with child labour.[41] Anthropological studies on nomadic societies in the Sahel region stress the existence of ideas about generation-specific work. At the age of ten or eleven, young Fulbe start working as herdsmen. This is part of a training project to educate them in the art of herding. In this context, work and play are closely linked.[42]

V.

A global perspective on the history of work and labour does not mean attempts to simply expand or complicate Western labour history, nor to direct the focus exclusively to the non-European world. Work and labour could provide tools for capturing more concretely the ways in which the West and the rest have influenced each other. One of the central merits of global labour history is to stress that free and unfree, paid and unpaid labour should be dealt with equally, and that there is no unilinear way from unfree labour to free labour. In fact, while it is easy to show how labour regimes and working practices in the Americas, Africa and Asia have been shaped by European influences, it is far more difficult to demonstrate how Europe has been influenced by its colonial experiences and practices. However, this article has tried to identify a number of paths that could be followed. In this context, future research on global labour issues should avoid the impulse 'to subordinate the rich histories of labour, generated on multiple scales of social space, to the trajectory of globalization'.[43] Frederick Cooper has warned us about the dangers of 'doing history backward' and to limit ourselves to identifying only the flows and nodal points of globalization.[44] It is no accident, for instance, that recent research very much focused on seamen and other mobile sectors of the African and Asian labour force, which contributed to the emergence of global commodity and labour markets.[45] However, we take the risk of neglecting large parts of the workforce – non-plantation rural labour, for instance – and tend to miss out on the contradictions and unevenness of processes of global incorporation. The 'globalization' of labour not only meant unbounded mobility, but spatial immobility as well.

Notes

1. See Dirk Hoerder, *Cultures in Contact. World Migration in the Second Millennium* (Durham: Duke University Press, 2002).
2. Sebastian Conrad, *Globalisierung und Nation im deutschen Kaiserreich* (Munich: Beck, 2006). Recent studies on the global history of commodities such as cotton also stress the link between globalization and the rise of the nation state. See, for instance, Sven Beckert, 'Emancipation and Empire: Reconstructing the Worldwide Web of Cotton Production in the Age of the American Civil War', in *American Historical Review* 109 (2004): 1405–38.
3. See Patrick Manning, *Navigating World History* (New York: Palgrave, 2003); Anthony G. Hopkins (ed.), *Globalization in World History* (Cambridge: Norton, 2003); Christopher A. Bayly, *The Birth of the Modern World, 1750–1914. Global Connections and Comparisons* (Oxford: Blackwell Publishing, 2004); Sebastian Conrad and Shalini Randeria (eds), *Jenseits des Eurozentrismus. Postkoloniale Perspektiven in den Geschichts- und Kulturwissenschaften* (Frankfurt: Campus, 2002); Sebastian Conrad, Andreas Eckert and Ulrike Freitag (eds), *Globalgeschichte. Theorien, Ansätze, Themen* (Frankfurt: Campus, 2007).
4. My thinking about this field has been deeply influenced by the many contributions to a series of conferences on 'Labour in a Global Perspective', which I co-organized with Jürgen Kocka at the Social Science Research Centre Berlin (WZB) in 2005 and 2006. As general introductions, see Marcel van der Linden, 'Global Labor History and "The Modern World System". Thoughts at the Twenty-Fifth Anniversary of the Fernand Braudel Center', in *International Review of Social History* 46 (2001): 423–459; Jan Lucassen (ed.), *Global Labour History* (Berne: Lang, 2005); and Marcel van der Linden, *Workers of the World. Essays toward a Global Labor History* (Leiden: Brill, 2008).
5. These are central aspects of global history, at least according to Bruce Mazlish, 'Comparing Global History to World History, *Journal for Interdisciplinary History* 28 (1998): 385–95.

6. Jürgen Kocka and Claus Offe, 'Einleitung', in Kocka and Offe (eds), *Geschichte und Zukunft der Arbeit* (Frankfurt: Campus, 2000), pp. 9–15.
7. See, for instance, Bénédicte Zimmermann, Claude Didry and Peter Wagner (eds), *Le travail et la nation. Histoire croisée de la France et de l'Allemagne* (Paris: Editions de la Maison des Sciences de l'Homme, 1999); Jürgen Kocka's contribution to this volume, above pp. 1–16.
8. See Christian Topalov, *Naissance du chômeur* (Paris: Belin, 1984); Bénédicte Zimmermann, *La constitution du chômage en Allemagne. Entre professions et territoires* (Paris: Maison des Sciences de l'Homme, 2000); Jürgen Kocka, 'Arbeit früher, heute, morgen. Zur Neuartigkeit der Gegenwart', in Kocka and Offe (eds), *Geschichte und Zukunft der Arbeit*, pp. 476–92, 480.
9. See R.J. Steinfield, *The Invention of Free Labor. The Employment Relation in English and American Law and Culture* (Chapel Hill: University of North Carolina Press, 1991); Robert Castel, *Die Metamorphosen der sozialen Frage. Eine Chronik der Lohnarbeit* (Konstanz: UVK, 2000; French edn, 1995).
10. See Reinhart Kößler and Hans Wienold, 'Arbeit und Vergesellschaftung. Eine aktuelle Erinnerung an die klassische Gesellschaftstheorie', in *Peripherie* 85/86 (2002): 162–83; see Gerd Spittler's contribution to this volume.
11. This diagnosis, framed among others by Hannah Arendt, *The Human Condition* (Chicago: Chicago University Press, 1958; German edn, *Vita Activa*, Munich: Piper, 1981) became very popular during the 1980s. See for instance Ralf Dahrendorf, 'Wenn der Arbeitsgesellschaft die Arbeit ausgeht', in Joachim Matthes (ed.), *Krise der Arbeitsgesellschaft? Verhandlungen des 21. Soziologentages in Bamberg 1982* (Frankfurt: Campus, 1983); André Gorz, *Kritik der ökonomischen Vernunft. Sinnfragen am Ende der Arbeitsgesellschaft* (Hamburg: Rotbuch Verlag, 1989); also Jürgen Habermas, *Die neue Unübersichtlichkeit* (Frankfurt: Suhrkamp, 1985).
12. Klaus Tenfelde (ed.), *Arbeiter und Arbeiterbewegung im Vergleich* (Munich: Oldenbourg, 1986).
13. Jürgen Kocka, 'Arbeit als Problem der europäischen Geschichte', in Manfred Bierwisch (ed.), *Die Rolle der Arbeit in verschiedenen Epochen und Kulturen* (Berlin: Akademie Verlag, 2003), p. 71; also see above pp. 1–16.
14. Marcel van der Linden, *Transnational Labour History. Explorations* (Aldershot: Ashgate, 2003), p. 2.
15. Ibid. According to William Sewell, Jr, this 'crisis' is due to the fact that labour history is too wedded in the meta-narrative of proletarianization. This thesis brings together, as Sewell points out, a number of processes and, while acknowledging variation, treats the overall trend as universal: cultivators and artisans are deprived of access to means of production; they move to cities or are forced into insecure wage labour jobs on farms; their skills are devalued, and even tighter forms of managerial control are devised. Meanwhile, workers acquire a sense of their collective identity as the sellers of labour power; their tradition of artisanal autonomy or republican assertiveness are re-channelled into class identity; they build organizations; they go on strike; and they collectively challenge capital. Sewell criticizes that this proletarianization thesis pays 'insufficient attention to the profoundly uneven and contradictory character of changes in productive relations, not to mention the role of discourse and politics in labour history'. See William Sewell, Jr, 'Toward a Post-materialist Rhetoric for Labor History', in Lenard A. Berlanstein (ed.), *Rethinking Labor History: Essays in Discourse and Class Analysis* (Urbana: University of Illinois Press, 1993), pp. 15–38 (quote: p. 18). On this, see also Frederick Cooper,

Decolonization and African Society. The labor question in French and British Africa (Cambridge: Cambridge University Press, 1996), pp. 12f. On the 'crisis' of labour history see also, among many others, Marcel van der Linden (ed.), *The End of Labor History* (Cambridge: Cambridge University Press, 1993); Thomas Welskopp, 'Von der verhinderten Heldengeschichte des Proletariats zur vergleichenden Sozialgeschichte der Arbeit – Perspektiven der Arbeitergeschichtsschreibung in den 1990er Jahren', in *1999. Zeitschrift für Sozialgeschichte des 19. und 20. Jahrhunderts* 8/3(1994): 34–53; John Belchem, 'Reconstructing Labour History', in *Labour History Review* 62 (1997): 147–52.

16. Gerd Spittler is the exception confirming this rule. See his *Hirtenarbeit. Die Welt der Kamelhirten und Ziegenhirtinnen von Timia* (Cologne: Köppe, 1998). See also Spittler, 'Arbeit. Transformation von Objekten oder Interaktion mit Subjekten', in *Peripherie* 85/86 (2002): 9–31. With a focus on wage labour, see the review article by Sutti Ortiz, 'Laboring in the Factories and in the Fields', in *Annual Review of Anthropology* 31 (2002): 395–417.
17. See, for instance, Günther Schmid, *Wege in eine Vollbeschäftigung. Übergangsarbeitsmärkte und aktivierende Arbeitsmarktpolitik* (Frankfurt: Campus, 2002).
18. See Alain Supiot, *Beyond Employment. Report for the European Commission* (Oxford: Oxford University Press, 2001).
19. See the comprehensive overviews by, Marcel van der Linden, 'Die Geschichte der Arbeiterinnen und Arbeiter in der Globalisierung', in *Sozial.Geschichte* 18/1 (2003): 10–40; idem, 'Vorläufiges zur transkontinentalen Arbeitergeschichte', in *Geschichte und Gesellschaft* 28/2 (2002): 291–304; idem, 'Transnationale Arbeitergeschichte', in Gunilla Budde, Sebastian Conrad and Oliver Janz (eds), *Transnationale Geschichte. Themen, Tendenzen und Theorien* (Göttingen: Vandenhoeck and Ruprecht, 2006), pp. 265–74. Over the last fifteen years many important monographs on South Asian labour history have appeared, among them Samita Sen, *Women and Labour in Late Colonial India. The Bengal Jute Industry* (Cambridge: Cambridge University Press, 1999); Rajnarayan Chandavarkar, *The Origins of Industrial Capitalism in India: Business Strategies and the Working Classes in Bombay, 1900–1940* (Cambridge: Cambridge University Press, 1994); Chitra Joshi, *Lost Worlds of Labour. Culture and Community in North India* (Delhi: Permanent Black, 2002); for an assessment of these and other studies, see Ravi Ahuja, 'Erkenntnisdruck und Denkbarrieren. Anmerkungen zur indischen Arbeiterhistoriographie', in Shalini Randeria, Martin Fuchs and Antje Linkenbach (eds), *Konfigurationen der Moderne: Diskurse zu Indien* (Baden-Baden: Nomos, 2004), pp. 349–66.
20. John D. French, 'The Latin American Labor Studies Boom', in *International Review of Social History* 45 (2000): 279–308; John Womack, Jr, 'Doing Labor History. Feeling, Work, Material Power', in *Journal of the Historical Society* 5/3 (2005): 255–96.
21. See for instance Bill Freund, *The Making of Contemporary Africa. The Development of African Society since 1800* (London: Macmillan Press, 1998). For historiographical overviews, see Bill Freund, 'Labor and Labor History in Africa. A Review of the Literature', in *African Studies Review* 27 (1984): 1–58; Andreas Eckert, 'Geschichte der Arbeit und Arbeitergeschichte in Afrika', in *Archiv für Sozialgeschichte* 39 (1999): 502–530. Among the numerous more recent monographs focusing on labour are Lisa A. Lindsay, *Working with Gender. Wage Labor and Social Change in Southwestern Nigeria* (Portsmouth, NH: Heinemann, 2003); Isaïe Dougnon, *Travail de Blanc, travail de Noir. La migration des paysans dogon vers l'Office du Niger et du Ghana (1910–1980)* (Paris/Amsterdam: Karthala, 2007).
22. Van der Linden, *Transnational Labour History*, p. 3.

23. See Shalini Randeria, 'Geteilte Geschichte und verwobene Moderne', in Jörn Rüsen (ed.), *Zukunftsentwürfe. Ideen für eine Kultur der Veränderung* (Frankfurt: Campus, 1999), pp. 87–96.
24. Ann Laura Stoler and Frederick Cooper, 'Between Metropole and Colony. Rethinking a Research Agenda', in idem (eds), *Tensions of Empire. Colonial Cultures in a Bourgeois World* (Berkeley: University of Chicago Press, 1997), p. 1.
25. See David Eltis (ed.), *Coerced and Free Migrations. Global Perspectives* (Stanford: Stanford University Press, 2002).
26. See, among many others, Paul E. Lovejoy and Nicolas Rogers (eds), *Unfree Labour in the Development of the Atlantic World* (London: Routledge, 1994).
27. Paul E. Lovejoy, *Transformations in Slavery. A History of Slavery in Africa* (2nd edn, Cambridge: Cambridge University Press, 2000).
28. Sidney W. Mintz, *Sweetness and Power. The Place of Sugar in Modern History* (New York: Penguin, 1985); Albert Wirz, *Sklaverei und kapitalistisches Weltsystem* (Frankfurt: Suhrkamp, 1984).
29. Ravi Ahuja, 'Geschichte der Arbeit jenseits des kulturalistischen Paradigmas. Vier Anregungen aus der Südasienforschung', in *Geschichte und Zukunft der Arbeit*, pp. 121–34; idem, 'Die Lenksamkeit des "Lacars". Regulierungsszenarien eines transnationalen Arbeitsmarktes in der ersten Hälfte des zwanzigsten Jahrhunderts', in *Geschichte und Gesellschaft* 31/3 (2005): 323–53.
30. See David Washbrook, 'Progress and Problems. South Asian Economic and Social History, c.1720–1860', *Modern Asian Studies* 22 (1988): 72; Ahuja, 'Geschichte der Arbeit', p. 124. For a case study, see Ahuja, *Die Erzeugung kolonialer Staatlichkeit und das Problem der Arbeit. Eine Studie zur Sozialgeschichte der Stadt Madras und ihres Hinterlandes zwischen 1750 und 1800* (Stuttgart: Franz Steiner Verlag, 1999); idem, 'Labour Relations in an Early Colonial Context: Madras, 1750–1800', in *Modern Asian Studies* 32/4 (2002): 793–826.
31. Ahuja, 'Geschichte der Arbeit', p. 125.
32. Douglas Hay and Paul Cravan (eds), *Masters, Servants, and Magistrates in Britain and the Empire, 1582–1955* (Chapel Hill: University of North Carolina Press, 2004).
33. See Ravi Ahuja, 'Arbeit und Kolonialherrschaft im neuzeitlichen Südasien. Eine Einführung', in Dietmar Rothermund and Karin Preisendanz (eds), *Südasien in der Neuzeit* (Vienna: Promedia, 2003), p. 200; Ranajit Das Gupta, *Labour and Working Class in Eastern India. Studies in Colonial History* (Calcutta: K.P. Bagchi, 1994); Marina Carter, *Voices from Indenture. Experiences of Indian Migrants in the British Empire* (London/New York: Leicester University Press, 1996).
34. Syed H. Alatas, *The Myth of the Lazy Native* (London: Routledge, 1977).
35. Frederick Cooper, 'Africa in a Capitalist World', in Darlene Clark Hine and Jacqueline McLeod (eds), *Crossing Boundaries. Comparative History of Black People in the Diaspora* (Bloomington: University of Chicago Press, 1999), p. 401.
36. Sebastian Conrad, 'Circulation, "National Work" and Identity Debates about the Mobility of Work in Germany and Japan, 1890–1914', in Wolf Lepenies (ed), *Entangled Histories and Negotiated Universals. Centers and Peripheries in a Changing World* (Frankfurt: Campus, 2003), pp. 260–80.
37. Sebastian Conrad, '"Eingeborenenpolitik" in Kolonie und Metropole. "Erziehung zur Arbeit" in Ostafrika und Ostwestfalen", in Sebastian Conrad and Jürgen Osterhammel (eds), *Das Kaiserreich transnational. Deutschland in der Welt 1871–1914* (Göttingen: Vandenhoeck and Ruprecht, 2004), pp. 107–28; Conrad, *Globalisierung*, Chapter 2.

38. Gaston Donnat, *Afin que nul n'oublie. L'itinéraire d'un anti-colonialiste. Algérie – Cameroun – Afrique* (Paris: L'Harmattan, 1986); Elisabeth Schmidt, *Cold War and Decolonization in Guinea, 1946–1958* (Athens, OH: Ohio University Press, 2007).
39. See Cooper, *Decolonization.*
40. Georg Elwert, 'Jede Arbeit hat ihr Alter. Arbeit in einer afrikanischen Gesellschaft', in *Geschichte und Zukunft der Arbeit*, pp. 175–93.
41. For a recent excellent case study see Beverly C. Grier, *Invisable Hands. Child Labor and the State in Colonial Zimbabwe* (Portsmouth,NH: Heinemann, 2006). A brief overview is provided by Andreas Eckert, 'Familie, Sklaverei, Lohnarbeit: Kinder und Arbeit in Afrika im 19. und 20. Jahrhundert', in *Sozialwissenschaftliche Informationen* 28/2 (1999): 131–36.
42. See the articles in Kurt Beck and Gerd Spittler (eds), *Arbeit in Afrika* (Hamburg: Lit. Hirschberg, 1996).
43. Ravi Ahuja, 'Scenarios of Labour Regulation and Transterritorial History. Some Preliminary Observations', Opening Lecture to the Conference *Rethinking Labour History from a Global Perspective*, 12 October 2006.
44. Frederick Cooper, *Colonialism in Question. Theory, Knowledge, History* (Berkeley: University of California Press, 2005), Chapter 4.
45. See, for instance, Golan Balanchandran, 'Searching for the Sardar: The State, Pre-capitalist Institutions and Human Agency in the Maritime Labour Market, Calcutta, 1880–1935', in Burton Stein and Sanjay Subrahmanyam (eds), *Institutions and Economic Change in South Asia* (Dehli: Oxford University Press, 1999), pp. 206–36; Diana Frost, *Work and Community among West African Migrant Workers since the Nineteenth Century* (Liverpool: Liverpool University Press, 1999).

Bibliography

Abu-Lughod, L. 1986. *Veiled Sentiments: Honor and Poetry in a Bedouin Society.* Berkeley: University of California Press.

Ahuja, R. 1999. *Die Erzeugung kolonialer Staatlichkeit und das Problem der Arbeit. Eine Studie zur Sozialgeschichte der Stadt Madras und ihres Hinterlandes zwischen 1750 und 1800.* Stuttgart: Franz Steiner Verlag.

———, 2000. 'Geschichte der Arbeit jenseits des kulturalistischen Paradigmas. Vier Anregungen aus der Südasienforschung', in J. Kocka and C. Offe (eds), *Geschichte und Zukunft der Arbeit.* Frankfurt am Main: Campus, pp. 121–34.

———, 2002. 'Labour Relations in an Early Colonial Context: Madras, 1750–1800', in *Modern Asian Studies* 32/4: 793–826.

———, 2003. 'Arbeit und Kolonialherrschaft im neuzeitlichen Südasien. Eine Einführung', in D. Rothermund and K. Preisendanz (eds), *Südasien in der Neuzeit.* Vienna: Promedia, pp. 194–212.

———, 2004. 'Erkenntnisdruck und Denkbarrieren. Anmerkungen zur indischen Arbeiterhistoriographie', in S. Randeria et al. (eds). *Konfigurationen der Moderne: Diskurse zu Indien.* Baden-Baden: Nomos, pp. 349–66.

———, 2005. 'Die Lenksamkeit des "Lakars". Regulierungsszenarien eines transnationalen Arbeitsmarktes in der ersten Hälfte des zwanzigsten Jahrhunderts', in *Geschichte und Gesellschaft* 31/3: 323–53.

———, 2006, 'Scenarios of Labour Regulation and Transterritorial History. Some Preliminary Observations', Opening Lecture to the Conference *Rethinking Labour History from a Global Perspective.* 12 October 2006.

Alatas, S.H. 1977. *The Myth of the Lazy Native.* London: Routledge.

Alston, J.P. 1986. *The American Samurai. Blending American and Japanese Practices.* New York: de Gruyter.

'An die feiernden Buchdrucker' ('For the striking printers'), in *Das Volk* 30 (19 August 1848): 119f.

Applebaum, H. 1992. *The Concept of Work. Ancient, Medieval, and Modern.* Albany, NY: State University of New York Press.

Arendt, H. 1958. *The Human Condition.* Chicago: University of Chicago Press. German edn 1981. *Vita Activa.* Munich: Piper.

Arnold-Kanamori, H. 1998. *Der Menschentyp als Produktivkraft. Max-Weber-Studien des japanischen Wirtschaftshistorikers Ôtsuka Hisao (1907–1996).* Hamburg: Kovac.

Arrow, K. 1974. *The Limits of Organization.* New York: W.W. Norton and Company.

Aßländer, M. 2005. *Von der vita activa zur industriellen Wertschöpfung. Eine Sozial- und Wirtschaftsgeschichte menschlicher Arbeit.* Marburg: Metropolis.

Avdela, E. 1999. 'Work, Gender and History in the 1990s and Beyond', in *Gender and History,* 11(3): 528–41.

Bade, K. 2000. *Europa in Bewegung. Migration vom späten 18. Jahrhundert bis zur Gegenwart.* Munich: Beck.

Baier, A. 1994. *Moral Prejudices: Essays on Ethics.* Cambridge, MA: Harvard University Press.

Balanchandran, G. 1999. 'Searching for the Sardar: The State, Pre-capitalist Institutions and Human Agency in the Maritime Labour Market, Calcutta, 1880–1935' in B. Stein and S. Subrahmanyam (eds), *Institutions and Economic Change in South Asia.* Dehli: Oxford University Press, pp. 206–36.

Baron, A. 1991. 'Gender and Labor History. Learning from the Past, Looking to the Future', in A. Baron (ed.), *Work Engendered: Toward a New History of American Labor.* Ithaca: Cornell University Press, pp. 1–46.

———, (ed.). 1991. *Work Engendered: Toward a New History of American Labor.* Ithaca and London: Cornell University Press.

Bartov, O. 1985. *The Eastern Front 1941–1945: German Troops and the Barbarisation of Warfare.* Basingstoke: Macmillan.

Baudry, B. 1998. 'Trust in Inter-Firm Relations', in N. Lazaric and E. Lorenz (eds), *Trust and Economic Learning.* Cheltenham: Edward Elgar, pp. 64–77.

Bayly, Ch.A. 2004. *The Birth of the Modern World, 1750–1914. Global Connections and Comparisons.* Oxford: Blackwell Publishing.

Bebel, A. 1979. *Die Frau und der Sozialismus.* Berlin: Dietz.

———, 1986. *Aus meinem Leben,* Berlin and Bonn: J.H.W. Dietz Nachf.

Beck, K. and G. Spittler (eds). 1996. *Arbeit in Afrika.* Hamburg: Lit. Hirschberg.

Beck, U. (ed.). 1999. *Schöne neue Arbeitswelt.* Frankfurt: Suhrkamp.

Beckert, S. 2004. 'Emancipation and Empire: Reconstructing the Worldwide Web of Cotton Production in the Age of the American Civil War', in *American Historical Review* 109: 1405–38.

Beckmann, G. M. 1969. *Genji Okubo. The Japanese Communist Party 1922–1945.* Stanford: Stanford University Press.

Belchem, J. 1997. 'Reconstructing Labour History', in *Labour History Review* 62: 147–152.

Bellah, R. 1985. *Tokugawa Religion. The Cultural Roots of Modern Japan.* New York: Free Press.

Bellamy, E. 1917. *Looking Backward: 2000 to 1887.* New York: Random House.

Berg, M. 1985. *The Age of Manufactures, 1700–1820.* London: Fontana Press.

———, 1994. *The Age of Manufactures, 1700–1820,* 2nd edn. London: Routledge.

Berghoff, H. 2004. 'Die Zähmung des entfesselten Prometheus? Die Generierung von Vertrauenskapital und die Konstruktion des Marktes im Industrialisierungs- und Globalisierungsprozeß', in H. Berghoff and J. Vogel (eds), *Wirtschaftsgeschichte als Kulturgeschichte.* Frankfurt: Campus, pp. 143–68.

———, 2004. 'Wozu Unternehmensgeschichte? Erkenntnisinteressen, Forschungsansätze und Perspektiven des Faches', in *Zeitschrift für Unternehmensgeschichte* 49: 131–48.

'Beschlüsse der ersten National-Buchdrucker-Versammlung', in D. Dowe and T. Offermann (eds), *Deutsche Handwerker- und Arbeiterkongresse, 1848–1852.* Berlin: Dietz, p. 423.

Biener, C. 1930. 'Entstehungsgeschichte des Weißkunigs', in *Mitteilungen des Österreichischen Instituts für Geschichtsforschung* 44: 83–102.

Biernacki, R. 1995. *The Fabrication of Labor. Germany and Britain 1690–1914.* Berkeley: University of California Press.

Bierwisch, M. 2003. 'Arbeit in verschiedenen Epochen und Kulturen. Einleitende Bemerkungen', in M. Bierwisch (ed.), *Die Rolle der Arbeit in verschiedenen Epochen und Kulturen.* Berlin: Akademie Verlag, pp. 7–18.

———, (ed.). 2003. *Die Rolle der Arbeit in verschiedenen Epochen und Kulturen.* Berlin: Akademie Verlag.

Blackburn, R. 1997. *The Making of New World Slavery: From the Baroque to the Modern, 1492–1800.* London: Verso.

Blumenberg, W. 1993. *Das Leben geht weiter. Der letzte Film des Dritten Reiches.* Berlin: Rowohlt.

Bock, G. 1983. 'Historische Frauenforschung. Fragestellungen und Perspektiven', in K. Hausen (ed.), *Frauen suchen ihre Geschichte. Historische Studien zum 19. und 20. Jahrhundert.* Munich: C.H. Beck, pp. 22–60.

———, 1988. 'Geschichte, Frauengeschichte, Geschlechtergeschichte', in *Geschichte und Gesellschaft* 14: 364–91.

———, 1989. 'Women's History and Gender History: Aspects of an International Debate', in *Gender and History* 1: 7–30.

———, 1991. 'Antinatalism, Maternity and Paternity in National Socialist Racism', in G. Bock and P. Thane (eds), *Maternity and Gender Policies. Women and the Rise of the European Welfare States 1880s–1950s.* London: Routledge, pp. 233–55.

———, 1991. 'Challenging Dichotomies. Perspectives on Women's History', in K. Offen et al. (eds), *Writing Women's History. International Perspectives.* Indianapolis: Indiana University Press, pp. 1–23.

———, 1993. 'Gleichheit und Differenz in der nationalsozialistischen Rassenpolitik', in *Geschichte und Gesellschaft* 19: 277–310.

Bock, G. and P. Thane (eds). 1991. *Maternity and Gender Policies. Women and the Rise of the European Welfare States 1880s–1950s.* London: Routledge.

Böll, H. 2001. *Briefe aus dem Krieg,* ed. Jochen Schubert. Cologne: Kiepenheuer and Witsch.

Boris, E. and A. Janssens. (eds). 1999. 'Complicating Categories: Gender, Class, Race and Ethnicity', in *International Review of Social History:* Supplement 7. Cambridge, Cambridge University Press.

Born, S. 1898. *Erinnerungen eines Achtundvierzigers.* 3rd edn Leipzig: Vorwärts.

Bourke, J. 1998. *An Intimate History of Killing: Face-to-face Killing in Twentieth-Century Wars.* London: Basic Books.

Bracke, W. 1876, *Nieder mit den Sozialdemokraten!* Braunschweig: Bracke.

Brant, S. 1986, *Narrenschiff,* Manfred Lemmer, ed. Tübingen: Max Niemeyer Verlag.

Bräuer, H. 1997. *Der Leipziger Rat und die Bettler. Quellen und Analysen zu Bettlern und Bettelwesen bis in das 18. Jahrhundert.* Leipzig: Leipziger Universitätsverlag.

Bräuer, H. and E. Schlenkrich. 2002. *Armut und Armutsbekämpfung. Schriftliche und bildliche Quellen bis um 1800 aus Chemnitz, Dresden, Freiberg, Leipzig und Zwickau. Ein sachthematisches Inventar.* Leipzig: Leipziger Universitätsverlag.

Browning, C. 1992. *Ordinary Men: Reserve Police Battalion 101 and the Final Solution in Poland.* New York: Harper Perennial.

Bruch, R. vom. 1985. 'Bürgerliche Sozialreform im deutschen Kaiserreich', in R. vom ruch (ed.), *Bürgerliche Sozialreform in Deutschland vom Vormärz bis zur Ära Adenauer.* Munich: Beck, pp. 61–179.

Brüggemeier, F.-J. 1983. *Leben vor Ort: Ruhrbergleute und Ruhrbergbau 1889–1919.* Munich: Beck.

'Buchdruckerversammlung in Heidelberg, 23.4.1848', in D. Dowe and T. Offermann (eds), *Deutsche Handwerker- und Arbeiterkongresse,* Berlin: Dietz, p. 393.

Bücher, K. 1893. *Die Entstehung der Volkswirtschaft.* Tübingen: Laupp.

———, 1896. *Arbeit und Rhythmus.* Leipzig: Reinicke.

———, 1901. *Industrial Evolution.* New York: H. Holt and Company.

Buchner, R. et al. (eds). 1956. *Kaiser Maximilian I. Weisskunig.* 2 vols. Stuttgart: W. Kohlhammer.

Budde, G. (ed.). 1997. *Frauen arbeiten. Weibliche Erwerbstätigkeit in Ost- und Westdeutschland nach 1945.* Göttingen: Vandenhoeck and Ruprecht.

Burawoy, M. 1979. *Manufacturing Consent: Changes in the Labor Process under Monopoly Capitalism.* Chicago: Chicago University Press.

Burke, P. 1995. 'The Invention of Leisure in Early Modern Europe', in *Past and Present,* 146: 136–50.

Burnett, J. 1994. *Idle Hands. The Experience of Unemployment 1790–1990.* London: Routledge.

Campbell, J. 1989. *Joy in Work, German Work. The National Debate 1800–1945.* Princeton: Princeton University Press.

Canning, K. 1992. 'Gender and the Politics of Class Formation. Rethinking German Labor History', in *American Historical Review* 97: 736–68.

———, 1996. *Languages of Labor and Gender. Female Factory Work in Germany, 1850–1914.* Ithaca and London: Cornell University Press.

———, 2006. *Gender History in Practice: Historical Perspective on Bodies, Class, and Citizenship.* Ithaca and London: Cornell University Press.

Carter, M. 1996. *Voices from Indenture. Experiendes of Indian Migrants in the British Empire.* London and New York: Leicester University Press.

Castel, R. 2000. *Die Metamorphosen der sozialen Frage. Eine Chronik der Lohnarbeit.* Konstanz: UVK; French edn 1995.

Catalog 1969. Ausstellung 'Maximilian I., Innsbruck: Tyrolia.

Chandavarkar, R. 1994. *The Orignis of Industrial Capitalism in India: Business Strategies and the Working Classes in Bombay, 1900–1940.* Cambridge: Cambridge University Press.

Chuhei, S. 1994. *Origins of Economic Thought in Modern Japan.* London: Routledge.

Churchill, W. 1974. *The River War: An Historical Account of the Reconquest of the Soudan,* vol. 3 in *The Collected Works of Sir Winston Churchill,* 34 vols. London: Longmans, Green and Co.

———, 1992. *War Correspondent, 1895–1900,* Frederick Woods, ed. London: Leo Cooper.

Clasen, C.P. 1981. *Die Augsburger Weber: Leistungen und Krisen des Textilgewerbes um 1600.* Augsburg: Jan Thorbecke.

Clausen, L. 1988. *Produktive Arbeit – destruktive Arbeit. Soziologische Grundlagen.* Berlin: de Gruyter.

Coleman, J. 1982. 'Systems of Trust', in *Angewandte Sozialforschung* 10: 277–99.

———, 1990. *Foundations of Social Theory.* Cambridge: Harvard University Press.

Conrad, S. 2003. 'The Opened and the Closed Country. Conflicting Views of Japan's Position in the World', in B. Stuchtey and E. Fuchs (eds), *Writing World History 1800–2000.* Oxford: Oxford University Press, pp. 327–51.

———, 2003. 'Circulation, "National Work" and Identity Debates about the Mobility of Work in Germany and Japan, 1890–1914', in W. Lepenies (ed.), *Entangled Histories and Negotiated Universals. Centers and Peripheries in a Changing World.* Frankfurt am Main: Campus, pp. 260–80.

———, 2004. '"Eingeborenenpolitik" in Kolonie und Metropole. "Erziehung zur Arbeit" in Ostafrika und Ostwestfalen', in S. Conrad and J. Osterhammel (eds), *Das Kaiserreich transnational. Deutschland in der Welt 1871–1914.* Göttingen: Vandenhoeck and Ruprecht, pp. 107–128

———, 2006. *Globalisierung und Nation im Deutschen Kaiserreich.* Munich: Beck.

Conrad, S. and S. Randeria. 2002. 'Geteilte Geschichten. Europa in einer postkolonialen Welt', in idem (eds), *Jenseits des Eurozentrismus. Postkoloniale Perspektiven in den Geschichts- und Kulturwissenschaften.* Frankfurt am Main: Campus, pp. 9–49.

Conrad, S., A. Eckert and U. Freitag (eds). 2007. *Globalgeschichte. Theorien, Ansätze, Themen.* Frankfurt am Main: Campus.

Conze, W. 1972. 'Arbeit', in O. Brunner et al. (eds), *Geschichtliche Grundbegriffe. Historisches Lexikon zur politisch-sozialen Sprache in Deutschland,* vol. 1. Stuttgart: Klett, pp. 154–215.

Cooper, F. 1996. *Decolonization and African Society. The labor question in French and British Africa.* Cambridge: Cambridge University Press.

———, 1999. 'Africa in a Capitalist World', in D. Clark Hine and J. McLeod (eds), *Crossing Boundaries. Comparative History of Black Peaple in the Diaspora.* Bloomington: University of Chicago Press, pp. 391–418.

———, 2005. *Colonialism in Question. Theory, Knowledge, History.* Berkeley: University of California Press.

Dahlmann, D. and G. Hirschfeld (eds). 1999, *Lager, Zwangsarbeit, Vertreibung und Deportation. Dimensionen der Massenverbrechen in der Sowjetunion und in Deutschland 1933–1945.* Essen: Klartext-Verlag.

Dahrendorf, R. 1983. 'Wenn der Arbeitsgesellschaft die Arbeit ausgeht', in J. Matthes (ed.), *Krise der Arbeitsgesellschaft? Verhandlungen des 21. Soziologentages in Bamberg 1982.* Frankfurt am Main: Campus.

Daniel, U. 1995, *Klassengesellschaft in der Kriegsgesellschaft.* Göttingen: Vandenhoeck and Ruprecht.

Danker, U. et al. (eds). 2001. *'Ausländereinsatz in der Nordmark'. Zwangsarbeitende in Schleswig-Holstein 1939–1945.* Bielefeld: Verlag für Regionalgeschichte.

Darnton, R. 1984. 'Workers Revolt: The Great Cat Massacre of the Rue Saint-Severin', in R. Darnton (ed.), *The Great Cat Massacre and Other Episodes in French Cultural History.* London: Vintage, pp. 75–104. German edn 1989. *Das große Katzenmassaker. Streifzüge durch die französische Kultur vor der Revolution.* Munich: Hanser.

Das Gupta, R. 1994. *Labour and Working Class in Eastern India. Studies in Colonial History.* Calcutta: K.P. Bagchi.

Davidoff, L. 1974. 'Mastered for Life. Servant and Wife in Victorian and Edwardian England', in L. Davidoff, 1995, *Worlds Between: Historical Perspectives on Gender and Class.* London: Polity, pp. 18–40.

Davidoff, L. and C. Hall. 1987. *Family Fortunes: Men and Women of the English Middle Class, 1780–1850.* London: Routledge.

Davis, J.M. 2006. *In Hostile Skies: An American B-24 Pilot in WW II,* D.L. Snead (ed.), Denton: Texas A and M University Press.

Deist, W. 1992. 'Verdeckter Militärstreik im Kriegsjahr 1918?', in W. Wette (ed.), *Der Krieg des kleinen Mannes. Eine Militärgeschichte von unten.* Munich and Zurich: Piper, pp. 146–67.

Deutschmann, C. 1987. 'Der "Betriebsclan". Der japanische Organisationstypus als Herausforderung an die soziologische Modernisierungstheorie', in *Soziale Welt* 39: 133–48.

Diderot, D. et al. (eds). 1765. *Encyclopéédie ou dictionnaire raisonné des sciences, des arts et des métiers,* vol. 16. Neufchatel: Samuel Fauche.

Dirlik, A. 2002. 'Modernity as History. Post-revolutionary China, Globalization and the Question of Modernity', in *Social History* 27: 16–39.

Disselkamp, A. 1994. *L'Ethique protestante de Max Weber.* Paris: Presses universitaires de France.

Distelrath, G. 1996. *Die japanische Produktionsweise. Zur wissenschaftlichen Genese einer stereotypen Sicht der japanischen Wirtschaft.* Munich: Iudicium.

Donnat, G. 1986. *Afin que nul n'oublie. L'itinéraire d'un anti-colonialiste. Algérie – Cameroun – Afrique.* Paris: L'Harmattan.

Dore, R. 1996. 'Confucianism, Economic Growth and Social Development', in J. Kreiner (ed.), *The Impact of Traditional Thought on Present-Day Japan,* Munich: Iudicium, pp. 17–30.

Dougnon, I. 2007. *Travail de Blanc, traveil de Noir. La migration des paysans dogon vers l'Office du Niger et du Ghana (1910–1980).* Paris and Amsterdem: Karthala.

Dowe, D. and T. Offermann (eds). 1983. 'Beschlüsse der ersten National-Buchdrucker-Versammlung zu Mainz am 11., 12., 13. und 14. Juni 1848', in *Deutsche Handwerker- und Arbeiterkongresse 1848–1852. Protokolle und Materialien.* Berlin and Bonn: J.H.W. Dietz Nachf.

Drescher, S. 1997. 'Capitalism and Slavery after Fifty Years', in *Slavery and Abolition* 18: 212–27.

Duara, P. 1995. *Rescuing History from the Nation: Questioning Narratives of Modern China.* Chicago: University of Chicago Press.

Duby, G. 1966. *Die Zeit der Kathedralen.* Frankfurt: Suhrkamp.

———, 1981. *Die drei Ordnungen. Das Weltbild des Feudalismus.* Frankfurt: Suhrkamp.

Dülmen, R. van. 1988. 'Prostestantismus und Kapitalismus. Max Webers These im Licht der neueren Sozialgeschichte', in C. Gneuss and J. Kocka (eds), *Max Weber. Ein Symposium.* Munich: Deutscher Taschenbuch Verlag, pp. 88–101.

———, 2000. '"Arbeit" in der frühneuzeitlichen Gesellschaft', in J. Kocka and C. Offe (eds), *Geschichte und Zukunft der Arbeit.* Frankfurt am Main: Campus, pp. 80–87.

Eckert, A. 1999. 'Familie, Sklaverei, Lohnarbeit: Kinder und Arbeit in Afrika im 19. und 20. Jahrhundert', in *Sozialwissenschaftliche Informationen* 28/2: 131–36.

———, 1999. 'Geschichte der Arbeit und Arbeitergeschichte in Afrika', in *Archiv für Sozialgeschichte* 39: 502–530.

Ehmer, J. 1998. 'Traditionelles Denken und neue Fragestellungen zur Geschichte von Handwerk und Zunft', in F. Lenger (ed.), *Handwerk, Hausindustrie und die historische Schule der Nationalökonomie.* Bielefeld: Verlag für Regionalgeschichte, pp. 19–77.

———, 2001. 'History of Work', in *International Encyclopedia of the Social and Behavioral Sciences,* vol. 24. London: Elsevier, pp. 16,569–175.

———, 2003. 'Die Geschichte der Arbeit als Spannungsfeld von Begriff, Norm und Praxis', in *Bericht über den 23. Österreichischen Historikertag in Salzburg, Veröffentlichungen des Verbandes Österreichischer Historiker und Geschichtsvereine,* vol. 32, Salzburg: Verb. Österr. Historiker und Geschichtsvereine, Österr. Staatsarchiv, pp. 25–44.

Ehmer, J. and P. Gutschner. 1998. 'Befreiung und Verkrümmung durch Arbeit', in R. van Dülmen (ed.), *Erfindung des Menschen. Schöpfungsträume und Körperbilder 1500–2000.* Wien: Böhlau Verlag, pp. 283–303.

Ei, W. 1976. *Teihon Tomioka nikki*. Tokyo: Sôjusha.

Eifert, C. 1993. *Frauenpolitik und Wohlfahrtspflege. Zur Geschichte der sozialdemokratischen 'Arbeiterwohlfahrt'.* Frankfurt am Main: Campus.

Eltis, D. (ed.) 2002. *Coerced and Free Migration. Global Perspectives.* Stanford: Stanford University Press.

Elwert, G. 2000. 'Jede Arbeit hat ihr Alter. Arbeit in einer afrikanischen Gesellschaft', in J. Kocka and C. Offe (eds), *Geschichte und Zukunft der Arbeit.* Frankfurt am Main: Campus, pp. 175–93.

Engels, F. 1887. *The Condition of the Working Class in England.* New York: John W. Lowell Co.

Erker, P. 2002. '"A New Business History"? Neuere Ansätze und Entwicklungen in der Unternehmensgeschichte', in *Archiv für Sozialgeschichte* 42: 557–604.

Fiedler, M. 2000. 'Netzwerke des Vertrauens', in D. Ziegler (ed.), *Großbürger und Unternehmer.* Göttingen: Vandenhoeck and Ruprecht, pp. 93–115.

———, 2001. 'Vertrauen ist gut, Kontrolle ist teuer: Vertrauen als Schlüsselkategorie wirtschaftlichen Handelns', in *Geschichte und Gesellschaft* 27: 576–92.

Fourier, C. 1829. *Le Nouveau Monde industriel et sociétaire.* Paris: Bossange.

Foviaux, J. 1990. 'Discipline et réglementation des activités professionelles à travers les arrêts du Parlement de Paris (1257–1382)', in J. Hamesse and C. Muraille–Samaran (eds), *Le travail au moyen âge. Une approche interdisciplinaire.* Louvain–la–Neuve: Publications de l'Institut d'Etudes Médiévales, p. 239.

Freedman, P. 1999. *Images of the Medieval Peasant.* Stanford: Stanford University Press.

French J.D. 2000. 'The Latin American Labor Studies Boom', in *International Review of Social History* 45: 279–308.

Freund, B. 1984. 'Labor and Labor History in Africa. A Review of the Literature', in *African Studies Review* 27: 1–58.

———, 1998. *The Making of Contemporary Africa. The Development of African Society since 1800.* London: Macmillan Press.

Freund, F. et al. 2004. *Zwangsarbeiter und Zwangsarbeiterinnen auf dem Gebiet der Republik Österreich 1939–1945.* Munich: Oldenbourg.

Frevert, U. 1991. 'Klasse und Geschlecht – Ein deutscher Sonderweg?', in L. Barrow et al. (eds), *Nichts als Unterdrückung? Geschlecht und Klasse in der englischen Sozialgeschichte.* Münster: Verlag Westfälisches Dampfboot, pp. 259–76.

———, 2000. 'Vertrauen. Historische Annäherungen an eine Gefühlshaltung', in C. Benthien et al. (eds), *Emotionalität: Zur Geschichte der Gefühle.* Cologne: Böhlau Verlag, pp. 179–84.

Frevert, U. et al. 1991. 'Historical Research on Women in the Federal Republic of Germany', in K. Offen et al. (eds), *Writing Women's History. International Perspectives.* London: Macmillan, pp. 291–331.

Frieser, K.-H. 2005. *The Blitzkrieg Legend: The 1940 Campaign in the West.* Annapolis: Naval Institute Press.

Frost, D. 1999. *Work and Community among Wast African Migrant Workers since the Nineteenth Century.* Liverpool: Liverpool University Press.

Fukuyama, F. 1995. *Trust: The Social Virtues and the Creation of Prosperity.* New York: Simon and Schuster.

Fussel, P. 1975. *The Great War and Modern Memory.* Oxford: Oxford University Press.

Gambetta, D. 1988. 'Mafia: The Price of Distrust', in D. Gambetta (ed.), *Trust: Making and Breaking Cooperative Relations.* Oxford: Basil Blackwell, pp. 158–75.

Garon, S. 1987. *The State and Labor in Modern Japan.* Berkeley: University of California Press.

Gay, P. 1999. 'Menschen im therapeutischen Netz', in U. Frevert and H.-G. Haupt (eds), *Der Mensch des 20. Jahrhunderts.* Frankfurt am Main: Campus, pp. 324–43.

Geremek, B. 1990. 'Le refus du travail dans la société urbaine du bas moyen âge', in J. Hamesse and C. Muraille-Samaran (eds), *Le travail au moyen âge. Une approche interdisciplinaire.* Louvain-la-Neuve : Publications de l'Institut d'Etudes Médiévales, pp. 379–94.

Gerhards, J. 1988. *Soziologie der Emotionen. Fragestellungen, Systematik und Perspektiven.* Weinheim: Beltz.

Geyer, M. 1995. 'Von einer Kriegsgeschichte, die vom Töten spricht', in T. Lindenberger and A. Lüdtke (eds), *Physische Gewalt.* Frankfurt am Main: Suhrkamp, pp. 136–61.

Gollwitzer, H. 1962. *Die Gelbe Gefahr. Geschichte eines Schlagworts. Studien zum imperialistischen Denken.* Göttingen: Vandenhoeck and Ruprecht.

Gordon, A. 1991. *Labor and Imperial Democracy in Prewar Japan.* Berkeley: University of California Press.

———, 1998. 'The Invention of Japanese-Style Labor Management', in S. Vlastos (ed.), *Mirror of Modernity. Invented Traditions of Modern Japan.* Berkley: University of California Press, pp. 19–36.

Gordon, S. 1990. 'Social Structural Effects on Emotions', in T.D. Kemper (ed.), *Research Agendas in the Sociology of Emotions.* Albany: SUNY Press, pp. 145–79.

Gorz, A. 1989. *Kritik der ökonomischen Vernunft. Sinnfragen am Ende der Arbeitsgesellschaft.* Hamburg: Rotbuch Verlag.

———, 2000. *Arbeit zwischen Misere und Utopie.* Frankfurt: Suhrkamp.

Grebing, H. et al. (eds). 1993. *Das HolzArbeiterbuch. Die Geschichte der Holzarbeiter und ihrer Gewerkschaften.* Cologne: Bund-Verlag.

Grieger, M. and H. Mommsen. 1996. *Das Volkswagenwerk und seine Arbeiter im Dritten Reich.* Düsseldorf: Econ.

Grier, B.C. 2006. *Invisable Hands. Child Labor and the State in Colonial Zimbabwe.* Portsmouth, NH: Heinermann.

Grimm, J. und W. Grimm. 1854. 'Arbeit', in *Deutsches Wörterbuch,* vol. 1. Leipzig: S. Hirzel, pp. 538–41.

Grimmer-Solem, E. 2005. 'German Social Science, Meiji Conservatism, and the Peculiarities of Japanese History', in *Journal of World History* 16: 187–222.

Groot, G. de and Marlou Schrover (eds). 1995. *Women Workers and Technological Change in Europe in the Nineteenth and Twentieth Century.* London: Taylor and Francis.

Gudmundsson, B.I. 1989. *Storm Troop Tactics: Innovation in the German Army, 1914–1918.* New York and London: Praeger Press.

Guinnane, T. 2001. 'Cooperatives as Information Machines: German Rural Credit Cooperatives, 1883–1914', in *Journal of Economic History* 61: 366–89.

Habermas, J. 1985. *Die neue Unübersichlichkeit.* Frankfurt am Main: Suhrkamp.

Hachtmann, R. 1989. *Industriearbeit im 'Dritten Reich'. Untersuchungen zu den Lohn- und Arbeitsbedingungen in Deutschland 1933–1945.* Göttingen: Vandenhoeck and Ruprecht.

———, 1993. 'Industriearbeiterinnen in der deutschen Kriegswirtschaft 1936–1944/45', in *Geschichte und Gesellschaft*, 19: 332–61.

Hagemann, K. 1990. *Frauenalltag und Männerpolitik. Alltagsleben und gesellschaftliches Handeln von Arbeiterfrauen in der Weimarer Republik.* Bonn: J.W.H. Dietz Nachf.

———, 2006. 'Between Ideology and Economy: The "Time Politics" of Child Care and Public Education in the Two Germanys', in *Social Politics: International Studies in Gender, State and Society* 13: 217–60.

Hamburger Institut für Sozialforschung (ed.). 2001. *Verbrechen der Wehrmacht: Dimensionen des Vernichtungskrieges 1941–1944.* Hamburg: Hamburger Edition.

Hamesse, J. and C. Muraille-Samaran (eds). 1990. *Le travail au moyen âge. Une approche interdisciplinaire.* Louvain-la-Neuve: Publications de l'Institut d'Etudes Médiévales.

Hammermann, G. 2002. *Zwangsarbeit für den 'Verbündeten'. Die Arbeits- und Lebensbedingungen der italienischen Militär-Internierten in Deutschland 1943–1945.* Tübingen: Max Niemeyer.

Hanau, P. et al. (eds). 1985. *Die Arbeitswelt in Japan und in der Bundesrepublik Deutschland- ein Vergleich.* Neuwied: Luchterhand Verlag.

Harazim, A. 2005. 'Bergbau nahe Auschwitz. Der Einsatz von Konzentrationslagerhäftlingen auf oberschlesischen Zechen', in K. Tenfelde and H.-C. Seidel (eds), *Zwangsarbeit im Bergwerk, Der Arbeitseinsatz im Kohlenbergbau des Deutschen Reiches und der besetzten Gebiete im Ersten und Zweiten Weltkrieg*, vol. 1. Essen: Klartext Verlag, pp. 411–32.

Hareven, T. 1982. *Family Time and Industrial Time: The Relationship between the Family and Work in a New England Industrial Community.* Cambridge, MA: University Press of America.

Haubrichs, W. 2006. 'Das Wortfeld "Arbeit" und "Mühe" im Mittelhochdeutschen', in: V. Postel (ed.), *Arbeit im Mittelalter, Vorstellungen und Wirklichkeiten.* Berlin: Akademie Verlag, pp. 91–106.

Hauch, G. (ed.). 1993. *Geschlecht-Klasse-Ethnizität, 28. Tagung der Historikerinnen und Historiker der Arbeiterinnen- und Arbeiterbewegung.* Vienna: Europaverlag.

Hauch, G. et al. (eds). 2003. *Industrie und Zwangsarbeit im Nationalsozalismus. Mercedes – VW – Reichswerke Hermann Göring in Linz und Salzgitter.* Innsbruck: Studien-Verlag.

Haupert, B. and F.J. Schäfer. 1991. *Jugend zwischen Kreuz und Hakenkreuz.* Frankfurt am Main: Suhrkamp.

Hausen, K. 1993. 'Wirtschaften mit der Geschlechterordnung. Ein Essay', in K. Hausen (ed.), *Geschlechterhierarchie und Arbeitsteilung. Zur Geschichte ungleicher Erwerbschancen von Männern und Frauen.* Göttingen: Vandenhoeck and Ruprecht, pp. 40–67.

———, 1997. 'Arbeiterinnenschutz, Mutterschutz und gesetzliche Krankenversicherung im Deutschen Kaiserreich und in der Weimarer Republik. Zur Funktion von Arbeits- und Sozialrecht für die Normierung und Stabilisierung der Geschlechterverhältnisse', in U. Gerhard (ed.), *Frauen in der Geschichte des Rechts. Von der Frühen Neuzeit bis zur Gegenwart.* Munich: C.H. Beck, pp. 713–43.

———, 1997. 'Frauenerwerbstätigkeit und erwerbstätige Frauen. Anmerkungen zur historischen Forschung', in Gunilla Budde (ed.), *Frauen arbeiten. Weibliche Erwerbstätigkeit in Ost- und Westdeutschland nach 1945.* Göttingen: Vandenhoeck and Ruprecht, pp. 19–45.

Hay, D. and P. Cravan (eds) 2004. *Masters, Servants, and Magistrates in Britain and the Empire, 1582–1955.* Chapel Hill: University of North Carolina Press.

Heer, H. (ed.). 1996. *"Stets zu erschießen sind Frauen, die in der Roten Armee dienen": Geständnisse deutscher Kriegsgefangener über ihren Einsatz an der Ostfront.* Hamburg: Hamburger Edition.

Heerma van Voss, L. and M. van der Linden (eds) 2002. *Class and Other Identities. Gender, Religion and Ethnicity in the Writing of European Labour History.* New York: Berghahn Books.

Heilbroner, R.L. 1985. *The Act of Work.* Washington: Library of Congress.

Heit, K. 2000. *Fukoku yûtokuron.* Tokyo: Chôôkôronsha.

Heita, K. 1991. *Nihon bunmei to kindai seiyô.* Tokyo: NHK Books.

Hennock, E.P. 2007. *The Origin of the Welfare State in England and Germany, 1850–1914. Social Policies Compared.* Cambridge: Cambridge University Press.

Herbert, U. 1999. *Fremdarbeiter. Politik und Praxis des 'Ausländer-Einsatzes' in der Kriegswirtschaft des Dritten Reiches.* 2nd edn Essen: Klartext-Verlag.

———, 2001. 'Zwangsarbeit im "Dritten Reich". Kenntnisstand, offene Fragen, Forschungsprobleme', in N. Reimann (ed.), *Zwangsarbeit in Deutschland 1939–1945. Archiv- und Sammlungsgut, Topographie und Erschließungsstrategien.* Bielefeld: Verlag für Regionalgeschichte, pp. 16–37.

———, (ed.). 1991. *Europa und der 'Reichseinsatz. Ausländische Zivilarbeiter, Kriegsgefangene und KZ-Häftlinge in Deutschland 1938–1945.* Essen: Klartext.

Herbst, E. 1921. *Der Taylorismus als Hilfe in unserer Wirtschaftsnot.* 3rd edn Leipzig: Anzengruber.

Hirschfeld, G. (ed.). 2003. *Enzyklopädie Erster Weltkrieg.* Paderborn: Schöningh.

Hirschmeier, J. and T. Yui. 1975. *The Development of Japanese Business 1600–1973.* London: Harper Collins.

Hisao, O. 1969. 'Kyôdôtai no kiso riron', in *Otsuka Hisao chosakushû*, vol. 7. Tokyo: Iwanami Shoten, pp. 1–104.

Hochschild, A. 1979. 'Emotionwork, Feeling Rules, and Social Structure', in *American Journal of Sociology* 85: 551–75.

Hochschild, A. 1983. *The Managed Heart: Commercialization of Human Feelings.* Berkeley: University of California Press.

———, 1990. 'Ideology and Emotion Management', in T.D. Kemper (ed.), *Research Agendas in the Sociology of Emotions.* Albany: SUNY Press, pp. 117–42.

Hoerder, D. 2002. *Culture in Contact. World Migration in the Second Millennium.* Durham: Duke University Press.

Homze, E. 1967. *Foreign Labor in Nazi Germany.* Princeton: Princeton University Press.

Hopkins, A.G. (ed.). 2002. *Globalization in World History.* London: W.W. Norton.

Hornung, E. et al. 2004. *Zwangsarbeit in der Landwirtschaft in Niederösterreich und dem nördlichen Burgenland.* Munich: Oldenbourg.

Hoston, G. 1992. *Marxism and the Crisis of Development in Prewar Japan.* Princeton: Princeton University Press.

Hsu, F. 1975. *Iemoto. The Heart of Japan.* New York: John Wiley and Sons. Hull, I. 2005. *Absolute Destruction: Military Culture and the Practices of War in Imperial Germany.* Ithaca, London: Cornell University Press.

Humburg, M. 1998. *Das Gesicht des Krieges: Feldpostbriefe von Wehrmachtssoldaten aus der Sowjetunion 1941–1944.* Opladen: Westdeutscher Verlag.

Ichirô, T. 1996. 'Nashonarizumu- Modanizumu- Koroniarizumu. Okinawa kara no shiten', in I. Toshio and S. Tôru (eds), *Nihon shakai to imin. Kôza gaikokujin teijû mondai*, vol. 1. Tokyo: Attashi Sholen, pp. 129–64.

———, 1990. *Kindai Nihon shakai to 'Okinawajin'.* Tokyo: Nihon Keizai Hyôronsha.

Jahn, P. and U. Schmiegelt, U. (eds). 2000. *Foto-Feldpost: geknipste Kriegserlebnisse 1939–1945.* Berlin: Elefantenpress.

Janka, W. 1992. *Spuren eines Lebens.* Reinbek: Rowohlt.

Janssens, A. (ed.). 1998. *The Rise and Decline of the Male Breadwinner Family? International Review of Social History*, Supplement 5, Cambridge: Cambridge University Press.

Jaritz, G. and K. Sonnleitner (eds). 1995. *Wert und Bewertung der Arbeit im Mittelalter und in der frühen Neuzeit.* Graz: Institut für Geschichte.

———, 2006. 'Der Kontext der Repräsentation oder: Die "ambivalente" Verbildlichung von Arbeit im Spätmittelalter', in V. Postel (ed.), *Arbeit im Mittelalter. Vorstellungen und Wirklichkeiten.* Berlin: Akademie Verlag, pp. 245–63.

Joshi, Chitra 2002. *Lost Worlds of Labour. Culture and Community in North India.* Delhi: Permanent Book.

Joyce, P. 1980. *Work, Society and Politics: The Culture of the Factory in Later Victorian England.* Brighton: Harvester.

———, (ed.). 1987. *The Historical Meanings of Work.* Cambridge: Cambridge University Press.

Jünger, E. 1929. *Storm of Steel.* London: Chatto & Windus.

———, 1932. *Der Arbeiter: Herrschaft und Gestalt.* Stuttgart: Klett-Cotta.

Kaienburg, H. 1996. 'Jüdische Arbeitslager an der "Straße der SS"', in *1999. Zeitschrift für Sozialgeschichte* 11: 13–39.

Kaiser, J.C. (ed.). 2005. *Zwangsarbeit in Diakonie und Kirche 1939–1945.* Stuttgart: Kohlhammer.

Karner, S. and P. Ruggenthaler 2004. *Zwangsarbeit in der Land- und Forstwirtschaft auf dem Gebiet Österreichs 1939 bis 1945.* Vienna: Oldenbourg.

Kassel, B. 1997. *Frauen in einer Männerwelt. Frauenerwerbsarbeit in der Metallindustrie und ihre Interessenvertretung durch den Deutschen Metallarbeiter-Verband 1891–1933.* Cologne: Bund.

Katznelson, I. and A. Zolberg (eds). 1986. *Working-Class Formation: Nineteenth-Century Patterns in Western Europe and the United States.* Princeton: Princeton University Press.

Kazuo, O. 1955. *Nihon no rôdôsha kaikyû.* Tokyo: Týyô Keizai Shinpôsha.

Kern, H. and M. Schumann. 1984. *Das Ende der Arbeitsteilung? Rationalisierung in der industriellen Produktion.* Munich: Beck.

Kern, M. and C. Sottas. 2003. 'The Abolition of Forced or Compulsory Labour', in *Fundamental Rights at Work and International Labour Standards,* International Labour Office (ed.), Geneva: International Labor Office, pp. 33–55.

Kessler-Harris, A. 2002. 'Two Labour Histories or One?' in L. Heerma van Voss and M. van der Linden (eds), *Class and Other Identities: Gender, Religion, and Ethnicity in the Writing of European Labour History.* New York: Berghahn Books, pp. 133–49.

———, 2004. 'Reframing the History of Women's Wage Labor: Challenges of a Global Perspective', in *Journal of Women's History* 15,4: 186–206.

Kinzley, D.W. 1991. *Industrial Harmony in Modern Japan. The Invention of a Tradition.* London: Routledge.

Kleinschmidt, C. 2002. *Der produktive Blick. Wahrnehmung amerikanischer und japanischer Management- und Produktionsmethoden durch deutsche Unternehmer 1950–1985.* Berlin: Akademie Verlag.

Kloft, H. 1984. 'Arbeit und Arbeitsverträge in der griechisch-römischen Welt', in *Saeculum* 35: 200–21.

Koch, M. 2004. '"… wenn der Tod mit seinen furchtbaren Arten seine Ernte holt". Deutungen physischer Gewalt am Beispiel des Wehrmachtsgefreiten Hermann Rombach', in *Historische Anthropologie* 12: 179–98.

Kocka, J. 1975. *Unternehmer in der deutschen Industrialisierung.* Göttingen: Vandenhoeck and Ruprecht.

———, 1990. *Arbeitsverhältnisse und Arbeiterexistenzen. Grundlagen der Klassenbildung im 19. Jahrhundert.* Bonn: Verlag J.H.W. Dietz Nachf.

———, 1990. *Weder Stand noch Klasse. Unterschichten um 1800.* Bonn: Dietz.

———, 1992. 'Klasse und Geschlecht', in *Geschichte und Gesellschaft* 18/2: pp. 137–47.

———, 2000. 'Arbeit früher, heute, morgen. Zur Neuartigkeit der Gegenwart', in J. Kocka and C. Offe (eds), *Geschichte und Zukunft der Arbeit.* Frankfurt am Main: Campus, pp. 476–92.

———, 2001. *Das lange 19. Jahrhundert. Arbeit, Nation und bürgerliche Gesellschaft.* Stuttgart: Klett.

———, 2003. 'Arbeit als Problem der europäischen Geschichte', in M. Bierwisch (ed.), *Die Rolle der Arbeit in verschiedenen Epochen und Kulturen.* Berlin: Akademie Verlag, pp. 77–92.

———, 2005. 'Mehr Last als Lust. Arbeit und Arbeitsgesellschaft in der europäischen Geschichte', in *Jahrbuch für Wirtschaftsgeschichte/Economic History Yearbook 2*: pp.186–206.

Kocka, J. and C. Offe (eds). 2000. *Geschichte und Zukunft der Arbeit.* Frankfurt am Main: Campus.

Köhler, H. 1967. *Arbeitsdienst in Deutschland. Pläne und Verwirklichungsformen bis zur Einführung der Arbeitsdienstpflicht im Jahre 1935.* Berlin: Duncker and Humblot.

Kôji, T. 1970. *Economic Development and the Labor Market in Japan.* New York: Columbia University Press.

Kolbe, W. 2002. *Elternschaft im Wohlfahrtsstaat. Schweden und die Bundesrepublik im Vergleich 1945–2000.* Frankfurt am Main: Campus.

Koselleck, R. 1967. *Preußen zwischen Reform und Revolution. Allgemeines Landrecht, Verwaltung und soziale Bewegung von 1791 bis 1848.* Stuttgart: Klett Cotta.

Kößler, R. 1990. 'Arbeit und Revolution. Sozialistische Perspektiven', in H. König et al. (eds), *Sozialphilosophie der industriellen Arbeit.* Opladen: Westdeutscher Verlag, pp. 96–113.

Kößler, R. and H. Wienold, 'Arbeit und Vergesellschaftung. Eine aktuelle Erinnerung an die klassische Gesellschaftstheorie', in *Peripherie* 85/86: 162–183.

Kranig, A. 1983. *Lockung und Zwang. Zur Arbeitsverfassung im Dritten Reich.* Stuttgart: Deutsche Verlagsanstalt.

Kroener, B. et al. 1999. *Das Deutsche Reich und der Zweite Weltkrieg,* vol. 5: *Organisation und Mobilisierung des Deutschen Machtbereichs,* part 2: *Kriegsverwaltung, Wirtschaft und personelle Ressourcen 1942–1944/45.* Stuttgart: DVA.

Krupp, A. 1877. *Ein Wort an die Angehörigen meiner gewerblichen Anlagen.* Essen: Buchdr. d. Krupp'schen Etabl..

Kühne, T. 2003. 'Vertrauen und Kameradschaft. Soziales Kapital im "Endkampf" der Wehrmacht', in U. Frevert (ed.), *Vertrauen.* Göttingen: Vandenhoeck and Ruprecht, pp. 245–78.

———, 2006. *Kameradschaft: die Soldaten des nationalsozialistischen Krieges und das 20. Jahrhundert.* Göttingen: Vandenhoeck and Ruprecht.

Kulawik, T. 1999. *Wohlfahrtsstaat und Mutterschaft. Schweden und Deutschland 1870–1912.* Frankfurt am Main: Campus.

Kundrus, B. 1995. *Kriegerfrauen. Familienpolitik und Geschlechterverhältnisse im Ersten und Zweiten Weltkrieg.* Hamburg: Christians.

Landes, D. 1998. *The Wealth and Poverty of Nations: Why Some Are So Rich and Some So Poor.* New York: W.W. Norton.

Latzel, K. 2000. *Deutsche Soldaten – nationalsozialistischer Krieg?: Kriegserlebnis –Kriegserfahrung; 1939–1945.* Paderborn: Schöningh.

Le Goff, J. 1980. *Time, Work and Culture in the Middle Ages.* Chicago: Chicago University Press.

Leed, E.J. 1979. *NoMan's Land: Combat and Identity in World War I.* Cambridge: Cambridge University Press.

Lehmann, H. 1988. 'Asketischer Protestantismus und ökonomischer Rationalismus. Die Weber-These nach zwei Generationen', in W. Schluchter (ed.), *Max Webers Sicht des okzidentalen Christentums. Interpretation und Kritik.* Frankfurt am Main: Suhrkamp, pp. 529–53.

Lenk, W. 1978. *'Ketzer'lehren und Kampfprogramme. Ideologieentwicklung im Zeichen der frühbürgerlichen Revolution in Deutschland.* Berlin: Akademie Verlag.

Levenstein, A. 1912. *Die Arbeiterfrage. Mit besonderer Berücksichtigung der sozialpsychologischen Seite des modernen Großbetriebes und der psycho-physischen Einwirkungen auf die Arbeiter.* Munich: Ernst Reinhardt. *Liederbuch für Handwerkervereine* (1859).

Lincoln, J.R. and A.L. Kalleberg. 1990. *Culture, Control, and Commitment. A Study of Work Organization and Work Attitudes in the United States and Japan.* Cambridge: Cambridge University Press.

Linden, M. van der (ed.). 1993. *The End of Labour History? International Review of Social History,* Supplement 1, Cambridge: Cambridge University Press.

———, 2001. 'Global Labor History and "The Modern World System". Thoughts at the Twenty-Fifth Anniversary of the Fernand Braudel Center', in *International Review of Social History* 46: 423–59.

———, 2002. 'Vorläufiges zur transkontinentalen Arbeitergeschichte' in *Geschichte und Gesellschaft* 28/2: 291–304.

———, 2003. *Transnational Labour History. Explorations.* Aldersho: Ashgate.

———, 2003. 'Die Geschichte der Arbeiterinn und Arbeiter in der Globalisierung', in *Sozial.Geschichte* 18/1: 10–40.

———, 2006. 'Transnationale Arbeitergeschichte' in G. Budde et al. (eds), *Transnationale Geschichte. Themen, Tendenzen und Theorien.* Göttingen: Vandenhoeck und Ruprecht, pp. 265–74.

———, 2008. *Workers of the World. Essays Toward a Global Labor History.* Leiden: Brill.

Lindsay, L.A. 2003. *Working with Gender. Wage Labor and Social Change in Southwestern Nigeria.* Portsmouth, NH: Heinemann.

Linhart, S. 1988. 'From Industrial to Postindustrial Society. Changes in Japanese Leisure-Related Values and Behaviour', in *Journal of Japanese Studies* 14: 271–307.

Linhart, S. and W. Manzenreiter. 1999. 'Japan: Von der Arbeitsgesellschaft zur Freizeitgesellschaft', in *Minikomi. Informationen des Akademischen Arbeitskreis Japan* 1: 5–11.

Lipburger, P.M. 1988. '"Quoniam si quis nun vult operari, nec manducet..." Auffassungen von der Arbeit vor allem im Mittelalter', in *Mitteilungen der Gesellschaft für Salzburger Landeskunde* 128: 47–86.

Lippert, W. 1979. *Entstehung und Funktion einiger chinesischer marxistischer Termini. Der lexikalisch-begriffliche Aspekt der Rezeption des Marxismus in Japan und China.* Wiesbaden: 183–86.

Lorenz, E. 1988. 'Neither Friends nor Strangers: Informal Networks of Subcontracting in French Industry', in D. Gambetta (ed.), *Trust: Making and Breaking Cooperative Relations.* Oxford: Basil Blackwell, pp. 194–210.

Lovejoy, P.E. 2000. *Transformations in Slavery. A History of Slavery in Africa.* 2nd edn Cambridge: Cambridge University Press.

Lovejoy, P.E. and N. Rogers (eds) 1994. *Unfree Labour in the Development of the Atlantic World.* London: Routledge.

Lucassen, J. (ed.). 2005. *Global Labor History.* Berne: Lang.

Lüdtke, A. 1986. '"Deutsche Qualitätsarbeit", "Spielereien" am Arbeitsplatz und "Fliehen" aus der Fabrik: Industrielle Arbeitsprozesse und Arbeiterverhalten in den 1920er Jahren', in Friedhelm Boll (ed.), *Arbeiterkulturen zwischen Alltag und Politik.* Vienna: Europa Verlag, pp. 155–97.

———, 1993. 'Arbeit, Arbeitserfahrungen und Arbeiterpolitik', in A. Lüdtke, *Eigen-Sinn. Arbeiter, Arbeitserfahrungen und Politik vom Kaiserreich bis in den Faschismus.* Hamburg: Ergebnisse Verlag, pp. 351–440.

———, 1993. 'Polymorphous Synchrony', in *International Review of Social History 38*, Supplement 1: 39–84.

———, 2003. '"Fehlgreifen in der Wahl der Mittel". Optionen im Alltag militärischen Handelns', in *Mittelweg* 36: 61–73.

Luhmann, N. 1968. *Vertrauen: Ein Mechanismus der Reduktion sozialer Komplexität.* Stuttgart: Enke.

———, 1988. 'Familiarity, Confidence, Trust: Problems and Alternatives', in D. Gambetta (ed.), *Trust: Making and Breaking Cooperative Relations.* Oxford: Basil Blackwell, pp. 94–107.

Lutz, B. 2005. 'Integration durch Aufstieg. Überlegungen zur Verbürgerlichung der deutschen Facharbeiter in den Jahrzehnten nach dem Zweiten Weltkrieg', in M. Hettling and B. Ulrich (eds), *Bürgertum nach 1945.* Hamburg: Hamburger Edition, pp. 284–309.

Lutz, C. and L. Abu-Lughod (eds). 1990. *Language and the Politics of Emotion.* Cambridge: Cambridge University Press.

MacKinnon, M.H. 1993. 'The Longevity of the Thesis. A Critique of the Critics', in H. Lehmann and G. Roth (eds), *Weber's Protestant Ethic. Origins, Evidence, Contexts.* Cambridge: Cambridge University Press, pp. 211–43.

Malaparte, C. 1989. *Die Wolga entspringt in Europa.* Cologne: Kiepenheuer and Witsch.

Malinowski, B. 1912. 'The Economic Aspect of the Intichiuma Ceremonies', in *Festskrift tillegnad Edvard Westermarck.* Helsingsfors: J. Simelii Arvinjars, pp. 81–108.

———, 1925. 'Labour and Primitive Economics', in *Nature* 116: 926–30.

———, 1925. 'Magic, Science and Religion', in J. Needham (ed.), *Science, Religion and Reality.* London: Sheldon Press, pp. 20–84.

———, 1935. *Coral Gardens and Their Magic.* 2 vols, New York: American Book Co.

Manning, P. 2003. *Navigating World History.* New York: Palgrave.

Mansfield, M. et al. (eds). 1994. *Aux sources du chômage (1880–1914).* Paris: Belin.

Marshall, B.K. 1967. *Capitalism and Nationalism in Prewar Japan. The Ideology of the Business Elite, 1868–1941.* Stanford: Stanford University Press.

Marshall, G. 1982. *In Search of the Spirit of Capitalism. An Essay on Max Weber's Protestant Ethic Thesis.* London: Blackwell Publishing.

Marshall, S.L.A. 1947. *Men Against Fire: The Problem of Battle Command in Future War.* New York: University of Oklahoma Press.

Marwitz, F. von der. (1836) 1965. 'Von der Schrankenlosigkeit', reprint in C. Jantke and D. Hilger (eds), *Die Eigentumslosen. Der deutscher Pauperismus und die Emanzipationskrise in Darstellungen und Deutungen der zeitgenössischen Literatur.* Freiburg and Munich: Alber, pp. 134–48.

Marx, K. 1867. *Das Kapital,* vol. 1. Berlin: Dietz.

———, 1932. *Ökonomisch-philosophische Manuskripte.* Stuttgart: Kröner.

———, 1959. *Outlines of a Critique of Political Economy.* Moscow: Foreign Language Publishing House.

———, 1932. *Die deutsche Ideologie.* Stuttgart: Kröner.

———, 1939. *Grundrisse der Kritik der Politischen Ökonomie.* Moskau: Foreign Language Publishing House.

———, 1959. *Economic and Philosophical Manuscripts of 1844.* Moscow: Foreign Language Publishing House.

———, 1965. *Das Kapital.* 3 vols, Berlin: Dietz.

———, 1985. 'Randglossen zum: Programm der deutschen Arbeiterpartei (1875)', in *Karl Marx – Friedrich Engels Gesamtausgabe (MEGA),* vol. 25: *Artikel, Entwürfe Mai 1875 bis Mai 1883.* Berlin (GDR): Dietz.

Marx, K. and F. Engels. 1964. *The German Ideology.* Moscow: Progress Publishers.

———, 1976. *Marx Engels Collected Works,* vol. 5: *The German Ideology.* London: Lawrence and Wishart.

———, 1986. *Marx Engels Collected Works,* vol. 28: *Outlines of a Critique of Political Economy.* London: Lawrence and Wishart.

Masaaki, S. (ed.). 1989. *Meiji no kotoba jiten.* Tokyo: Tôkyôdô, pp. 603–605.

Masao, M. 1958. 'Shôkai. Berâ 'Tokugawa jidai no shûkyô', in *Kokka gakkai zasshi* 72: 437–58.

Mason, T. 1978. *Sozialpolitik im Dritten Reich. Arbeiterklasse und Volksgemeinschaft*, 2nd edn Opladen: Westdeutscher Verlag.

Mattes, M. 2005. *'Gastarbeiterinnen' in der Bundesrepublik. Anwerbepolitik, Migration und Geschlecht in den 50er bis 70er Jahren.* Frankfurt: Campus Verlag.

Matthes, J. (ed.). 1982. *Krise der Arbeitsgesellschaft? Verhandlungen des 21. Deutschen Soziologentages in Bamberg.* Frankfurt am Main: Campus.

Mauser, W. and B. Becker-Cantarino. 1991. *Frauenfreundschaft – Männerfreundschaft: Literarische Diskurse im 18. Jahrhundert.* Tübingen: Niemeyer.

Mawdsley, E. 2005. *Thunder in the East: The Nazi-Soviet War 1941–1945.* London: Hodder Arnold.

Mazlish, B. 1998. 'Comparing Global History to World History' in *Journal for Interdisciplinary History* 28: 385–395.

McIvor, A. 2001. *A History of Work in Britain, 1880–1950.* Basingstoke and New York: Palgrave.

McPherson, C.B. (ed.). 1982. *Thomas Hobbes, Leviathan.* Harmondsworth: Penguin.

Mehnert, U. 1995. *Deutschland, Amerika und die 'Gelbe Gefahr'. Zur Karriere eines Schlagworts in der Großen Politik, 1905–1917.* Stuttgart: Steiner.

Meier, C. 2003. 'Griechische Arbeitsauffassungen in archaischer und klassischer Zeit', in: Bierwisch, M. (ed.), *Die Rolle der Arbeit in verschiedenen Epochen und Kulturen.* Berlin: Akademie Verlag, 2003, pp. 19–76.

Mengersen, O. von. 2004. 'Zwangsarbeit im kolonialen Kontext. Ideologie und Praxis britischer Arbeitspolitik in Nigeria 1900–1930', in O. von Mengersen et al. (eds), *Personen. Soziale Bewegungen. Parteien. Beiträge zur neuesten Geschichte. Festschrift für Hartmut Soell.* Heidelberg: Manutius, pp. 177–201.

Menzer, P. (ed.). 1924. *Immanuel Kant, Eine Vorlesung Kants über Ethik.* Berlin: Pan Verlag Rolf Heise.

Mercier, L.-S. 1982. *Das Jahr 2440. Ein Traum aller Träume*, trans. Christian Felix Weiße. Frankfurt am Main: Suhrkamp.

Michio, M. 1982. *Why Has Japan Succeeded? Western Technology and the Japanese Ethos.* Cambridge: Cambridge University Press.

Militaergeschichtliches Forschungsamt (ed.). 1983–1999. *Das Deutsche Reich und der Zweite Weltkrieg*, vols 4 and 5. Stuttgart/Munich: Deutsche Verlagsanstalt.

Mintz, S.W. 1992. *Die süße Macht. Kulturgeschichte des Zuckers.* Frankfurt am Main: Campus. Engl. edn 1985. *Sweetness and Power. The Place of Sugar in Modern History.* New York: Penguin.

Misztal, B. 1996. *Trust in Modern Societies: The Search for the Bases of Social Order.* Cambridge: Polity Press.

Moeller, R.G. 1993. *Protecting Motherhood. Women and the Family in the Politics of Postwar Germany.* Berkeley: University of California Press.
Moingeon, B. and A. Edmondson. 1998. 'Trust and Organisational Learning', in N. Lazaric and E. Lorenz (eds), *Trust and Economic Learning.* Cheltenham: Edward Elgar, pp. 247–65.
Morris-Suzuki, T. 1989. *A History of Japanese Economic Thought.* London: Routledge.
More, T. 1975. *Utopia* (1516). *A New Translation, Backgrounds, Criticism*, trans. and ed. R. Adams. New York: W.W. Norton.
Müller, J.D. 1996. 'Zwischen Repräsentation und Regierungspraxis: Transformation des Wissens in Maximilians Weiskunig', in G. Scholz Williams and S. Schindler (eds), *Knowledge, Science, and Literature in Early Modern Germany.* Chapel Hill: University of North Carolina Press, pp. 49–70.
Murakami, Y. 1984. 'Ie Society as a Pattern of Civilisation', in *Journal of Japanese Studies* 10: 281–363.
Musson, A. 2004. 'Reconstructing English Labor Laws: A Medieval Perspective', in M. Uebel and K. Robertson (eds), *The Middle Ages at Work.* New York: Palgrave Macmillan, pp. 113–32.
Neyer, G. 1997. 'Die Entwicklung des Mutterschutzes in Deutschland, Österreich und in der Schweiz von 1877 bis 1945', in U. Gerhard (ed.), *Frauen in der Geschichte des Rechts. Von der Frühen Neuzeit bis zur Gegenwart.* Munich: C.H. Beck, pp. 744–58.
Niehuss, M. 2001. *Familie, Frau und Gesellschaft. Studien zur Strukturgeschichte der Familie in Westdeutschland 1945–1960.* Göttingen: Vandenhoeck and Ruprecht.
Nienhaus, U. 1995. *Vater Staat und seine Gehilfinnen. Die Politik mit der Frauenarbeit bei der deutschen Post 1864–1945.* Frankfurt am Main: Campus.
Nippel, W. 2000. 'Erwerbsarbeit in der Antike', in J. Kocka and C. Offe (eds), *Geschichte und Zukunft der Arbeit.* Frankfurt am Main: Campus, pp. 54–66.
Nitzsche, M. 1904. 'Die Japanische Konkurrenz', in *Preußische Jahrbücher* 117: 225–43.
Nolan, M. 1994. *Visions of Modernity: American Business and the Modernization of Germany.* Oxford: Oxford University Press.
O'Brien, T. 1998. *The Things They Carried.* New York: Broadway.
Oertzen, C. von. 1999. *Teilzeitarbeit und die Lust am Zuverdienen. Geschlechterpolitik und gesellschaftlicher Wandel in Westdeutschland 1948–1969.* Göttingen: Vandenhoeck and Ruprecht.
Oertzen, C. and A. Rietzschel. 1997. 'Das "Kuckucksei" Teilzeitarbeit. Die Politik der Gewerkschaften im deutsch-deutschen Vergleich', in G. Budde, *Frauen arbeiten. Weibliche Erwerbstätigkeit in Ost- und Westdeutschland nach 1945.* Göttingen: Vandenhoeck and Ruprecht, pp. 212–51.
Oexle, O.G. 1988. 'Die funktionale Dreiteilung als Deutungsschema der sozialen Wirklichkeit in den ständischen Gesellschaften des Mittelalters', in W. Schulze (ed.), *Ständische Gesellschaft und soziale Mobilität.* Munich: Oldenbourg, pp. 19–51.

———, 2000. 'Arbeit, Armut, "Stand" im Mittelalter', in J. Kocka and C. Offe (eds), *Geschichte und Zukunft der Arbeit.* Frankfurt am Main: Campus, pp. 67–79.

Offe, C. 1984. *Arbeitsgesellschaft. Strukturprobleme und Zukunftsperspektiven.* Frankfurt am Main: Campus.

———, 1999. 'How Can We Trust Our Fellow Citizens?', in M. Warren (ed.), *Democracy and Trust.* Cambridge: Cambridge University Press, pp. 42–87.

———, et al. (eds). 2000. *Geschichte und Zukunft der Arbeit.* Frankfurt am Main: Campus.

Oltmer, J. 2002. 'Flucht, Vertreibung und Asyl im 19. und 20. Jahrhundert', in K. Bade (ed.), *Migration in der europäischen Geschichte seit dem späten Mittelalter.* Osnabrück: IMIS.

Oltmer, J. 2004. 'Migration, Integration und Krieg im Europa des "Jahrhunderts der Flüchtlinge"', in *Geschichte, Politik und ihre Didaktik. Zeitschrift für historisch-politische Bildung* 32: 90–100.

Oltmer, J. 2005. *Migration und Politik in der Weimarer Republik.* Göttingen: Vandenhoeck and Ruprecht.

Oltmer, J. (ed.). 2002. *Migrationsforschung und interkulturelle Studien: 10 Jahre IMIS.* Osnabrück: Rasch.

Ortiz, S. 2002. 'Laboring in the Factories and in the Fields', in *Annual Review of Anthropology* 31: 395–417.

Ostwald, W. 1909. *Energetische Grundlagen der Kulturwissenschaft.* Leipzig: Dr. Klinkhardt.

Otto, R. 1998. *Wehrmacht, Gestapo und sowjetische Kriegsgefangene im deutschen Reichsgebiet 1941/42.* Munich: Oldenbourg.

Ouchi, W.G. 1981. *Theory Z. How American Business Can Meet the Japanese Challenge.* New York: Avon Books.

Overmanns, R. 2005. 'Die Kriegsgefangenenpolitik des Deutschen Reiches 1939–1945', in J. Echternkamp (ed.), *Die deutsche Kriegsgesellschaft.* Stuttgart: DVA, pp. 729–875.

Patel, K. 2003. *'Soldaten der Arbeit'. Arbeitsdienste in Deutschland und den USA 1933–1945.* Göttingen: Vandenhoeck and Ruprecht.

Pearson, P. and D. Richardson, D. 2001. 'Business Networking in the Industrial Revolution', in *Economic History Review* 54: 657–79.

Penter, T. 2005. 'Zwangsarbeit – Arbeit für den Feind. Der Donbass unter deutscher Okkupation (1941–1943)', in *Geschichte und Gesellschaft* 31: 68–100.

———, 2005. 'Zwischen Hunger, Terror und einer "glücklichen Zukunft". Der Arbeitseinsatz im Steinkohlenbergbau des Donezbeckens unter deutscher Besatzung 1941 bis 1943', in K. Tenfelde and H.-C. Seidel (eds), *Zwangsarbeit im Bergwerk, Der Arbeitseinsatz im Kohlenbergbau des Deutschen Reiches und der besetzten Gebiete im Ersten und Zweiten Weltkrieg,* vol. 1. Essen: Klartext Verlag, pp. 433–66.

Peppler, K. (ed.). 1940. *Die 'Deutsche Arbeitskunde'.* Leipzig: Bibliographisches Institut.

Pfister, P. (ed.). 2001. *Katholische Kirche und Zwangsarbeit. Stand und Perspektiven der Forschung.* Regensburg: Schnell and Steiner.

Piquet, N. 2005. '"Privilegierte" Zwangsarbeiter. Sowjetische und serbische Arbeitskräfte im nordfranzösischen und belgischen Steinkohlenbergbau während der deutschen Besatzung', in K. Tenfelde and H.-C. Seidel (eds), *Zwangsarbeit im Bergwerk, Der Arbeitseinsatz im Kohlenbergbau des Deutschen Reiches und der besetzten Gebiete im Ersten und Zweiten Weltkrieg*, vol. 1. Essen: Klartext Verlag, pp. 467–93.

Pleij, H. 1997. *Der Traum vom Schlaraffenland.* Frankfurt: S. Fischer.

Pomeranz, K. 2000. *The Great Divergence. Europe, China, and the Making of the Modern World Economy.* Princeton: Princeton University Press.

Popitz, H. 1976. *Technik und Industriearbeit: Soziologische Untersuchungen in der Hüttenindustrie.* Tübingen: Mohr Siebeck.

Postel, V. (ed.). 2006. *Arbeit im Mittelalter. Vorstellungen und Wirklichkeiten.* Berlin: Akademie Verlag.

Prak, M. 1996. 'Individual, Corporation and Society: The Rhetoric of Dutch Guilds (Eighteenth Century)', in M. Boone and M. Prak (eds), *Individual, Corporate and Judicial Status in European Cities (Late Middle Ages And Early Modern Period).* Louvain: Apeldorn, pp. 255–79.

Putnam, R. 1983. *Making Democracy Work: Civic Traditions in Modern Italy.* Princeton: Princeton University Press.

———, 2000. *Bowling Alone: The Collapse and Revival of American Community.* New York: Simon and Schuster.

Rabinbach, A. 1990. *The Human Motor. Energy, Fatigue, and the Origins of Modernity.* New York: Basic Books Inc.

Randeria, S. 1999. 'Geteilte Geschichte und verwobene Moderne', in J. Rüsen et al. (eds), *Zukunftsentwürfe. Ideen für eine Kultur der Veränderung.* Frankfurt: Campus, pp. 87–96.

———, 1999. 'Jenseits von Soziologie und soziokultureller Anthropologie. Zur Ortsbestimmung der nichtwestlichen Welt in einer zukünftigen Sozialtheorie', in *Soziale Welt* 50: 373–82.

Ranft, P. 2006. *The Theology of Work. Peter Damian and the Medieval Religious Renewal Movement.* New York: Palgrave Macmillan.

Rantzsch, P. and E. Uitz (1991). 'Historical Research on Women in the German Democratic Republic', in K. Offen et al. (eds), *Writing Women's History. International Perspectives.* Indianapolis: Indiana University Press, pp. 333–54.

Rass, C. 2003. *'Menschenmaterial': Deutsche Soldaten an der Ostfront. Innenansichten einer Infanteriedivision, 1939–1945.* Paderborn: Schöningh.

Rathgen, K. 1891. *Japans Volkswirtschaft und Staatshaushalt.* Leipzig: Duncker and Humblot.

Rathkolb, O. (ed.). 2001. *NS-Zwangsarbeit. Der Standort Linz der Reichswerke Hermann Göring AG Berlin 1938–1945.* 2 vols, Vienna: Böhlau.

Rawe, K. 2005. '*... Wir werden sie schon zur Arbeit bringen!' Ausländerbeschäftigung und Zwangsarbeit im Ruhrkohlenbergbau während des Ersten Weltkrieges.* Essen: Klartext Verlag.

Redding, G. 1993. *The Spirit of Chinese Capitalism.* New York: de Gruyter.

Reddy, W.M. 2001. *The Navigation of Feeling: A Framework for the History of Emotions.* Cambridge: Cambridge University Press.

Reibert, W. 1940. *Der Dienstunterricht im Heere: Ausgabe der Schützenkompanie.* Berlin: E.S. Mittler.

Richert, D. 1989. *Beste Gelegenheit zum Sterben: Meine Erlebnisse im Kriege 1914–1918,* A. Tramitz and B. Ulrich (eds), Munich: Knesebeck.

Rieff, P. 1966. *The Triumph of the Therapeutic.* New York: Harper and Row.

Riehl, H. 1854. *Die Familie.* Stuttgart: Klett-Cotta.

———, 1861. *Die deutsche Arbeit.* Stuttgart: Klett-Cotta.

Rifkin, J. 1995. *The End of Work.* New York: Little, Brown and Company.

Rippberger, T. 1998. *Ökonomik des Vertrauens.* Tübingen: Mohr Siebeck.

Ritter, G. 1983. *Sozialversicherung in Deutschland und England. Entstehung und Grundzüge im Vergleich.* Munich: Beck.

Ritter, G.A. (ed.). 2002. *Geschichte der Arbeiter und der Arbeiterbewegung in Deutschland seit dem Ende des 18. Jahrhunderts.* Bonn: Dietz Verlag.

Roeck, B. 1985. *Elias Holl. Architekt einer europäischen Stadt.* Regensburg: Friedrich Pustet.

Roper, L. 1989. *The Holy Household. Women and Morals in Reformation Augsburg.* Oxford: Oxford University Press. German edn 1995. *Das fromme Haus. Frauen und Moral in der Reformation.* Frankfurt am Main: Campus.

Rose, S.O. 1992. *Limited Livelihoods: Gender and Class in Nineteenth-Century England.* Berkeley: University of California Press.

———, 1993. 'Gender and Labour History. The Nineteenth-Century Legacy', in M. van der Linden (ed.), *The End of Labour History? International Review of Social History,* Supplement 1: 145–62.

Roth, G. and C. Wittich (eds). 1968. *Economy and Society.* 3 vols, New York: Bedminster.

Rouette, S. 1993. *Sozialpolitik als Geschlechterpolitik. Die Regulierung der Frauenarbeit nach dem Ersten Weltkrieg.* Frankfurt am Main: Campus Verlag.

Ruch, C. et al. 2001. *Geschäfte und Zwangsarbeit. Schweizer Industrieunternehmen im 'Dritten Reich'.* Zürich: Chronos.

Rutar, S. 2005. 'Arbeit und Überleben in Serbien. Das Kupfererzbergwerk Bor im Zweiten Weltkrieg', in *Geschichte und Gesellschaft* 31: 101–34.

Saage, R. 1991. *Politische Utopien der Neuzeit.* Darmstadt: WBG.

Sabel, C. and J. Zeitlin. 1985. 'Historical Alternatives to Mass Production: Politics, Markets and Technology in 19th Century Industrialization', in *Past and Present* 108: 133–76.

Sachse, C. 1990. *Siemens, der Nationalsozialismus und die moderne Familie. Eine Untersuchung zur Sozialen Rationalisierung in Deutschland im 20. Jahrhundert.* Hamburg: Rasch und Röhrig.

———, 2002. *Der Hausarbeitstag. Gerechtigkeit und Gleichberechtigung in Ost und West. 1939–1994*. Göttingen: Wallstein.

Sahlins, M. 1972. *Stone Age Economics*. New York: Aldine Transaction.

———, 1994. 'Cosmologies of Capitalism. The Trans-Pacific Sector of "The World System"', in N.B. Dirks et al. (eds), *Culture/Power/History. A Reader in Contemporary Social Theory*. Princeton: Princeton University Press, pp. 412–56.

Schäfer, A. 2000. *Zwangsarbeiter und NS-Rassenpolitik. Russische und polnische Arbeitskräfte in Württemberg 1939–1945*. Stuttgart: Kohlhammer.

Scheutz, M. et al. (eds).1997. *Wiener Neustädter Handwerksordnungen (1432 bis Mitte des 16. Jahrhunderts). Fontes Rerum Austriacarum, Fontes Juris*, vol. 13, Vienna: Böhlau.

Schieder, W. 1963. *Anfänge der deutschen Arbeiterbewegung. Die Auslandsvereine im Jahrzehnt nach der Julirevolution von 1830*. Stuttgart: Klett-Cotta.

Schluchter, W. 1988. 'Religion, politische Herrschaft, Wirtschaft und bürgerliche Lebensführung. Die okzidentale Sonderentwicklung', in idem (ed.), *Max Webers Sicht des okzidentalen Christentums. Interpretation und Kritik*. Frankfurt am Main: Suhrkamp, pp. 11–128.

Schmid, G. 2002. *Beyond Employment. Report for the European Commission*. Oxford: Oxford University Press.

Schmidt, E. 2007. *Cold War and Decolonization in Guinea. 1946–1958*. Athens, OH: Ohio University Press.

Schmitt, S. 1995. '"All these Forms of Women's Work which Endanger Public Health and Public Welfare": Protective Labor Legislation for Women in Germany, 1878–1914', in A. Kessler-Harris et al. (eds), *Protecting Women. Labor Legislation in Europe, the United States, and Australia, 1880–1920*. Chicago: University of Illinois Press, pp. 125–49.

———, 1995. *Der Arbeiterinnenschutz im deutschen Kaiserreich. Zur Konstruktion der schutzbedürftigen Arbeiterin*. Stuttgart and Weimar: J.B. Metzler.

Schmitz, W. 2004. *Nachbarschaft und Dorfgemeinschaft im archaischen und klassischen Griechenland*. Berlin: Akademie Verlag.

Schnabel, J.G. 1997. *Insel Felsenburg* (1731–1743), vols 1–4. Frankfurt: Zweitausendeins.

Schöck-Quinteros, E. 1998. 'Heimarbeiterschutz für die "Mütter des arbeitenden Volkes". Deutschland 1896–1914', in *L'Homme. Zeitschrift für Feministische Geschichtswissenschaft* 9: 183–215.

Scholl, S. and F. Hartnagel. 2005. *Damit wir uns nicht verlieren. Briefwechsel 1937–1943*, edited by T. Hartnagel. Frankfurt am Main: S. Fischer.

Schörken, R. 1984. *Luftwaffenhelfer und Drittes Reich: Die Entstehung eines politischen Bewusstseins*. Stuttgart: Klett-Cotta.

Schröder, H.J. 1992. *Die gestohlenen Jahre. Erzählgeschichten und Geschichtserzählung im Interview: Der Zweite Weltkrieg aus der Sicht ehemaliger Mannschaftssoldaten*. Tübingen: Niemeyer.

Schröder, H.-C. 1995. 'Max Weber und der Puritanismus', in *Geschichte und Gesellschaft* 21: 459–78.

Schubert, V. (ed.). 1986. *Der Mensch und seine Arbeit. Eine Ringvorlesung der Universität Munich*, St. Ottilien: Eos Verlag.

Schulte, T. 1989. *The German Army and Nazi Policies in Occupied Russia.* New York: Berg.

Schulze, W. 1987. *Deutsche Geschichte im 16. Jahrhundert 1500–1618.* Frankfurt am Main: Suhrkamp.

Schwentker, W. 1998. *Max Weber in Japan. Eine Untersuchung zur Wirkungsgeschichte 1905–1995.* Tübingen: Mohr Siebeck.

———, 1999. 'Der "Geist" des japanischen Kapitalismus. Die Geschichte einer Debatte', in W. Mommsen and W. Schwentker (eds), *Max Weber und das moderne Japan.* Göttingen: Vandenhoeck and Ruprecht, pp. 270–98.

Scott, J. 1974. *The Glassworkers of Carmaux.* Cambridge, MA: Harvard University Press.

Scott, J. Wallach. 1986. 'Gender: A Useful Category of Historical Analysis', in *American Historical Review* 91: 1,053–75.

Sewell, W. Jr. 1993. 'Toward a Post-materialist Rhetoric for Labor History', in L.A. Berlanstein (ed.), *Rethinking Labor History: Essays in Discourse and Class Analysis.* Urbana: University of Illinois Press, pp. 15–38.

Seibt, F. 1981. 'Vom Lob der Handarbeit', in H. Mommsen and W. Schulze (eds), *Vom Elend der Handarbeit.* Stuttgart: Klett Cotta, pp. 158–81.

Seidel, H.-C. 2005. 'Arbeitseinsatz und Zwangsarbeit im europäischen Steinkohlenbergbau unter deutscher Herrschaft', in J. Bähr and R. Banken (eds), *Das Europa des 'Dritten Reiches'. Recht, Wirtschaft, Besatzung.* Frankfurt: Klostermann, pp. 259–86.

———, 2005. 'Der "Russenstreb". Die betriebliche Organisation des Ausländer- und Zwangsarbeitereinsatzes im Ruhrbergbau während des Zweiten Weltkrieges', in *Geschichte und Gesellschaft* 31: 8–37.

Sen, S. 1999. *Women and Labour in Late Colonial India. The Bengal Jute Industry.* Cambridge: Cambridge University Press.

Seyfahrt, C. and W.M. Sprondel (eds). 1973. *Seminar: Religion und gesellschaftliche Entwicklung. Studien zur Protestantismus-Kapitalismus-These Max Webers.* Frankfurt am Main: Suhrkamp.

Shakai seisaku gakkai shiryô shûsei hensan iinkai (ed.). 1978. *Shakai seisaku gakkai shiryô shûsei.* Tokyo: Ochanomizu Shobô.

Shapiro, S. 1987. 'The Social Control of Impersonal Trust', in *American Journal of Sociology* 93: 623–58.

Shepherd, B. 2003. 'The Continuum of Brutality: Wehrmacht Security Divisions in Central Russia, 1942', in *German History* 21: 49–81.

Shumpei, U. 1990. *Nihon bunmeishino kôsô. Juyô to sôzô no kiseki.* Tokyo: Kadokawa Shoten.

Sider. G. 1976. 'Christmas Mumming and the New Year in Outport Newfoundland', in *Past and Present* 71: 102–25.

Sieberg, H. 1985. *Colonial Development. Die Grundlegung moderner Entwicklungspolitik durch Großbritannien 1919–1949.* Stuttgart: Steiner.

Simmel, G. 1992. *Soziologie: Untersuchungen über die Formen der Vergesellschaftung.* Frankfurt: Suhrkamp.

Simon-Muscheid, K. 2004. '"Ein rebmesser hat sine frowe versetzt für 1 ß brotte". Armut in den oberrheinischen Städten des 15. und 16. Jahrhunderts', in H. Bräuer (ed.), *Arme – ohne Chance? Kommunale Armutund Armutsbekämpfung vom Spätmittelalter bis zur Gegenwart.* Leipzig: Leipziger Universitätsverlag, pp. 39–70.

Skinner, Q. 1989. 'Ambrogio Lorenzetti: The Artist as Political Philosopher', in H. Belting and D. Blume (eds), *Malerei und Stadtkultur in der Dantezeit. Die Argumentation der Bilder.* Munich: Hirmer, pp. 85–103.

Smith, A. 1967. *An Inquiry into the Nature and Causes of the Wealth of Nations,* vol. 1. Oxford : Oxford University Press.

Smith, T.C. 1988. 'Peasant Time and Factory Time in Japan', in T.C. Smith (ed.), *Native Sources of Japanese Industrialization, 1750–1920.* Berkeley: University of California Press, pp. 199–235.

Solow, B. and S. Engermann (eds). 1987. *British Capitalism and Caribbean Slavery. The Legacy of Eric Williams.* Cambridge: Cambridge University Press.

Sonenscher, M. 1983. 'Work and Wages in Paris in the Eighteenth Century', in: M. Berg, P. Hudson and M. Sonenscher (eds), *Manufacturer in Town and Country before the Factory.* Cambridge: Cambridge University Press, pp. 147–72.

Spiliotis, S. 2003. *Verantwortung und Rechtsfrieden. Die Stiftungsinitiative der deutschen Wirtschaft.* Frankfurt am Main: Fischer.

Spittler, G. 1998. *Hirtenarbeit. Die Welt der Kamelhirten und Ziegenhirtinnen von Timia.* Cologne: Köppe.

———, 2001. 'Work: Anthropological Aspects', in *International Encyclopedia of the Social and Behavioral Sciences,* vol. 24, pp. 16,565–16,568.

———, 2002. 'Arbeit. Transformation von Objekten oder Interaktion mit Subjekten', in *Peripherie* 85/86: 9–31.

———, 2008. *Founders of the Anthropology of Work. German Social Scientists of the 19th and Early 20th Centuries and the First Ethnographers.* Berlin. Lit.

Spittler, G. and K. Beck (eds). 1996. *Arbeit in Afrika.* Münster: Lit.

Spittler, G. et al. (eds). 2003. *Le travail en Afrique noire – Représentations et pratiques à l'époque contemporaine.* Paris: Karthala.

Spoerer, M. 2001. 'NS-Zwangsarbeiter im Deutschen Reich. Eine Statistik vom 30. September 1944 nach Arbeitsamtsbezirken', in *Vierteljahreshefte für Zeitgeschichte* 49: 665–84.

———, 2001. *Zwangsarbeit unter dem Hakenkreuz. Ausländische Zivilarbeiter, Kriegsgefangene und Häftlinge im Deutschen Reich und im besetzten Europa 1939–1945.* Stuttgart: Deutsche Verlagsanstalt.

Spoerer, M. and J. Fleischhacker. 2002. 'Forced Laborers in Nazi Germany. Categories, Numbers, and Survivors', in *Journal of Interdisciplinary History* 23: 169–204.

Stader, I. (ed.). 2006. *"Ihr daheim und wir hier draußen." Ein Briefwechsel zwischen Ostfront und Heimat, Juni 1941–März 1943*. Cologne: Böhlau.

Stearns, P. 1986. *Anger. The Struggle for Emotional Control in America's History*. Chicago: University of Chicago Press.

———, 1989. 'Suppressing Unpleasant Emotions: The Development of a Twentieth-Century American Style', in A. Barnes and P. Stearns (eds), *Social History and Issues in Human Consciousness*. New York: New York University Press, pp. 230–61.

———, 1994. *American Cool. Constructing a Twentieth-Century Emotional Style*. New York: New York University Press.

———, (ed.). 1988. *Emotion and Social Change: Toward a New Psychohistory*. New York: Holmes and Meier.

Stearns, P. and T. Haggerty 1991. 'The Role of Fear: Transitions in American Emotional Standards for Children, 1850–1950', in *American Historial Review* 96: 63–94.

Stearns, P. and C. Stearns. 1985. 'Emotionology: Clarifying the History of Emotions and Emotional Standards', in *American Historical Review* 90: 813–30.

Stedman Jones, G. 1983. *Languages of Class. Studies in English Working-Class History 1832–1982*. Cambridge: Cambridge University Press.

Stefanski, V. 2005. 'Nationalsozialistische Volkstums- und Arbeitseinsatzpolitik im Regierungsbezirk Kattowitz 1939–1945', in *Geschichte und Gesellschaft* 31: 38–67.

Steinfield, R.J. 1991. *The Invention of Free Labor. The Employment Relation in English and Ameican Law and Culture*. Chapel Hill: University of North Carolina Press.

Stiftung Bibliothek des Ruhrgebiets. (ed.). 2006. *Suche nach Wahrheit. Aufarbeitung von Zwangsarbeit und Unrecht im 20. Jahrhundert*. Essen: Klartext.

Stoler, A.L. and F. Cooper 1997. 'Between Metropole and Colony. Rethinking a Research Agenda', in idem (eds), *Tensions of Empire Colonial Cultures in a Bourgeois World*. Berkeley: University of Chicago Press.

Stollberg-Rilinger, B. 1986. *Der Staat als Maschine: Zur politischen Metaphorik des absoluten Fürstenstaats*. Berlin: Duncker and Humblot.

Stouffer, S. 1949. *The American Soldier: Combat and Its Aftermath*. Princeton: Princeton University Press.

Stråth, B. (ed.). 2000. *After Full Employment. European Discourses on Work and Flexibility*. Brussels: Peter Lang Publishing.

Subrahmanyam, S. 2005. *Explorations in Connected History*. 2 vols, Oxford: Oxford University Press.

Supiot, A. (ed.). 1999. *Au-delà de l'emploi. Transformation du travail et devenir du droit du travail en Europe*. Paris: Flammarion.

Szompka, P. 1996. 'Trust and Emerging Democracy: Lessons from Poland', in *International Sociology* 11: 37–62.

Takebayashi, S. 2003. *Die Entstehung der Kapitalismustheorie in der Gründungsphase der deutschen Soziologie. Von der historischen Nationalökonomie zur historischen Soziologie Werner Sombarts und Max Webers.* Berlin: Duncker and Humblot.

Takeyoshi, K. 1950. *Nihon shakai no kazokuteki kôzô.* Tokyo: Nihon Hyôron Shinsha.

Tamanoi, M.A. 1998. *Under the Shadow of Nationalism. Politics and Poetics of Rural Japanese Women.* Honolulu: University of Hawaii Press.

Tamotsu, A. 1996. *Der Japandiskurs im historischen Wandel. Zur Kultur und Identität einer Nation.* Munich: Iudicium.

Tenfelde, K. 1979. 'Ländliches Gesinde in Preußen. Gesinderecht und Gesindestatistik 1810 bis 1861', in *Archiv für Sozialgeschichte* 19: 189–229.

———, 1985. 'Dienstmädchengeschichte. Strukturelle Aspekte im 19. und 20. Jahrhundert', in H. Pohl and B. Brüninghaus (eds), *Die Frau in der deutschen Wirtschaft.* Stuttgart: Steiner, pp. 105–19.

———, (ed,). 1986. *Arbeiter und Arbeiterbewegung im Vergleich.* Munich: Oldenbourg.

Tenfelde, K. and G. Ritter. 1994. *Arbeiter im Deutschen Kaiserreich 1871–1914.* Bonn: Dietz.

Tenfelde, K. and H.-C. Seidel (eds). 2005. *Zwangsarbeit im Bergwerk, Der Arbeitseinsatz im Kohlenbergbau des Deutschen Reiches und der besetzten Gebiete im Ersten und Zweiten Weltkrieg.* Essen: Klartext Verlag.

———, (eds). 2007. *Zwangsarbeit im Europa des 20. Jahrhunderts.* Essen: Klartext.

Thomas, K. (ed.). 1999. *The Oxford Book of Work.* Oxford: Oxford University Press.

Thorwart, F. (ed.). 1910. *Hermann Schulze-Delitzsch's Schriften und Reden,* vol. 2. Berlin: Guttentag Thoß, B. and H.-E. Volkmann (eds). 2002. *Erster Weltkrieg – Zweiter Weltkrieg: ein Vergleich.* Paderborn: Schöningh.

Thurnwald, R. 1923. 'Die Gestaltung der Wirtschaftsentwicklung aus ihren Anfängen heraus', in M. Paly, *Erinnerungsgabe für Max Weber,* vol. i. Munich: Duncker and Humblot, pp. 273–333.

———, 1932. *Werden, Wandel und Gestaltung der Wirtschaft im Lichte der Völkerforschung.* Berlin: de Gruyter.

———, 1932. *Economics in Primitive Communities.* Oxford: Oxford University Press.

Tilgher, A. 1977. *Work: What It Has Meant to Men through the Ages.* New York: Harcourt Brace and Co.

Tille, A. 1904. *Der Wettbewerb weißer und gelber Arbeit in der industriellen Produktion.* Berlin: Elsner.

Topalov, Ch. 1984. *Naissance du chômeur.* Paris: Belin.

Tsurumi, E.P. 1990. *Factory Girls. Women in the Thread Mills of Meiji Japan.* Princeton: Princeton University Press.

Tsutsui, W.M. 1998. *Manufacturing Ideology. Scientific Management in Twentieth-Century Japan.* Princeton: Princeton University Press.

Uebel, M. 2004. 'Introduction: Conceptualizing Labor in the Middle Ages', in M. Uebel and K. Robertson (eds), *The Middle Ages at Work*. New York: Palgrave Macmillan.

Uebel, M. and K. Robertson (eds). 2004. *The Middle Ages at Work*. New York: Palgrave Macmillan.

Usborne, C. 1992. *The Politics of the Body in Weimar Germany. Women's Reproductive Rights and Duties*. London: Macmillan.

Velez-Ibanez, C. 1983. *Bands of Mutual Trust: The Cultural System of Rotating Credit Associations among Urban Mexicans and Chicanos*. New Brunswick: Rutgers University Press.

Ven, F. van der. 1972. *Sozialgeschichte der Arbeit*. 3 vols, Munich: dtv.

Vogel, A. 1997. *Das Pflichtjahr für Mädchen. Nationalsozialistische Arbeitseinsatzpolitik im Zeichen der Kriegswirtschaft*. Frankfurt am Main: Lang.

Wagner, P. 2005. *Bauern, Junker und Beamte. Lokale Herrschaft und Partizipation im Ostelbien des 19. Jahrhunderts*. Göttingen: Wallstein.

———, et al. (eds). 2000. *Arbeit und Nationalstaat. Frankreich und Deutschland in europäischer Perspektive*. Frankfurt am Main: Campus.

Wallerstein, I. 1999. 'Eurocentrism and its Avatars. The Dilemmas of Social Science', in I. Wallerstein (ed.), *The End of the World as We Know It. Social Science for the 21st Century*. Minnesota: University of Minnesota Press.

Walter, R. and R. Otto. 1998. 'Das Massensterben der sowjetischen Kriegsgefangenen und die Wehrmachtsbürokratie. Unterlagen zur Registrierung der sowjetischen Kriegsgefangenen 1941–1945 in deutschen und russischen Archiven', in *Militärgeschichtliche Mitteilungen* 57: 149–80.

Walther, R. 1990. 'Arbeit – Ein begriffsgeschichtlicher Überblick von Aristoteles bis Ricardo', in H. König et al. (eds), *Sozialphilosophie der industriellen Arbeit*. Opladen: Westdeutscher Verlag, pp. 3–25. 'Was wir wollen und sollen', in *Deutsche Arbeiterhalle* 14 (27 July 1868).

Washbrook, D. 1988. 'Progress and Problems. South Asian Economic and Social History, c. 1720–1860', in *Modern Asian Studies* 22: 57–96.

Weber, M. 1904. 'Die Protestantische Ethik und der Geist des Kapitalismus', in *Archiv für Sozialwissenschaft und Sozialpolitik* 20: 1–54; 1905. *Archiv für Sozialwissenschaft und Sozialpolitik* 21: 1–110; expanded version in 1920. *Gesammelte Aufsätze zur Religionssoziologie*, vol. 1. Tübingen: Mohr.

———, 1908. 'Zur Psychophysik industrieller Arbeit', in M. Weber, *Gesammelte Aufsätze zur Soziologie und Sozialpolitik*. Tübingen: Mohr, pp. 61–255.

———, 1920. 'Die Protestantische Ethik und der Geist des Kapitalismus', erweiterte Fassung, in *Gesammelte Aufsätze zur Religionssoziologie*, vol. 1. Tübingen: Mohr, pp. 17–206.

———, 1920/21. *Gesammelte Aufsätze zur Religionssoziologie*. 3 vols, Tübingen: Mohr.

———, 1951. *The Religion of China: Confucianism and Taoism*, trans. and ed. Hans G. Gerth. New York: The Free Press.

———, 1952. *Ancient Judaism*, trans. and ed. H. Gerth. New York: The Free Press.

———, 1958. *The Religion of India: Hinduism and Buddhism*, trans. and ed. H. Gerth and D. Martindale. New York: The Free Press.

———, 1968. '"Energetische" Kulturtheorien', in *Archiv für Sozialwissenschaft und Sozialpolitik* 29: pp. 575–98 reprint in 1985 *Gesammelte Aufsätze zur Wissenschaftslehre*, Tübingen: Mohr, pp. 400–26.

———, 1972. *Wirtschaft und Gesellschaft*. Tübingen: Mohr.

———, 1993. *Die protestantische Ethik und der 'Geist' des Kapitalismus*, K. Lichtblau and J. Weiß (eds) Bodenheim: Athenäum-Hain-Hanstein.

———, 2002. *The Protestant Ethic and the Spirit of Capitalism*, trans. S. Kalberg. Los Angeles: Roxbury.

Wei-ming, T. 1996. 'The Confucian Dimension in the East Asian Development Model', in J. Kreiner (ed.), *The Impact of Traditional Thought on Present-Day Japan*. Munich: Iudicium, pp. 31–48.

Weisbrod, B. 2000. 'Military Violence and Male Fundamentalism: Ernst Jünger's Contribution to the Conservative Revolution', *History Workshop Journal* 49: 69–94.

Weitling, W. 1971. *Die Menschheit wie sie ist und wie sie sein sollte* (1838/9), ed. W. Schäfer, Reinbek: Rowohlt.

Welskopp, T. 1998. 'Klasse als Befindlichkeit? Vergleichende Arbeitergeschichte vor der kulturhistorischen Herausforderung', in *Archiv für Sozialgeschichte* 38: 301–36.

———, 2000. *Das Banner der Brüderlichkeit. Die deutsche Sozialdemokratie vom Vormärz bis zum Sozialistengesetz*. Bonn: Verlag J.H.W. Dietz Nachf.

———, 1994. *Arbeit und Macht im Hüttenwerk. Arbeits- und industrielle Beziehungen in der deutschen und amerikanischen Eisen- und Stahlindustrie von den 1860er bis zu den 1930er Jahren*. Bonn: J.H.W. Dietz Nachf.

———, 1994. 'Von der verhinderten Heldengeschichte des Proletariats zur vergleichenden Sozialgeschichte der Arbeit – Perspektiven der Arbeitergeschichtsschreibung in den 1990er Jahren', in *1999. Zeitschrift für Sozialgeschichte des 19. und 20. Jahrhunderts* 8/3: 34–52.

———, 2004. '"Manneszucht" und "Selbstbeherrschung". Zivilgesellschaftliche Werte in der deutschen Sozialdemokratie, 1848–1878', in R. Jessen et al. (eds), *Zivilgesellschaft als Geschichte. Studien zum 19. und 20. Jahrhundert*. Wiesbaden: VS Verlag für Sozialwissenschaften, pp. 65–88.

———, 2004. 'Markt und Klasse in der deutschen Sozialdemokratie, 1848–1878', in *Marx–Engels Jahrbuch 2004*: pp. 9–30.

Weltecke, D. 2003. 'Gab es "Vertrauen" im Mittelalter?', in U. Frevert (ed.), *Vertrauen: Historische Annäherungen*. Göttingen: Vandenhoeck and Ruprecht, pp. 81–88.

Wetterer, A. 2002. *Arbeitsteilung und Geschlechterkonstruktion. 'Gender at Work' in theoretischer und historischer Perspektive*. Konstanz: Universitäts Verlag Konstanz.

Weule, K. 1908. *Negerleben in Ostafrika. Ergebnisse einer ethnologischen orschungsreise.* Leipzig: F.A. Brockhaus.

———, 1909. *Native Life in East Africa. The Results of an Ethnological Research Expedition.* London: Sir Isaac Pitman and Sons.

———, 1912. *Die Urgesellschaft und ihre Lebensfürsorge.* Stuttgart: Kosmos.

Wheatcroft, S. 1999. 'Ausmaß und Wesen der deutschen und sowjetischen Repressionen und Massentötungen 1930–1945', in D. Dahlmann and G. Hirschfeld (eds), *Lager, Zwangsarbeit, Vertreibung und Deportation. Dimensionen der Massenverbrechen in der Sowjetunion und in Deutschland 1933–1945.* Essen: Klartext-Verlag, pp. 67–109.

Wiedemann, K. 1979. *Arbeit und Bürgertum. Die Entwicklung des Arbeitsbegriffs in der Literatur Deutschlands an der Wende zur Neuzeit.* Heidelberg: Carl Winter Universitätsverlag.

Wierling, D. 1987. *Mädchen für alles: Arbeitsalltag und Lebensgeschichte städtischer Dienstmädchen um die Jahrhundertwende.* Berlin: Dietz.

Wiesflecker, H. 1986. *Kaiser Maximilian I. Das Reich, Österreich und Europa an der Wende zur Neuzeit,* vol. 5. Vienna: Verlag für Geschichte und Politik, pp. 315–17.

Williams, E. 1944. *Capitalism and Slavery.* Chapel Hill: University of North Carolina Press.

Wilmowsky, T. Freiherr von. 1950. *Warum wurde Krupp verurteilt? Legende und Justizirrtum.* Stuttgart: F. Vorwerk.

Wikander, U. et al. (eds)1995. *Protecting Women. Labor Legislation in Europe, the United States and Australia. 1880-1920.* Urbana and Chicago: University of Illinois Press.

Wirz, A. 1984. *Sklaverei und kapitalistisches Weltsystem.* Frankfurt: Suhrkamp.

Womack, J. 2005. 'Doing Labor History. Feeling, Work, Material Power', in *Journal of the Historical Society* 5/3: 255–96.

Work in the Life-Cycle. Economic History Yearbook 2008/1. Berlin: Akademieverlag.

Yeo, E. 2002, 'Gender in Labour and Working-Class History', in L. Heerma van Voss and M. van der Linden (eds), *Class and Other Identities: Gender, Religion, and Ethnicity in the Writing of European Labour History.* New York: Berghahn, pp. 73–87.

Zedler, J.H. 1732. *Grosses Vollständiges Universal Lexicon aller Wissenschafften und Künste,* vol. 2. Halle and Leipzig: Zedler.

———, 1746. *Grosses vollständiges Universal-Lexicon aller Wissenschafften und Künste,* vol. 48, Leipzig: Zedler.

Ziemann, B. 1998. 'Die Eskalation des Tötens in zwei Weltkriegen', in R. van Dülmen (ed.), *Erfindung des Menschen: Schöpfungsträume und Körperbilder 1500–2000,* exhibition catalogue, Vienna: Böhlau, pp. 411–29.

Zimmermann, B. et al (eds). 1999. *Le travail et la nation. Histoire croisée de la France et de l'Allemagne.* Paris: Maison des Sciences de l'Homme.

———, 2000. *La constitution du chômage en Allemagne. Entre professions et territories.* Paris: Maison des Sciences d l'Homme.

———, 2001. *La constitution du chômage en Allemagne. Entre professions et territories.* Paris: Editions de la Maison des Sciences de l'Homme.

———, 2001. 'Work and Labor. History of the Concept', in *International Encyclopedia of the Social and Behavioral Sciences*, vol. 24. London: Elsevier, pp. 16,561–65.

Zorn, W. 1986. 'Arbeit in Europa vom Mittelalter bis ins Industriezeitalter', in V. Schubert (ed.), *Der Mensch und seine Arbeit. Eine Ringvorlesung der Universität Munich.* St. Ottilien: Eos Verlag, pp. 181–212.

Zunkel, F. 1970. 'Die ausländischen Arbeiter in der deutschen Kriegswirtschaft des 1. Weltkrieges', in G. Ritter (ed.), *Entstehung und Wandel der modernen Gesellschaft.* Berlin: de Gruyter, pp. 280–311.

Notes on Contributors

Sebastian Conrad is Professor of Modern History at the European University Institute in Florence, Italy. He was a Fellow at the Center for Advanced Study (Wissenschaftskolleg) in Berlin. His publications include *Auf der Suche nach der verlorenen Nation. Geschichtsschreibung in Westdeutschland und Japan, 1945–1960* (1999); *Globalisierung und Nation im Deutschen Kaiserreich* (2006); *Deutsche Kolonialgeschichte* (2008) and the edited volumes *Globalgeschichte. Theorien, Ansätze, Themen* (2007, with Andreas Eckert, Ulrike Freitag) and *Competing Visions of World Order: Global Moments and Movements, 1880s–1930s* (2007, with Dominic Sachsenmaier).

Andreas Eckert is Professor of African History at Humboldt University Berlin. He holds visiting professorships in Bloomington, Harvard and the Maison des Sciences de l'Homme in Paris. He is a Fellow of the Royal Historical Society (U.K.), chair of the study group of modern social history (Arbeitskreis für Moderne Sozialgeschichte) and currently editor of the *Journal of African History*. His main research areas are nineteenth- and twentieth-century African history, colonialism, the history of historiography and global labour history. Among his recent publications are *Kolonalismus* (2006), *Herrschen und Verwalten. Afrikanische Bürokraten, staatliche Ordnung und Politik in Tanzania, 1920–1970* (2007) and *Vom Imperialismus zum Empire. Nicht-westliche Perspektiven auf die Globalisierung* (2009, edited with Shalini Randeria).

Josef Ehmer is Professor of Social and Economic History at the University of Vienna; he was Professor of Modern History at the University of Salzburg (1993–2005) and visiting professor at various European universities. His books include: *Familienstruktur und Arbeitsorganisation im frühindustriellen Wien* (1980); *Sozialgeschichte des Alters* (1990); *Heiratsverhalten, Sozialstruktur, ökonomischer Wandel. England und Mitteleuropa in der Formationsperiode des Kapitalismus* (1991); *Soziale Traditionen in Zeiten des Wandels. Arbeiter und Handwerker im 19. Jahrhundert* (1994); *Bevölkerungsgeschichte und Historische Demographie 1800–2000* (2003); and the edited volume *The Idea of Work from Antiquity to Modern Times* (2009, with Catharina Lis).

Ute Frevert has taught modern European History in Berlin, Constance and Bielefeld. In 2003, she was appointed Professor of German History at Yale University, U.S.A. Her visiting professorships have taken her to Jerusalem, Vienna, Paris and Dartmouth College, U.S.A. She has been a Fellow at the Wissenschaftskolleg zu Berlin and at the Center for Advanced Study in Stanford. Since January 2008, she has been Director at the Max Planck Institute for Human Development in Berlin, where she leads the 'History of Emotions' Research Centre. Her many publications include *Women in German History: From Bourgeois Emancipation to Sexual Liberation* (1989), *Men of Honour: A Social and Cultural History of the Duel* (1995) and *A Nation in Barracks: Modern Germany, Military Conscription and Civil Society* (2004).

Karin Hausen is Professor Emerita of the Technical University Berlin, where she was Professor for Economic and Social History (1978 to 1995) and Professor for Interdisciplinary Women's Studies and Founding Director of the Centre for Interdisciplinary Studies on Women and Gender (1995 to 2003). Most of her publications deal with gender history and the impact of social, economic and institutional structures as well as cultural norms and images on individuals and groups when they manage their daily life. She has also published on 'Kamerun' as a German colony, on the history of technology and on the Paris Commune.

Jürgen Kocka was Professor for the History of the Industrial World at the Free University Berlin and Research Professor at the Berlin Social Science Research Centre (WZB) until 2009. Now he holds a regular visiting appointment at UCLA. He has published widely in the field of modern history, particularly eighteenth- and twentieth-century social and economic history. He has also written on theoretical problems of history and the social sciences. His publications include: *White Collar Workers in America 1890-1940* (1980); *Les employés en Allemagne 1850–1980* (1989); *Facing Total War. German Society 1914–1918* (1984); *Arbeitsverhältnisse und Arbeiterexistenzen. Grundlagen der Klassenbildung im 19. Jahrhundert* (1990); *Industrial Culture and Bourgeois Society. Business, Labor, and Bureaucracy in Modern Germany* (1999); *Das lange 19. Jahrhundert* (2001) as well as *Civil Society and Dictatorship in Modern German History* (2010).

Alf Lüdtke, born in 1943, is Honorary Professor at the University of Erfurt and, retired Research Associate at the former Max-Planck-Institut for History, Göttingen. Among his publications on the history of domination and violence but also on the history of work and the visual are *Gemeinwohl, Polizei und Festungspraxis: Staatliche Gewaltsamkeit und innere Verwaltung in Preussen, 1815–1850* (1982; English, 1989); *Alltagsgeschichte. Zur Rekonstruktion historischer Erfahrungen und Lebensweisen* (1989; French, 1993; English, 1995; Korean, 2002); *Herrschaft als soziale Praxis* (1991); *Eigen-Sinn. Fabrikalltag, Arbeitererfahrungen und Politik vom Kaiserreich bis in den Faschismus* (1993); *Die*

DDR im Bild (2004); *The No Man's Land of Violence. Extreme Wars in the 20th Century* (2006); *Staats-Gewalt: Ausnahmezustand und Sicherheitsregimes* (2008).

Gerd Spittler, born in 1939, is Professor Emeritus of Social Anthropology at the University of Bayreuth. He was a Fellow of the Wissenschaftskolleg and the Wissenschaftszentrum in Berlin and Chairman of the German Association for African Studies. He is a Honorary Member of the German Anthropological Association. His publications on work include the books *Founders of the Anthropology of Work* (2008), *Le Travail en Afrique noire* (co-editor, 2003), *Hirtenarbeit* (1998), *Arbeit in Afrika* (1996 co-editor).

Klaus Tenfelde, born in 1944, is Professor of Social History and Social Movements at the Ruhr-University, Bochum. He received his Ph.D. at the University of Münster in 1975, and his 'Habilitation' at the University of Munich in 1981. From 1986, he taught at the University of Innsbruck, Austria, and from 1990 at the University of Bielefeld. In 1995, he became the Director of the Institute for Social Movements, and Chairman of the "Stiftung Bibliothek des Ruhrgebiets" at the Ruhr-University, Bochum. His publications include: *Sozialgeschichte der Bergarbeiterschaft an der Ruhr im 19. Jahrhundert* (1977, 1981); *Proletarische Provinz. Radikalisierung und Widerstand in Penzberg/Oberbayern 1900–1945* (1981, 1982); *Arbeiter im Deutschen Kaiserreich 1871–1914* (together with Gerhard A. Ritter, 1994); *Krupp bleibt doch Krupp* (2005).

Thomas Welskopp, born in 1961, is Professor for the History of Modern Societies at Bielefeld University. From 2003 to 2004 he was a Fellow at the Center for Advanced Study in the Behavioral Sciences, Stanford, California; from 2008 to 2009 a Fellow of the Historisches Kolleg in Munich. Major publications are: *Der Migros-Kosmos. Zur Geschichte eines außergewöhnlichen Schweizer Unternehmens* (co-editor, 2003); *Das Banner der Brüderlichkeit. Die deutsche Sozialdemokratie vom Vormärz bis zum Sozialistengesetz* (2000); *Geschichte zwischen Kultur und Gesellschaft. Beiträge zur Theoriedebatte* (Co-editor, 1997); *Arbeit und Macht im Hüttenwerk. Die deutsche und amerikanische Eisen- und Stahlindustrie von den 1860er bis zu den 1930er Jahren* (1994).

Index